HUMANITY:

THE WORLD BEFORE RELIGION, WAR & INEQUALITY

BARRY BROWN

HUMANITY:
THE WORLD BEFORE RELIGION, WAR & INEQUALITY
Copyright © 2017 by Barry Brown

No part of this publication may be reproduced, distributed, or transmitted in any form or by any means, including photocopying, recording, or other electronic or mechanical methods, without the prior written permission of the author, except in the case of brief quotations embodied in critical reviews and certain other non-commercial uses permitted by copyright law.

Tellwell Talent
www.tellwell.ca

ISBN
978-1-77302-227-7 (Hardcover)
978-1-77302-225-3 (Paperback)
978-1-77302-226-0 (eBook)

Table of Contents

ACKNOWLEDGEMENTS V

INTRODUCTION VII

CHAPTER 1
THE WORLD BEFORE WAR, RELIGION & INEQUALITY 1

CHAPTER 2
THE IMPORTANCE OF BEING BALANCED 19

CHAPTER 3
THE FIRST BOOK WAS A STATUE 29

CHAPTER 4
THE CLASS OF 10,000 BC. 39

CHAPTER 5
THE FIRST LOGO 49

CHAPTER 6
DIVISIONS. 55

CHAPTER 7
WAR COMES TO EDEN 65

CHAPTER 8
A GAME OF THRONES. 83

CHAPTER 9
WAR, RELIGION AND THE NEW WORLD ORDER 91

CHAPTER 10
THE AGE OF GOVERNMENT:
INDUS VALLEY DEMOCRACY 103

CHAPTER 11
MAN INVENTED THE DEVIL,
WOMAN CREATED RELIGION 137

CHAPTER 12
EXODUS: 3 REVOLUTIONS
THAT CHANGED THE WORLD................... 153

CHAPTER 13
GOLDEN COWS AND STONE COMMANDMENTS.....171

CHAPTER 14
JUSTICE, LAW AND RIGHTEOUS RULERS........... 187

CHAPTER 15
FRAGMENTS 201

CHAPTER 16
THE GREAT COLLAPSE:
TERRORISM AND UTOPIA..................... 255

CHAPTER 17
THE BIG WOMB THEORY...................... 279

TESTIMONIALS 299

SIMPLIFIED TIMELINE 303

SHALOMASTE...............................308

ACKNOWLEDGEMENTS

There are many people to thank for their ongoing support during the difficult and challenging years I spent researching and writing this book. First among them is Isabel Brown, my ex-wife, whose unflinching and enormously generous financial help made this possible. My old and dear friend Mark Shnier reappeared in my life just when he was needed. The heartfelt support he and his wife Mira offered enabled me to complete my writing and publish my book.

I give deep thanks and gratitude to editor, writer, singer, actor, filmmaker and dear friend, Sally Champlin, for her endless editorial help and constant encouragement. She pushed me to complete this book before I knew there was a book to write.

Thanks also go to my many friends and associates who helped me complete this work including Dr. Mayank Vahia of India's Tata Institute for Fundamental Research, Sister Catherine D.M. Yaskiw, Levi Lecompte, Geneticist Dr. Lalji Singh of Hindu University, Dr. Rev. J.J. Mastandrea, David Cooper, A.C. Bhaktivedanta Swami Prabhupada, Glyn Evans, James Musselman and Scott Bell Terry Williams, Victoria Ollers and John Cowie, Francois Bergeron of L'Express newspaper, Bhaktimarga Swami of Toronto's Hare Krishna Temple, D'Arcy Jennish, Jesse Cohoon, George Anthony, Anna and Allan Bloom, Kirk Douglas and the estate of Tony Curtis, my landlords John and Nick Kioussis, and Etymonline.com for all the word histories. All of them contributed to the successful completion of this book.

Finally, I would like to thank the history itself for helping me understand its story. I didn't know what this journey would reveal when I began my research. But along the way, I was led to this pathway through our history. So, as our ancient ancestors would say, I thank eternal living knowledge for guiding me to the completion of this book.

Cover Art: Barry Brown
Shalomaste Art: Barry Brown
Illustrations: Anthony Paul Morgan,
Alessandra Braganini and others

INTRODUCTION

Recent articles in *Scientific American* and other journals have noted there is no evidence of war between human communities anywhere on Earth before about 6,000 years ago. Even though individuals and small groups have killed other people from time to time, in the long stretch of human history even those local incidents of murder and lethal violence were extremely rare until recently.

The story of humanity begins 3 million years ago in Africa with the first, upright-walking tool-using human ancestor called "Lucy." Since that beginning, more than 99.99% of human history is the story of how people populated the planet, created languages and planned cities, established global trade and advanced science, technology and the arts in a world before war. Less than 0.01% of humanity's history has taken place in the last 6,000 years since the invention and spread of military violence.

Contrary to popular belief, humans are not born with a 'war gene.'

So, when and where was that first war? War is the result of social divisions so extreme that people are willing to kill over them. Yet, global human civilization could only have developed and spread through cooperation – the exchange of words to create a common language and other friendly trade. When and where did those divisions between people first begin and how was humanity changed by that first war?

To understand what happened in the distant past and how people arrived in the modern world, the journey must begin by asking "What made us human?"

Humanity is a global family. All life on Earth is the larger family and that life has diversified and expanded over the past 3.5 billion years since the first single-celled forms of life appeared in the first oceans.

Every human has a common and very distant set of simian ancestors who lived 5-8 million years ago and passed their genetic traits to two sets of offspring – one that began the family of apes and the other that began the family line of humans. It is important to note that humans are related to the apes but not directly descended from them. Humans and apes have a common heritage, but the ancestors of humans advanced as one branch of the family, while apes developed as a distinct species. What distinguished the human branch was the human brain kept growing long after birth. This advancement has been linked to a change in diet from leaf-eating to foraging for fruits and nuts. The apes continued as passive leaf-eaters. Their cousins, the ancestral humans, developed bigger brains because fruits and nuts are more nutritious and gathering them required more effort and retained knowledge.

"Lucy" and her tribe of tool-makers lived in what is now Ethiopia 3 million years ago. Since then, the family of people mingled and traded with various kinds of ancient humans across the globe without any concept of social or racial differences until about 6,000 years ago. Early humans had no words for race, religion, nationality or social status because those divisions did not exist in early human communities. Among the roaming bands of hunter-gatherers all people were seen as the same and yet unique as well. In the ancient Indian language of Sanskrit, this prehistoric concept would be expressed as *Achintya Bheda Abheda* or "inconceivable simultaneous oneness and difference." In other words, all things are an individual variation on the common theme of life.

For if all things were the same, there would be no differences to enable change. And if there was no universal commonality that provided a path for communication and cooperation between all things, evolution would be impossible. Therefore, everything must have characteristics that are both similar and unique to allow for the growth of community and the sharing of knowledge and skills.

Humanity's prehistoric culture grew from the exchange of words, gifts and genes because early humans were honest and depended on trust to expand their relationships. To facilitate trade and relationships, words were coined and traded as humanity's first currency. Prehistoric humans used their currency of words to establish regular, long-distance trade that prospered in Southern Africa 400,000 years ago. Those markets for trading shells and beads started and continued because human relationships were honest and reliable.

Until 300 years ago, the scientific method was called Natural Philosophy. It was rooted in an ancient concept that all things were related and everything had the ability to communicate. In prehistoric and early human society, knowledge itself was understood to be a living entity that also communicated. This sense of knowledge as a living presence inside all things and the source of their individual expression, was similar to the modern understanding of DNA, and was the inspiration for later concepts of the soul and a universal God. And, just as many religions teach the importance of a developing a personal relationship with the Deity, Natural Philosophers said knowledge was not discovered, it was revealed as people deepened their personal relationship with its living spirit.

Modern thinkers are often critical when people perceive human-like personalities in non-human beings such as plants, animals or God. The term used is anthropomorphic, which means to shape something into human form. Yet, if all things have individual qualities and personality-like characteristics, perhaps what is termed imagination is actually observation. All things are unique and engaged in a relationship with other distinct individuals, which means all things must communicate. The human ability to empathize with other kinds of people and other forms of life, together with pattern recognition, was the way early humans first gathered knowledge about their world. And that remains true today.

Human civilization did not begin with isolated groups battling over resources until one emerged victorious. There is no evidence for that model and humanity would not have survived if isolation, suspicion and violence dominated prehistoric human culture. Human relationships come in just three types. People can be friends, they can be neutrals or enemies. If early humans were worried about violence and aggression from other people, there would be evidence of it. Yet, the artifacts from 3 million years of Stone Age history show a variety of hunting and working tools but no war weapons. There are no defensive walls around villages or cities before about 5,000 years ago. So, for 99.99% of history, humans were not at war and had no fear of being attacked. If the original human culture was indifferent to others, humanity's early history would have been broken by isolated genetic families and the limited transfer of ideas and inventions. Yet, the genetic evidence shows all humans are descendants of the original first family, and almost every modern language is a descendent of four original base languages that grew from an even earlier single source.

If humans were not interested in learning from others, no one would be reading this book because human civilization – with a common culture and shared technologies - would never have come into existence. Huddled in small, far apart communities that had no contact with each other, humans would have died out like the Neanderthals – humanity's isolationist cousins.

But humanity didn't die out. Instead, one early form of human civilization gave birth to another as people, inventions, histories and ideas were transferred from one intermingled tribe to another across the globe. More than 94,000 years after humanity's prehistoric ancestors left Africa to populate the world, its urban centers and technologies had advanced to the point where large scale war was possible. When war came, it would change humanity forever. Thousands of years later, the dramatic division between humanity before war and after would be evoked in the Ancient Greek legend of Pandora who released evils into the world that hadn't existed before, and the fall of humanity from paradise in the Biblical story of Eden.

The first physically modern humans – the *Homo Sapiens* or "People with Insight," walked out of Northeast Africa 100,000 years ago to explore and settle the world. But they were not the first humans to seek out new lands. Aided by long periods of low ocean levels, humanity's ancestral cousins were able to walk between mainland Europe and England, and Southeast Asia and the islands leading to Australia. And they began settling those regions almost a million years ago. What made *Homo Sapiens* different was their new sense of identity. They had a stronger sense of individuality and a greater desire to form larger communities.

Homo Sapiens' drive to establish a knowledge-based human society shifted into high gear with the birth of a new generation of people – the *Homo Sapien Sapiens* or "People with Insight into Insight." Starting about 40,000 years ago, those New Humans set down the foundations of the modern world with the first complex expressions of human culture in painting, writing, global trade networks and planned communities.

HUMANITY: THE WORLD BEFORE RELIGION, WAR & INEQUALITY

By 20,000 years ago, humans were no longer limited to wandering, semi-settled groups trading polished beads and shells. They lived in communities and discussed complex ideas as shown by the popularity of the world's first book of philosophy – commonly known as the Venus statues. About 12,000 years ago, humanity's first university was built at a place called Gobekli in southeast Turkey. It was the students and faculty of this school who launched large-scale agriculture and spread the concept of a single, global human civilization around the world. For 4,000 years, people from many regions would gather on its campus and carry what they learned back to their homelands. It would profoundly influence the course of human civilization and inspire humanity's Age of Knowledge culture that took root in Ancient India about 7,000 years ago.

Around 5,000-6,000 years ago, a leading warrior Prince in the technologically advanced and well-populated civilization of Ancient India convinced his followers to join him in a military adventure to rule their known world. The result was the world's first war. The end of humanity's first pre-war civilization would be recalled in the Bible as the loss of Eden. For underneath its religious coating, the world-changing event of the original Garden story was the world before and after war.

When I began this journey, it wasn't to write a book. I only wanted to know if Aristotle was right. When I discovered all the evidence supporting his claim it revealed a lost family tie between the Eastern and Western World that brought together the histories of Ancient India, the Hebrew Bible and the first war.

Roughly 2,400 years ago, the Greek philosopher Aristotle told one of his students that the Jewish people were descended from the philosophers and Brahman priests of Ancient India. It is not known why Aristotle made this claim. He may have noticed similarities between the Brahmans of India and the Israelite priests, or he may have heard this from the Jewish community of his day.

My personal interest was sparked because I am Jewish and when I was younger, I spent three years as a Hare Krishna monk studying India's ancient language of Sanskrit and its ancient books of wisdom. During that time, I was initiated as a Brahman – a teacher of the old knowledge.

I am not a religious man, but I am an investigative reporter. Though Aristotle's claim seemed far-fetched, I wanted to see if there was any evidence that Biblical history began in Ancient India. So, I put on my fedora and picked up a Bible.

According to its story, human civilization began in the Garden of Eden. Putting aside everything else, where in the world was Eden? Chapter 2 of Genesis says Eden was in the eastern end of a land called Havilah by a river known as the Pichon. So, where was Havilah?

According to the 20-volume, 1906 Jewish Encyclopedia, the oldest traditions in Christianity and Judaism say that Havilah was India and the Pichon River is today called the sacred Ganges River. If Biblical history began in India, what happened there 6,000 years ago that could have started its story? The only apparent answer was India's tale of the world's first massive war - the Battle of Kurukshetra. If the downfall of Eden and India's history of an ancient war were two narratives of the same event, that would reveal a profound and wholly new perspective on the common origins of human civilization.

Humanity proceeds from two starting points – an exploration of human history before war, and how the post-war journey of humanity led from India to Western Civilization. To make my presentation easier to follow some ancient dates have been rounded, and India often means the larger region of its old civilization that spread across modern Pakistan, Afghanistan, Sri Lanka and Bangladesh. India's ancient texts are grouped together as the Vedas or "Books of Knowledge," rather than their usual subdivisions. As with all histories, some events are highlighted over others. Passages from the Bible and India's ancient stories are not used for religious argument but only as historical references. Finally, multiculturalism in the prehistoric and ancient world does not refer to a government policy, but the reality of many different people living in the same mixed and mobile communities. Scholars and experts in many fields have reviewed my work and their support and guidance has been invaluable.

Attempts were made to contact the legal rights holder of each image. Some rights holders could not be identified, others did not respond. Anyone claiming a specific image should notify the author for credit and compensation.

This is the story of how human civilization was created, and why human relationships changed over time. It's a tour of human history unlike any other.

Buckle up and get ready, the ride is about to begin.

CHAPTER 1

THE WORLD BEFORE WAR, RELIGION & INEQUALITY

The prehistoric world of humanity had no nations or borders

Was there a time in human history before divisive religions, armed war and social inequality? If there was, how did humanity first organize itself and what changed?

The world of humanity's earliest ancestors had no boundaries. People followed coastlines and waterways from one part of the world to another. Turn a map of the world upside down. Roll an imaginary ball from South Africa down the continent's East Coast to the intersection of the Mediterranean Sea and the Sinai Peninsula where the trail leads north to Europe and east to Asia. Some humans followed the eastern coastline of India and Southeast Asia to China, Siberia and the Americas. Those turning north migrated to Europe and Eurasia while others settled in the Middle East. This journey was not a continuous settlement. People would stop to form a new campsite. Later, some wandered off and set up a new camp farther along the trail. By 20,000 years ago, human settlements and trading posts had leap-frogged to every part of the world.

**All modern people are descended from the family of *Homo Sapiens*
who left Africa to explore the world 100,000 years ago**

The social divisions and conflicts that separate people in the modern world did not exist when humanity began. For millions of years, people lived in mobile communities without rulers, laws or social divisions. In hunter-gatherer societies, people were largely self-reliant and group responsibilities were interchangeable. People shared resources and invented words to describe things in the world. Those personal relationships deepened trust between people in those early human communities, and trust was the seed that sprouted human civilization.

In the June 29, 2012 issue of *Scientific American*, writer John Horgan wrote that even though most people believe humans are and have always been violent and selfish, the hard evidence does not support this. In *"Quitting the Hominid Fight Club,"* Horgan summarized his findings and laid out the expert testimony.

There is "no fossil or archaeological evidence" that humanity's prehistoric ancestors fought wars, he wrote.

Archaeologist Jonathan Haas of the Field Museum in Chicago told Horgan there is no fossil evidence of any military combat anywhere in the world before about 6,000 years ago. What some historians call battlefields are more accurately described as extremely rare prehistoric crime scenes. They show one group of armed people killing a group of unarmed people. That is evidence of individual psychopathology and murder, not a battle between warriors.

"If war was deeply rooted in our biology, then it's going to be there all the time. And it's just not," Haas said in the article.

Anthropologist Brian Ferguson of Rutgers University reflected on what he learned when he uncovered the remains of an 11,500 year old community that once flourished along the Euphrates River in what is now Iraq. People lived there for more than 4,000 years without leaving behind a single mark of violence, he told Horgan.

In a 2012 *Science* magazine article, *The Battle Over Conflict*, author Andrew Lawler noted that cave paintings in Europe from about 40,000 to 10,000 years ago show people organizing for animal hunts "but not human-on-human conflict. Archaeologists have found little evidence of murder and organized violence before the military empires of the Near East sprang up 4,000 years ago."

Indeed, contrary to popular belief, war is so detrimental to evolutionary success that among the roughly 9 million species of life on Earth, only three are known to engage in organized warfare. Those three are ants, some species of chimpanzees and humans. Among these three, humans are and have always been the least warlike. Measured against our closest ape relatives – the chimpanzees – humans are much less aggressive.

In the March, 2016 Atlantic Magazine article *Bonobos Just Want Everyone to Get Along*, writer Cari Romm cited a 2013 study from Emory University that found strong similarities between the emotional development of young bonobos and that of human children. Bonobos, or pygmy chimps, are related to the more common chimpanzee but separate from them in the same way humans are distinct from Neanderthals. Chimps live in male-dominated hierarchical societies and start wars with their neighbors, Romm wrote. But bonobos society is nurtured by strong females and so as a group bonobos "have no problem welcoming outsiders into the fold: They mate, share food, and readily form bonds with strangers. They're also great at defusing conflicts before they escalate—when bonobos stumble upon a new feeding ground, for example, they tend to celebrate with group sex before eating, a habit researchers believe is meant to relieve tension," she added.

This distinction between the two chimp cultures – those open to outsiders and those closed to them - may offer a clue to the origins of modern human characteristics. Our earliest, higher-thinking human-like simian ancestors first appeared in Africa 5-8 million years ago. Earlier generations of this family migrated from Africa and traveled across Asia to India and China. But their descendants would return to Africa before continuing their evolution into upright, tool-making humans. Those two groups – the genetically mixed and mobile simians who returned to Africa from Asia, and their less genetically-mixed cousins who stayed in Africa – are the ancestors of all humans, and they passed their distinct cultures to modern human society. The early humans who remained in Southern Africa were the first geographic and social introverts, while those in the North migrated out and partied with everyone. The North African humans were descendants of the mixed-mutt simians who'd returned from Asia, and like them, the Northern community set out to discover new lands and new people. The humans of those two cultures were separated by a geographic boundary between the open savannahs of Northern Africa and the woodlands and dense rain forests of the South. The region between them is called The Transition Zone.

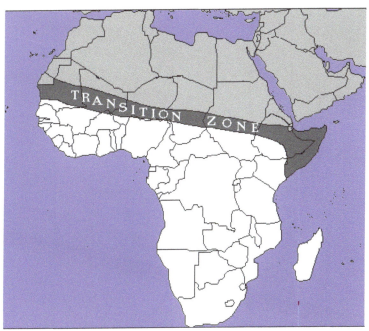

Africa's Transition Zone divided early humanity into the ethnically-mixed extroverts living in the North, and the less diverse introverts who remained in the South

In a May, 2016 article in the International Business Times, writer Avaneesh Pandey explained how climate change pushed the Asian simians back to Africa. Research from University of Kansas paleontologist K. Christopher Beard discovered that 34 million years ago there was a sudden drop in temperature and rainfall in many parts of the world. This forced humanity's primate ancestors to cluster around the equator and the tropics.

The severe cold and drought killed off the simian primates who'd settled far from the Equator, while others retreated to Africa where they found food and survived, Pandey explained. Without this global cooling event, the first humans might have evolved in Asia instead of Africa, the author noted. When the *Homo Sapiens* left Africa, they branched off into different families but continued to mix with each other and the shrinking population of older humans including Neanderthals and Denisovans.

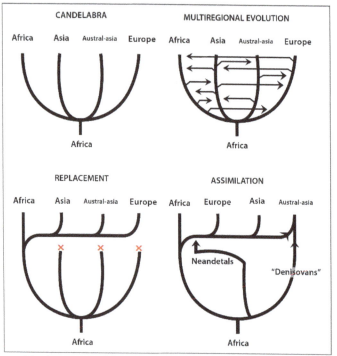

The history and family ties of modern and prehistoric humans seen in different ways

Research into the DNA of a 40,000 year old man who lived in Ice Age Europe showed the earliest Europeans had dark complexions and brown eyes. Humans with blue eyes arrived on the continent 14,000 years ago, followed by white-skinned people 7,000 years ago. The people who first brought blue eyes and white skin to Europe originally lived in Southwest Asia, the study found. In other words, light skin was not the result of living in northern environments. Research suggests the first large communities of lighter-skinned people were living in Southwest Asia before they migrated north.

Three hundred thousand years before *Homo Sapiens* came on the scene, ancestral human communities were conducting regular long distance trade in cosmetic clay and polished stones up and down the South African coast. The existence of those markets means that almost half a million years ago, humanity's ancestors already had a common language and a well-established culture of trade and travel. It appears the success of prehistoric human society was not the result of fierce competition. The human advantage was that people were friendly. *Homo Sapiens* were propelled to urban civilization and beyond because they were friendlier, more cooperative and greater risk-takers than earlier humans.

The secret of human success is that people like to party.

The word "party" originally meant a gathering where each person shared part of their food with a large group. Humanity flourished and human civilization was born because modern humans set out to meet new people, exchange gifts and information, trade local goods for foreign ones and intermarry. Earlier humans like Neanderthal isolated themselves in small communities. When conditions around them changed, they died out because they had limited contact with outsiders who might have helped, and no culture of innovation to search for a solution. Modern humans were more successful because they were better at networking. They shared and so they thrived.

"Good ideas took hold and spread just as they do today," Anthropology Professor Alison Brooks of the Columbian College of Arts and Sciences in Washington, D.C., told the 2012 World Science Festival in New York City. As people lived longer, more information was retained and passed from the older to the younger generations, she added.

Widespread human language was another milestone achieved through cooperation. By 40,000 years ago, four regional language groups had spread across humanity's vast trading areas and the descendants of those base languages can be found in almost every language in the modern world. A background check of almost any word will show its Indo-European, Afro-Asiatic, Austronesian or Sino-Tibetan origins.

The Sino-Tibetan family includes more than 400 languages including Chinese - they are second only to the Indo-European languages in terms of the number of native speakers

Today, Austronesian languages are spoken by nearly 400 million people

Afro-Asiatic languages are the world's fourth-largest group spoken by more than 350 million people – their ancient forms include Ancient Egyptian, Biblical Hebrew and Aramaic

Among early humans, words had a profound purpose. The development of language for trade, social interactions and the accumulation of reliable information meant words were more than just a common tool. Words were humanity's first money. Words allowed global trade to develop because words were highly valued. They were the currency each person minted on their own tongue. The importance early humans placed on words had to be very high because only words that were trusted were widely shared with others. Many old phrases reflect that heritage. A person's word was expected to be "as good as gold" and promises were always kept. In early human culture where words were valued like money, lying was non-existent. Lying was as unimaginable as stealing in the early human culture of honor and honesty.

The importance early humans placed on honesty in language shows up in the way the meaning of old words were changed to conform to a new culture. It is often assumed early humans were ignorant people who traded in imaginary falsehoods about gods of nature who created natural forces like thunder and lightning. However, humanity would not have survived or advanced if its founders were intellectually lazy or dishonest. It was only after the original culture of shared knowledge was lost and organized religions rose in its place that 'the gods did it' became the catch-all answer.

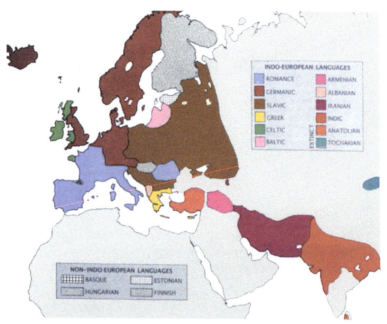

There are more than 400 Indo-European languages and dialects spoken by 3 billion people

The evolution of the word "thunder" shows this cultural change from individual observation to religious instruction. About 1,000 years ago, raiding Germanic tribes from Northern Europe spread the name of Thor - their god of storms - across the continent. Eventually, Thor's name was adopted as the new word for "thunder." But long before the Germanic invasion, the original word for "thunder" simply meant a big sound. In human history, individual investigation came before religious indoctrination.

Many people assume organized religion is one of the oldest, if not the oldest human practice. However, it is actually a very recent invention in the long history of human civilization. Sophisticated human expression began about 40,000 years ago when people started painting scenes of life and abstract symbols on rocks and inside caves. However, in the entire collection of 400 centuries of prehistoric cave art there is no representation of any god figure. For tens of thousands of years after the start of human painting, no portrait of a God or gods would be set down by any artist anywhere in the world. Assuming early humans did have a concept of a deity before the start of individual religious practices about 7,000 years ago, it is obvious the original concept of God was very different from that of modern times.

The lack of any representation of any deity makes one point clear – God had no special place as an actor in prehistoric human society. If early people had a concept of God, their Deity was like the air. The air surrounds and sustains all things, but no one praises the air twice a day or makes offerings to it. This spiritual sense without expression could be called a Formless Faith or an Invisible Religion.

Organized religion - the use of common rituals by several temples under a single leadership - began about 4,000 years ago. Before then, people improvised informal practices for their own reasons or they had no rituals because their faith was life. The first 3,000 years of Biblical history record that change. The first people of the Bible - the Ancient Hebrews - had no temples, religious laws or priests. It was the later Ancient Israelites who established their organized religion around 1300 BC. Organized religion was followed by the first Exclusive Religions that claimed superiority over others and the right to murder those who offended their God.

In modern religious sermons, the Deity is often described as a king and lawgiver. However, in the prehistoric world there were no kings or laws. So, how did the concept of God begin and why did it change? The way people perceived their Deity was a reflection of the world they lived in and understood. Peaceful societies imagined a peaceful, nurturing God, while warrior societies told stories of divine violence. The one common quality was that the Creator – however understood - was the source of knowledge.

In a world before books and teachers, people relied on their instincts to gather information about the world. They developed relationships with animals and plants in the natural world by asking them questions.

When early people heard answers as inner voices or through visual insights, those replies were thought to come from the living knowledge that unified all things and enabled their unique expression.

The concept of living knowledge was expressed in many early languages. In English, when people say "I have a book," the book is a thing with no life of its own. The Latin sentence *Est Mihi Liber* is typically translated as "I have a book." But the verb *est* expresses identity, being and life. So, "I have a book" actually carries the deeper meaning of "the book is sharing its knowledge with me."

Modern research has shown talking to animals may not be entirely one-sided. Studies of dogs have shown their brains process human words separately from intonation. In other words, they react to the meaning of specific words and ignore meaningless ones even when they are expressed with emotion.

The old Indo-European word for knowledge – Veda – has many descendant words in English. They include wisdom, spirit, visitor, stranger and guest. The combination of those meanings can be heard in the old Polish expression, "A guest has entered my house; God has entered my house." Here, the connection is made between all people - strangers and guests – and the spirit of knowledge (God) that lives within them.

Because early humans valued knowledge and shared insights as friends and neighbors, urban civilization and diverse markets were able to take root and thrive. Many people imagine "survival of the fittest" as another way of saying the strong will always dominate the weak. While that may be true in a one-on-one game of tennis, life would not have evolved and humanity would not have advanced without cooperation. Today, the word "competition" is used to mean a ruthless fight for supremacy with only one winner. However, the original meaning of competition was to "work together" and "come together." Competition meant the friendly rivalry of games, hunting matches and community building projects, not kill or be killed.

Working together for a common goal enabled people to share information and advance their skills, and complex human civilization was the long term result. Evolution is the story of success through cooperation. And it was kick-started when the earliest single-celled organisms began working together.

About 650-700 million years ago, Earth's entire climate suddenly changed from a globe of tropical seas to a giant Slurpee of icebergs and frigid water. Temperatures plunged worldwide, and Earth swirled like a gigantic slush ball for the next 120 million years. Deep ocean volcanoes continued to pump heat, creating energetic warm currents that pushed the sleety slurry around Snowball Earth. But for most of the single-celled organisms that had been swimming through a warm water paradise, life was over. It was the first great obliteration of almost all complex life on Earth – when complex life meant sponges.

In 2014, Malcolm Wallace, a professor of Earth Sciences at the University of Melbourne in Australia discovered strange clumps of fossils in remote regions of Australia and Namibia, Kate Ravilious wrote in her BBC article, *Earth Was a Frozen Snowball When Animals First Evolved.*

In the remains of ancient reefs, Wallace found 700 million year old bubble-shaped fossils that were connected in a network of finger-like strands, Ravilious wrote. That simple organization of cooperative organisms may have been the first stepping stone to multicellular animals and human life, Wallace told the BBC. Every sophisticated form of animal life that followed was made possible by the cooperative work of those long ago sponges.

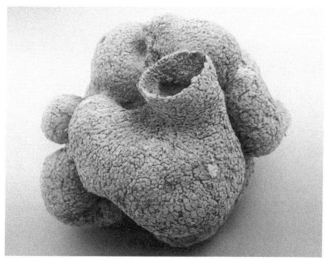

Simple cells advanced through cooperation - 600 million year old fossil of early sponge found in China (Photo: Science Magazine)

In the same article, Biology Professor Richard Boyle of the University of Southern Denmark in Odense said it is no coincidence complex life first appeared during and after the hardships of Snowball Earth. When the going gets tough, the tough work together and cells begin to specialize, he said.

Boyle thinks survival pressures caused by the 120 million year-long Slush Age gave rise to cell specialization. Specialization is a cell's way of giving up the freelance life and applying for a job. An individual cell abandons its 'me alone' attitude and picks up work as a full-time specialist in a larger company of cells with a common goal. Human blood cells, for example, go about their jobs while the digestive system provides them with nutrients, skin cells protect them and bones reproduce for them.

Cooperation among intelligent disease fighters inside the human body protects people from early death, and this sophisticated biotechnology was first created 400 million years ago. Before then, the population of Earth was mostly simple, grazing life forms that sucked up food in mouth openings without jaws. They vacuumed up the same food every day, so they had little need for a sophisticated internal protection force. When one of those early life forms accidentally sucked in something deadly, they accidentally died. Then a new kind of creature appeared, one with a hinged jaw that could rip up the body of its prey and swallow chunks of it as food.

A hinged jaw with teeth is basically a sword and a shield had to follow. With each bite, the attackers swallowed a multitude of potential dangers. The old system could not defend against so many possibilities. It needed allies and found them in its undigested food. Some immune defenders in the creature they were devouring managed to escape death and find a new purpose in the army of volunteers defending their new host. The descendants of that allied force of defenders remain at work as the adaptive immune system in humans.

Cross-species cooperation enabled sea plants to colonize the land. Four hundred and fifty million years ago, a beneficial fungi moved into the roots of some sea plants giving them the ability to breathe air and take root on land, according to authors Dianna and Mark McMenamin in their 1996 book, *Hypersea*.

Once established, plants continued their culture of cooperation. A 2015 article on the BBC web site assembled a variety of experts in plant intelligence. Suzanne Simard, a professor of forest ecology at the University of British Columbia, told the BBC every tree in a forest is linked to every other tree through their underground roots which form a "wood wide web." They use these pathways to talk with each other, she explained. Plants have social relationships, memories, the ability to solve problems and they are known to warn other plants of attack by insects.

Plants are intelligent "but they move much more slowly than animals so we need to record plant movement for many days," Prof. Stefano Mancuso, head of the International Laboratory for Plant Neurobiology at the University of Florence, told the BBC.

"We did an experiment with two climbing bean plants. If you put a single support between them, they compete for it. What is interesting is the behaviour of the loser: it immediately sensed the other plant had reached the pole and started to find an alternative. This was astonishing and it demonstrates the plants were aware of their physical environment and the behaviour of the other plant. In animals we call this consciousness," the professor said. Studies into plants suggest their main form of communication and knowledge gathering is by releasing and detecting different odors.

It is known that plants are much more sensitive to their environment than animals. The tip of a plant root can detect and measure 20 different physical and chemical properties including light, gravity, magnetic fields and pathogens. Does all this mean plants have individual personalities and the ability to reason without a brain?

In animals the main cells that transmit information to the rest of the body through electric signals are located in the brain. But plants have a kind of full body brain in which almost every cell is able to produce electrical signals, Prof. Mancuso explained.

Recently, scientists in Britain taught a group of bumblebees to pull a string to get to food and found the bees shared this knowledge with other bees. Clint Perry, one of the researchers from Queen Mary University of London, said this showed the ability to learn and pass along new knowledge is not limited to humans or a function of brain size.

There are more individual cells in the human body than there are stars in the Milky Way Galaxy. When cells work together they form tissues like human skin. When tissues advance, they combine and restructure to form organs like the heart. Organs cooperate through networks such as the skeleton and nervous system. And the teamwork of all those cells and living communities, along with billions of independent organisms living on and inside the human body, is what allows each person to go about their lives imagining they are independent.

Advanced evolution clearly favors cooperation and innovation over the go-it-alone, one size fits all strategy.

Early human society advanced quickly because men and women were free to form relationships with anyone or no one. Women's equality in prehistoric society enabled the rapid spread of knowledge and genes. Women acted as social lubricators encouraging the men they knew to become friends with each other. More importantly, women typically passed along more information about other people and what they were doing than men. So when women were able to move between groups of men, more information was shared with more people.

In a May 15, 2015 article in London's Guardian Newspaper, Science Writer Hannah Devlin said that despite the stereotype of macho cavemen dominating human culture until women demanded equality in recent times, the reverse is actually true. Equality between men and women was the starting point and gender inequality the later development. Mark Dyble, an anthropologist at University College London, told the Guardian that sexual equality was vital to early human social advancement and brain development. Social equality encouraged the transfer of information between people and spurred the development of complex language skills, he explained. Gender equality is a human trait that made people different from apes, Dyble told the paper.

"Chimpanzees live in quite aggressive, male-dominated societies with clear hierarchies" that are closed to unrelated outsiders, he said. Because of this resistance to change, apes don't share resources or seek out new ideas.

In the prehistoric world, the spread of knowledge through change and innovation happened slowly and not everywhere or all at once. It appeared and disappeared. But like bubbles in a slowly boiling pot of water, humanity was always moving.

Human appearance and human society has changed in many ways over the past 3 million years. But among all those changes, one stands out as the most important. It was an evolutionary development that took place over millions of years. The lack of it pushed humanity's ancestors out of the trees and onto the ground. And when it was fully formed, humanity would discover freedom, individuality and a new definition of what it meant to be human.

CHAPTER 2

THE IMPORTANCE OF BEING BALANCED

Hindu God Shiva - the Great Balancer of creation and destruction

The word "evolution" comes from two Indo-European words that date back more than 30,000 years. One is an ancient word for womb - *ulvam*, and the other is the word *wel* that means "to change" and "will."

At its root, evolution means "changes that take place in the womb as a result of individual will." Humans saw that all living things change in appearance and abilities as they are born, take shape and achieve maturity. The seed looks nothing like the plant that grows from it.

People observed that mastering skills for hunting and fishing changed the shape of their body with new muscles. That was the early concept of evolution – physical changes that resulted from the will to achieve a goal. That ancient logic has contemporary supporters. Modern research has shown that the mind can influence genetic expression in the womb and after birth. Large-scale evolutionary change is driven by large-scale events. When conditions are abundant, life combines and flourishes in a great explosion of diversity. When the environment is challenging and resources are scarce - such as after an asteroid strike – rapid adaptations take place to cope with the new reality.

The first stand-up, tool-using humans appeared about 3 million years ago. For the next 2.9 million years, little changed. At the start, there were at least six different species of humans that roamed the world. Some discovered how to hammer certain rocks against other stones so that chips would flake off. This left the rock with a sharp point they used as a hand axe and scraper. For a million years the primitive hand axe was humanity's only invention and they were happy that way. Humans wore no clothes, slept in the open and ate raw food. Prehistoric, Ice Age fruits and vegetables were dense with fibres, harder to chew and less nutritious than modern varieties. To improve their diet, people formed groups to hunt large animals and share the meat, bones and hides. This promoted skill development, planning and a group identity. Then, about 2 million years ago, some humans began a recycling program. They picked up the pointed chips that fell off when sharpening their axes and used them as needles for sewing. And so humans began to wear clothes.

By 400,000 years ago, human culture was well-established. Humans joined with each other through their use of language and the trading of gifts. Modern humans are called *Homo Sapien* ("People of Insight"), and when they appeared 100,000 years ago they entered a world populated by earlier humans called Neanderthals, Denisovans, the Cro-Magnons, *Homo Erectus* and Pygmy people.

The last of the old humans to die out was the Neanderthals. For nearly 300,000 years, their villages could be found in Europe, the Middle East and as far as China. Like other prehistoric humans, they had knowledge of herbal medicines and chewed the aspirin-like bark of poplar trees to relieve tooth aches. They made it through the Ice Age and survived in isolated pockets until as recently as 30,000 years ago. So, why did Neanderthal drop dead before the finish line and why did the *Homo Sapien* branch of humanity thrive? What made modern humans different?

People have always wanted to look their best - 100,000 years ago, abalone shells were a compact make-up kit for red ochre paste

The answer leads to the most profound change in human evolution. It was a small change to an inner structure behind the ear, near the brain. It changed the way humans perceived the world and their own identity. That change in perception resulted in the desire for larger communities, increased trade and new invention. Because of this development, the modern human identity of freedom, individual identity and urban society was born, and space travel was made possible.

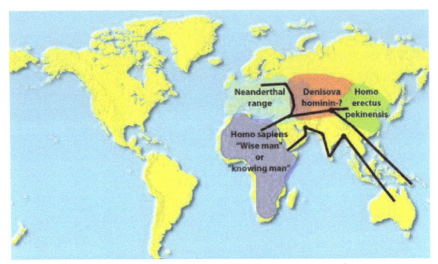

Ancient humans of many kinds began roaming the
world more than a million years ago

That change in the structure of the vestibular system – the circular canals and nerves behind the ear - gave modern humans a huge advantage over the older models. Modern humans were equipped with a new kind of software that changed the way they understood the world, the way they moved through it, and how they related to other people. The catalyst that propelled *Homo Sapiens* beyond humanity's earlier ancestors was an improved sense of balance.

It can be argued that a sense of balance exists within all things. Indeed, long before the appearance of humans, animals, birds and fish possessed sophisticated balancing systems. Research from the University of Alberta suggests the ancestors of two-legged dinosaurs like T-Rex developed better balance so they could stand upright and run faster. Modern research has suggested poor balance may have been why humanity's distant ancestors stopped living in trees – they kept falling down. And indeed, the fossil record shows a more primitive vestibular balance system that gradually grew sophisticated over millions of years as upright humans increased the distance of their walking, running and attempts at climbing.

As their balance improved, modern humans would grow taller and travel farther in the world than earlier humans like Neanderthal who had a less-developed sense of balance. When humans are physically fit, men have a V-shape from their chest to their waists and women have curves that roll out in and out again. No matter how many workouts Neanderthals took up, they could never look like a well-toned human. Neanderthals' rib cage flares out not in like a human. At their Hollywood best Neanderthals looked like a dense block of muscles with limbs attached. Their square structure was necessary because they had a less developed sense of balance. Without that sophisticated software, they had to rely on a square central mass and thick, muscular legs for stability. Poor balance skills determined Neanderthal culture and resulted in their extinction.

Like other humans, Neanderthals used stone tools, painted their bodies with red clay and buried their dead with ceremonies. They had larger brains than *Homo Sapiens* and Neanderthals left Africa much earlier than modern humans. However, their limited balance skills meant Neanderthals were risk averse. Without a perfect sense of balance, Neanderthals had to be more cautious about where they traveled and what physical feats they attempted. This influenced their outlook, and so Neanderthals resisted change because they feared new people and new ways would undermine the stability of their lives.

As a result of their introverted, risk-averse culture, Neanderthals did not develop interconnected communities or express their individuality with cave paintings, and poor balance kept them from exploring hard-to-access places. They were not driven to experiment or socialize. Instead, when the environment around them changed beyond their ability to cope, Neanderthals huddled together in isolated groups dying off one by one. When they could no longer access their traditional sources of food due to bad weather or the presence of modern humans, Neanderthals hid out in their remote villages scratching food from a shrinking supply and slowly starving to death. Neanderthal was not able to innovate, adapt or cooperate with others. In effect, they committed species suicide because they wouldn't change their diet.

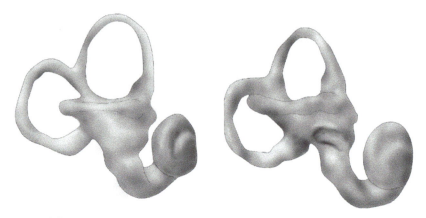

The simpler Neanderthal vestibular system shows they lacked good balance and that led to a cautious culture

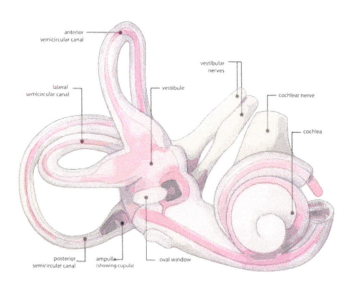

The modern vestibular system gave humans better balance and a new understanding of freedom and individuality

Genetic research shows humans were mating with Neanderthals and other ancient cousins and produced children. About 4 percent of modern people have Neanderthal ancestors. Traits including freckles, red hair and a high forehead all come from the Neanderthal line. This heritage is most common in Europe where Neanderthals had a large presence. The Neanderthal family line remains with modern people because humans embraced diversity from the start. The absence of human traits in Neanderthals shows the interbreeding was largely one-way. And indeed, genetic research has shown that Neanderthal genes in modern people were all inherited from Neanderthal women who mated with human men. Neanderthal men either avoided contact with human females or could not successfully reproduce with them. It appears human-Neanderthal children were accepted by humans because they reproduced and passed their genes along until the last of the Neanderthals died out about 30,000 years ago.

In contrast to the inward-looking Neanderthals, humans were wild adventurers who feared nothing. And that change from the old human identity to the new one was only made possible because modern humans were better balanced. In the modern world, there are common phrases such as "centre (balance) yourself," and "find your inner balance." Those concepts are unique to the modern human family. Earlier humans could not grasp that concept because they didn't have an individual sense of balance that moved and adjusted itself with the speed of modern humans and their new balancing software.

Each person's center of gravity now moved with them as they gyrated in any direction. That change stirred individual awareness and perceptions of the world in ways that had not been possible before.

Humans with better balance were bolder than their ancestors. For these new humans, no environment or passageway was inaccessible. They could climb upside down on rock faces, swing from vines like Tarzan or hand paddle a log across a rolling river and always be able to return to upright balance. This physical change in the way humans sensed the world produced the modern concepts of human freedom and individuality by giving people an unlimited scope of movement and a center of balance that moved with them. The high value early humans placed on balance was the foundation of human civilization in the same way stability was for Neanderthal. The culture of balance was expressed in human communities as they grew in size – bringing more people together with equal presence, sharing more information between communities and experimenting with constructions. By 30,000 years ago, humanity's grasp of balance led to the first manmade shelters assembled from tree bark, grass, mud and stones.

The cultural importance of balance in prehistoric human society was passed down to the modern world in symbols like the scales of justice and the many religions and philosophies that stress the importance of a balanced life.

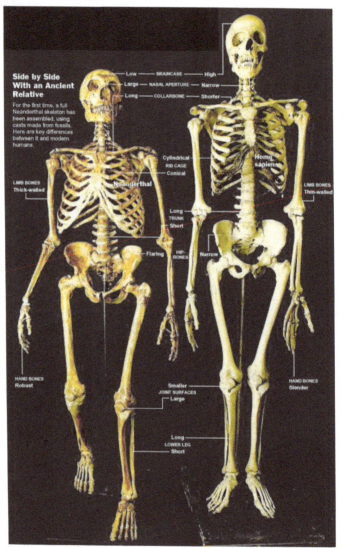

Balanced humans grew tall, but Neanderthal remained short and stocky

The last Neanderthals died out about 24,000 years ago. It's thought their final refuge was a cave in the island of Gibraltar where the skeletal remains of a Neanderthal family were found. They were trapped on the island when sea levels rose and they could not carve a boat, build a bridge or swim away from their secluded prison. They could not function in the human world that thrived on individual imagination and group innovation. When Neanderthals looked up and saw a bird flying in the sky, all they could perceive was something moving in the air. They could not imagine flying themselves because they lacked the balance software for understanding how a bird maneuvered. *Homo Sapiens* and their descendants however, could imagine soaring and turning in space because they had the same calculating software as the birds and the empathy to sense the possibility of flight and any other achievement of the natural world.

CHAPTER 3

THE FIRST BOOK WAS A STATUE

Human civilization picked up speed with expanded language, larger communities and the distribution of new skills and ideas. Around 40,000 years ago, people started experimenting with new ways to communicate. They created symbols to represent human activities, ideas and the world around them. Two of the oldest abstract symbols are the hashtag, a symbol for "human lands," and the asterisk which carried the meanings "spread out, create" and "to join." With the rise of organized religion, the asterisk became a symbol for God - the creator, joiner and multiplier." They appear alongside the 40,000 year old cave paintings of animals and human activities.

Another symbol of early human culture was the widespread use of friendship beads. First used as a universal greeting, this original human craft would later serve as a form of currency. But its enduring purpose was its value as a symbol of worldwide human trust.

Early human innovations were typically directed to one of two goals – improving their quality of life or making new friends. Shared words and language allowed more people to work together in their search for food, shelter and mates. However, words were not always useful when meeting new people or other humans. A more universal greeting was required to signal welcome. Humans wondered, what symbol or action would be universally recognized as a friendly greeting by all people? Physical gestures - whether a wave, a bow or a smile - could be misunderstood. So humans invented friendship beads.

In prehistoric settlements, the remains of polished shells and stone beads are everywhere. Most are punctured with a hole, indicating they were once worn as a necklace, anklet or bracelet. In some graves, thousands of beads and shells have been left behind along with the person's remains. Some researchers believe graves with lots of prehistoric bling indicate the deceased was a person of high rank and personal wealth. However, the early humans who made them were self-reliant hunters and gatherers who kept few possessions, and their communities had no social divisions.

Humanity's first universal greeting was a friendship offering - a necklace or bracelet of polished stones or decorative shells strung together

If the beads weren't a prehistoric status symbol, what did they signify? They were humanity's first common way of saying, "Let's exchange gifts and be friends." The craftwork of artistic beads and shells served as gift offerings in life, and after death they were used like flowers on a modern grave. The more flowers or shells, the more the deceased was loved by many people. Strings of stone beads, seashells and animal horns were used as the Stone Age version of a business card, credit card and social ice breaker. When early humans met, new styles of beads would be a topic of common interest because beads were the first fashion product that changed. Whenever they dropped into some prehistoric networking site, people would develop their social and language skills by complementing each other's beads.

"Hey, like your beads. Very pre-modern."

"You're too kind. I got them from a master bead polisher."

"The one with the matted hair who lives by the seaside and eats raw clams?"

"Yep. That's the one."

"Love his work."

"Well then, let me give you a necklace of beads."

"Oh no, I couldn't just take them."

"I insist. It's a gift."

"Thank you. Now you must come with me to my village. I have some ochre paste just in from the village down the road and it's fabulous."

"Cool. Let's go."

And so a system of personal introduction, economic development and the idea of a human commonwealth was born through the exchange of sea shells and cosmetics.

In the modern Western world, gift-giving is usually reserved for special occasions. But in the old tradition, people always brought a gift for their host when they visited someone. Modern people who carry on this practice are following the tradition that first joined humans with gifts of friendship. Modern companies that promote their "free gift" use the psychological bait of a prehistoric friendship offering, even though the reality of acceptance may be quite unfriendly.

Between 40,000 and 20,000 years ago, humanity's first painters crafted their work in caves and on rocks around the world. They produced so much creative expression that after first seeing prehistoric cave art, the Spanish artist Pablo Picasso lamented, "We have learned nothing in twelve thousand years."

Pablo Picasso saw the skill and perspective of prehistoric painters and said, humanity had learned nothing new about art in 12,000 years

By 20,000 years ago, most humans lived in round homes made from animal hides, bark, dirt, rocks and plant materials. They'd learned to make fabrics for clothes, rope for fish nets and thread for sewing.

In prehistoric and ancient human communities, women were seen as bearers of life who possessed a special knowledge separate from men. And so, the quality of wisdom was often personalized as a goddess. She was called Athena among the Ancient Greeks of 3,000 years ago and Inanna by the Sumerians and Akkadians of Mesopotamia 4,000 years ago. The high value placed on wise women and their insights into life may have inspired the world's first best-selling book at a time when humanity had not yet invented writing or paper.

From about 30,000 years ago to 20,000 years ago, a new invention suddenly appeared in human communities throughout Europe, the Middle East and Asia. But this innovation was not a tool. It was the world's first leisure commodity – a product unconnected to any known work or obligation. Today, those works of art are collectively known as the Venus Statues.

The 25,000 year old Venus of Willendorf was not a fertility goddess but the world's first book

These palm-sized statues typically depict a naked or semi-naked woman whose breasts and hips, legs and vulva are emphasised. There is much debate on the meaning and purpose of these small statues. So, what is known about them?

The Venus statues appeared at a time when many people were abandoning the life of wandering hunters for the benefits of living in or near an established urban center with its many goods and people. It was an era of prosperity and people had time for art and philosophy. The portable Venus figures were crafted from clay and limestone, animal bones and ivory and in their time, they were popular across the developing world. Like friendship beads, many statues have a thread hole indicating they were worn on a necklace and made to be portable. Although these figures have been found over a huge geographic area, the numbers of them are small. This suggests they were not commonly used as a decoration or traded as currency. Rather, people copied the figures as if they were a book in the public domain. This rush to read and replicate the first carved book of 30,000 BC, would be repeated when the first books with writing were popularized in Ancient Egypt around 2400 BC. And like all books when they first appeared, the Venus statues were a marvel of new technology mainly used by a particular group of people found in all communities – the wealthy and the educated.

The name, Venus statues, was given to them by modern researchers. The statues have no connection to the later Roman Goddess Venus or the planet named for her.

30,000-20,000 years ago, the Venus statues were the best-selling book in the prehistoric world

As the majority of known Venus Statues were created more than 20,000 years ago during a period of prosperity and gender equality in human society, what did they represent?

Most historians call this figure a fertility goddess. But, there are many problems with that interpretation. There are no representations of this alleged goddess anywhere else. She is not found in the cave paintings or among the rock drawings. There is also no evidence of any organized religion anywhere in human society 20,000 years ago, let alone one that united worshipers on multiple continents. There is no other example of a major deity figure that, like this Venus, has no known name, associated divine beings or legendary stories, and vanishes into history without leaving any trace of their existence in later religions.

If the statues weren't symbols of a deity, they were created as part of humanity's larger quest - to explore new knowledge and record their observations in a permanent form like the cave symbols and paintings. Because the Venus figures were used by people across the world, it must have embodied a widely understood meaning that expressed the highest values of human culture.

As they were not used for trade or worship, their portable size and imitated form indicate its use as a visual tool for meditation and intellectual reflection. Seen this way, the Venus Statues were the world's first book. A book is something that carries a fixed form of information the reader can return to repeatedly in their search for new insights.

The statue's design removes the common human features of feet and hands and focuses solely on uniquely feminine ones. This peculiar form of these statues may be a deliberate attempt to provoke thought association, like a 20,000 year old Rorschach test. The statues have similar exaggerated features. This is a book with a theme, but what is it? If the Venus statues were created to be read like a book, it is necessary to consider the way human understanding develops.

Intellectual development follows a predictable pattern as people grow out of a life of simple survival and enter one of increased self-awareness and deeper questions. Those steps are described by the American psychologist Abraham Maslow in his hierarchy of needs.

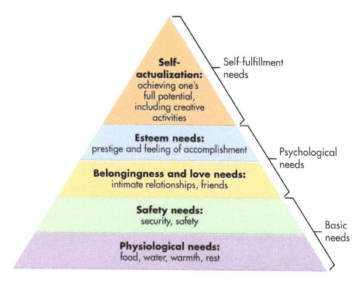

Maslow's Hierarchy of Needs explains why early humans created Venus as a book to 'read'

The peak of the pyramid is called "Self-Actualization." Self-actualization happens when people begin to ask deep questions.

"Who am I and what is the purpose of my life?"

That is the starting point of every philosophic quest. If the Venus statues were a book addressing those questions, then the title of humanity's first best-selling book was, *Ask a Woman*.

If the statues were a book representing female knowledge, then each exaggerated physical feature was a chapter meant to inspire insight. The statue's bulging breasts, hips, thighs and vulva were meant to steer the reader's thoughts away from the pleasures of sex and direct them to consider what a woman represented as a symbol of human life. She was meant to provoke questions – even if the answers would not be fully understood until modern times. What is the life-giving nature of mother's milk (chemistry)? Why is it white (physics)? What is the nature of the birthing machine of the hips and vulva (anatomy)? If different kinds of humans are born from women, is the secret of life in the birth canal or behind the stomach (genetics)? In most of the statues the woman's face is hidden behind a pattern of dots or lines. Those early binary symbols likely represent the creative thoughts of the female mind (psychology).

Despite their popularity, the Venus statues were a prehistoric fad. After about 10,000 years, people stopped using them and knowledge of their original purpose was lost. When the good times of leisure and literature ended, the statues were abandoned like a trinket that is no longer fashionable. And, hard times of bad weather did hit the human world in the post-Venus era of 20,000-12,000 years ago. Shifting climate patterns once again made finding food difficult in a colder and drier world. And until it reverted back to mild, most humans struggled to survive. There was little time for leisure and no interest in new ideas. The challenges of daily life were hard enough and even when better weather returned, the impulse for collective inventiveness remained frozen.

Fortunately, one group of people were determined to wake humanity from its intellectual apathy. Those pioneers of 12,000 years ago fanned the embers of civilization back to a glowing blaze that reinvigorated the human world. Their tremendous, collective effort would have far-reaching and unforeseen consequences. The long-lasting impact of their work would include humanity's first effort at mass education, the development of large-scale farming and the near-global spread of a genetic change that started a milk-drinking craze across most of the world.

To launch their revolution they built a prehistoric Wikipedia – a gathering place where people could access all the available knowledge in the world. It was a temple of learning meant to serve all humanity.

What they built was the world's first university.

CHAPTER 4

THE CLASS OF 10,000 BC

Gobekli Tepe is a 12,000 year old archeological site in Southeast Turkey. Its name means "Potbelly Hill," and refers to the 50 foot-high mountain ridge that is the site of its fantastic ruins. The first buildings may have been constructed 15,000 years ago, but the central site where 20 buildings once stood is more recent. The remains of winding stone walls and well-worn paths curve around more than a dozen circular rooms. Towering above the walls are elaborately carved T-shaped rock pillars. More than 200 of them have been recovered, and each one weighs between 7 and 50 tonnes. Prehistoric people cut out and hauled these boulders to the hilltop where they shaped and artistically decorated them with nothing more than simple stone tools. This stupendous feat of human cooperation and ingenuity took place 6,000 years before Stonehenge and 7,000 years before the construction of Ancient Egypt's Great Pyramid at Giza.

Whatever was happening at Gobekli 12,000 years ago, its buildings were planned, constructed and decorated by an unknown community of hunter-gatherers who dedicated themselves to its initial construction. Those founders and their descendants kept this institution going for 4,000 years. On the pillars, there are carvings of local animals like gazelles alongside alligators that must have been brought to this site in Turkey from thousands of miles away. Yet, the purpose of the images is unknown.

Gobekli sits at the northern tip and crossroads of the ancient lands called the Fertile Crescent. Despite its central location, there is little evidence of any large-scale, permanent settlement or burial grounds at this site. However, its growth from one building to twenty and its four thousand year lifespan indicates that at one time this was a major gathering spot for huge numbers of transient people. Why did so many people travel to this site, stay for a time and then leave? What was the attraction?

The 20,000 year old university at Gobekli Tepe was built at the northern crossroads of the Fertile Crescent (Courtesy: Bjoertvedt)

In a November 2008 article in *Smithsonian Magazine*, writer Andrew Curry explained the latest research. Eleven thousand years ago the hilltops near Gobekli were covered with barley and wild wheat, fruit and nut-bearing trees, and clear rivers and ponds that attracted geese and ducks, archaeologist Klaus Schmidt told Curry.

"This area was like a paradise," Schmidt said.

Many settlements dotted the regional landscape, but Gobekli was not connected to any of them. So, what was its purpose? Among archaeologists and historians, its buildings are routinely described as the remains of the world's oldest religious temple. Schmidt called Gobekli humanity's first "hilltop cathedral." Genetic analysis of modern wheat shows it was first cultivated for large-scale consumption at the same time as Gobekli and on hillsides close to it. Historians who call it a religious shrine believe so many worshipers were attending its services that a massive increase in food production and new agricultural technology was needed to feed them all. Whatever its original purpose, Stanford University archaeologist Ian Hodder told the *Smithsonian*, this prehistoric site may be the real starting point of multi-faceted, complex human society.

Despite the common consensus, Gobekli is not a relic of the world's first religious temple, but the world's oldest university. It could not have been a gathering spot for organized religious worshipers at that time because there were no organized religions 12,000 years ago. The site has no obvious religious purpose. There are no altars, images of gods or sacred symbols. More to the point, if it launched the era of community worship why did it take 7,000 years before anyone else built a temple?

Its pillar images include a crocodile or alligator. These are not local animals and the artist must have seen them, which means those reptiles were brought to Gobekli from their natural habitats in Egypt or China. If visitors came there to pray, why would they travel long distances with those animals? Was there a special seating section for dangerous reptiles?

A 12,000 year old pillar at Gobekli University shows a wild boar

If it was a religious site, it would have grown from a local culture as no one else used temples or conducted mass worship ceremonies that required them. Had that been the case, there would be no need to develop large-scale agriculture because visitors would have limited need for food during a brief visit. If it was a local temple, why wasn't it built near the community that wanted it? Why did its builders spend so much time, energy and effort on a distant shrine when no one else had temples of any kind?

Simply put, "Why would masses of people leave their homes and families and travel long distances to Gobekli, only to stand in a circle and worship an unfamiliar God in an unfamiliar way?"

Simply answered, "They wouldn't."

If the draw wasn't religious, what was the buzz that moved so many men and women to that isolated spot in southeast Turkey? It was the same excitement that drives people today. They came there to meet new people and discover new ways to improve their lives. Gobekli was a center of learning. Its pillars are the walls of world's first university built by the Class of 10,000 BC. It was a human library, the world's original site for mass socializing, and an emblem of humanity's Age of Knowledge.

Gobekli was the world's first university and its grounds were the first campus. Its establishment sparked the development of complex societies because it was a gathering spot where people shared all the knowledge available in the human world. It was a prehistoric Wikipedia, and it was built to spread human knowledge and establish the foundation of something new - global human civilization.

What evidence supports the thesis that it was the University of Gobekli?

Researchers including Stanford's Hodder have noted that the same innovations in technology such as building similarly-styled pens for animals began to appear around the region of Gobekli during its lifetime. While those developments could be coincidental, it does suggest a common, shared source of information.

Human culture in the Stone Age was created by people who swapped stories and useful bits of information with neighbors and visitors. Language use expanded because it was a useful tool for trade and to retain knowledge that could be passed down to younger generations. For most of human history, the sum of human knowledge was the number of living people, and those nodes of knowledge died with each person. If a family of skilled people perished, a library was lost. To remember what they'd learned and to help them teach others, people invented catchy phrases, rhymes and other memory aids. "Doe a deer, a female deer, ray a drop of golden sun," is a poem to remember the notes of the musical scale and it's based on that oldest of human devices for teachings and learning.

As people's skills and use of tools, crafts, medicinal plants and animals grew more complex and specialized, more mnemonics had to be learned. Memory and recall were strengthened as the human brain was rewired for higher learning. Gaining expertise in advanced skills required extra knowledge. Sometimes, that new information was supplied by traveling teachers who gathered seeds of information in one village and planted it in another. They were the freelance journalists of the Stone Age and they traveled from village to village sharing the latest gossip or practical information in exchange for a meal or some other gift. If these itinerant teacher used poetry to tell their stories, people might say they "sang for their supper."

Before the rise of Gobekli, changing weather spread hard times across the world. As a result, most traveling teachers were unemployed. Feeding those visitors was a luxury people could no longer afford. But, like the single celled sponges millions of years before, a determined group of those unemployed educators overcame the challenges of their time by joining together. They were intellectual entrepreneurs and they solved their problem by setting up the world's first school as a make-work project.

20-tonne T-shaped pillars stood beside the school's circular rooms

The teachers must have offered lessons in practical skills – hunting and fishing, medicine and the care of animals. The idea was to make each student a teacher who would share what they learned with their home community. This would spread knowledge across the world and promote the concept of a united and global human civilization. The plan to revive humanity's love of learning succeeded beyond their wildest dreams. As word of the new campus spread, waves of diverse people began flowing to Gobekli from across the Fertile Crescent.

Recent findings support this conclusion. People in this region are known to be the world's first large-scale farmers – cultivating wheat and other grains. While it was long assumed farming was invented by a single group of people, DNA analysis of those 10,000 year old farmers has shown they were a multicultural community that included people from Afghanistan, Pakistan and Iran, Dr. Garrett Hellenthal of University College London told the BBC in a July 2016 article.

By assembling and diffusing the sum of human understanding, Gobekli pioneered the concept that humanity was one family and its purpose was to spread its civilization and culture of knowledge around the world. It was those far-thinking teachers and students of 12,000 years ago who first envisioned and promoted the idea of an all-inclusive and interconnected human civilization as the model for humanity's future.

Because its purpose was global, not local, it was built away from established villages. To give their school visual importance they set it on a hilltop.

Young boys at school in Ancient Egypt - 7,000 years after Gobekli

Students, teachers, teachers' assistants, tourists, merchants and others traveled in and out of Gobekli in great caravans of people. Early entertainers may have had their first public performances at Gobekli.

New classrooms were built. Nearby tent cities must have flourished with excited locals and visitors from distant lands. New ideas were shared. This transfer of information makes sense if the site was a school, but has no relevance if Gobekli was a temple.

The cultivation of wheat and other grains was likely a development of the school's agriculture department spurred on by the increasing population of semi-permanent and transient people. The animal figures carved in the pillars may have been a teaching aid and coproduction of the departments of art and science. Foreign animals would have been brought to Gobekli for show and tell, and possibly left behind in its prehistoric zoo.

Gobekli's influence on the future course of human civilization was immeasurable. It was a center of knowledge and the world's first social networking site for people from around the world. It reawakened and accelerated humanity's intellectual progress, and set the template for every school that followed.

Beyond those impressive achievements, as people from East and West mingled on its campus relationships developed. As a result of that contact, the milk-drinking people living the Middle East and West Asia began their mass migration into the lands of the lactose intolerant people of Europe and North Africa. Until that crossbreeding of Western people with the Asian newcomers, most adult humans could not drink milk or digest most milk products. The enzyme that broke down milk sugars stopped working after infancy. If they tried to drink animal milk, the result would be muscle cramps and gas pain. However, large numbers of people living in the Middle East and West Asia were not lactose intolerant. They had an enzyme that kept working throughout life. And when a mass migration of those Eastern milk-drinking people began to move west, spreading their culture and mixing families, humanity's diet was forever changed.

There is a close time link between the era of Gobekli (12,000-8,000 years ago) and the western advancement of the Eastern cow culture (11,000-7,000 years ago). It may be that migration was initiated by contact between the two groups at Gobekli. Without that genetic mixing, most humans today would only be able to eat fermented milk products like yogurt and low sugar cheeses like Parmesan. The oldest evidence of cheese-making dates back about 7,000 years. So in the human diet of 12,000 years ago there was vegetarian food and meat, but no milk, butter or double dip ice cream.

There was also no finance capital or capitalism because the word "capital" was born from the cow culture. Capital - in the sense of property or possessions - comes from an ancient word for "cattle." The meaning of the Latin word for "great personal wealth" is "they have lots of cows." To have cows was to be wealthy, and to have herds of cows was the sign of a prosperous community.

Cows were honored and celebrated for the many benefits they brought to human society. They ploughed fields and carried loads. Cow dung was wet fertilizer and when dried, it was burned for fuel. Because cow dung is antiseptic, it was used for house cleaning and to protect wounds from infection. Much later, in the 1700s, the English doctor Edward Jenner noticed that milk maids – young women who milked cows and churned milk into butter and cheese – were not getting sick from the deadly smallpox virus. He used this knowledge to create the world's first vaccine – a word that also comes from a word for "cow."

Modern historians frequently say the incoming cow people displaced the lactose intolerant people already living in Europe. More accurately, the evidence shows the locals adopted the cow culture and mixed with the newcomers because they perceived the health benefits of milk and the advantages of keeping cows and bulls as livestock. As a result, the gene for lactose tolerance and the culture of bovine admiration spread across multiple continents.

Contemporary research has shown children who regularly drink milk grow taller than those who don't. The incoming people of the cattle culture likely towered over the non-milk-drinking Europeans who mixed with the short-statured Neanderthals. The locals may have been so awestruck by their height, they called these newcomers from the East, 'giants.' That migration of long-legged milk-lovers may have been the original inspiration for all the tall tales of giants that followed. And so the two groups mingled and Eastern cow culture spread over the Western lands of Europe and North Africa like cream cheese on a bagel.

There are two final things to consider about Gobekli.

It was there the first, long-lasting social division was created. The existence of the school gave birth to a new kind of language. Its teachers had to invent new words for innovative tools and techniques and so they coined words for the world's first academic language. At all schools, there are two speaking styles – the informal one of the campus and the specialized one of the classroom. The Proto Indo-European teaching language developed at Gobekli would be brought to India and later evolve into Sanskrit – the world's oldest known scholarly language.

India's ancient traditions claim its Age of Knowledge – the Vedic Era – was launched by families who brought their wisdom to India from a school in the "Arctic." It is generally thought "Arctic" referred to a cold place in central Asia - such as southeast Turkey. Genetic research supports the idea that the founders of Ancient India's earliest culture came from the region of Gobekli. One of the largest chromosomal families in the region of Turkey is Haplogroup R, which is also a major family group in India and, according to some research, Ancient Egypt as well.

That genetic trail suggests people who studied at Gobekli migrated to India where they established themselves as the region's first educated families, later called the Brahmans. Initially, the knowledge-wealthy families worked to ensure the benefits of education were widely shared. But later generations of Brahmans said they were born to rule forever. That generation of leaders was the first to restrict access to knowledge. Social rules made it difficult for lower-class people to associate with those of higher rank, and the high payments demanded by aristocratic teachers kept knowledge from spreading widely. The tool of knowledge for all was reshaped into private property and a source of social conflict.

The level playing field of the Stone Age was fading. Specialized knowledge brought with it new community divisions. Like a stone tossed in the water, the effects of Gobekli rippled over the human world. The fissures of social separation and technological advancement that first appeared there, would eventually explode in a history-changing eruption of war. But before humanity could fly apart into hostile fragments, it first had to be united in peace.

CHAPTER 5
THE FIRST LOGO

The hip humans of 10,000 BC were buzzing about a new idea – human civilization. As people from around the known world made new friendships and gathered new knowledge on the campus grounds of Gobekli, a new idea of humanity was born. Tribe and geography faded as people embraced a common mission - to advance and spread human civilization across the globe. This notion must have inspired many people, because someone decided this secular crusade needed a symbol that represented its ideals. Like friendship offerings, it had to be easily and universally understood by all people. But unlike beads and shells, this symbol would be an abstract image. And the artist who created it intended its meaning to be obvious. It would convey the idea of a global human family without differences united by a worldwide civilization of travel and trade.

The jump to fashioning the world's first logo was not a large one. Since the time of the first cave painters 40,000 years ago, humans had been experimenting with early forms of symbolic writing. Genevieve von Petzinger, a University of Victoria (Canada) graduate student in anthropology, studied more than 120 prehistoric cave sites in France.

As her book, *The First Signs,* notes, many of those letter-like symbols were used for thousands of years by widely separated people.

Among humanity's many prehistoric symbols, one stands out. It was not used by the cave painters of 40,000-20,000 years ago. It was created during the era of Gobekli, and its design suggests it was crafted for a deliberate purpose. This ancient symbol is more than 10,000 years old, and it has been found at prehistoric sites in Europe and Africa, the Middle East and India, China and Japan, Siberia and the Americas. Because this symbol was so widely adopted, it must have had a powerful and unifying message that all humans were willing to embrace.

That global symbol was the swastika. And it was humanity's first purposefully-designed logo.

The oldest known swastika was found in the Ukraine where it was set down 12,000 years ago. Since then, this symbol traveled around the world where it has been used as a sacred icon by cultures on every continent. It can be found in religious shrines and buildings, on roadside pillars and set alongside the Star of David in the ruins of 1,600 year old Jewish synagogues. To promote the use of this symbol far beyond its unknown starting point to people in every corner of the world, someone or some group of Stone Age salespeople did a lot of walking and a lot of talking.

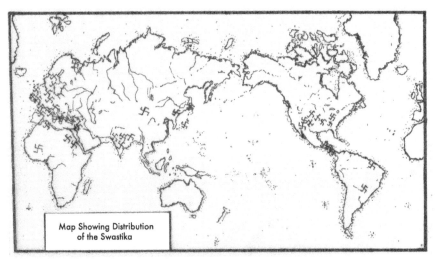

The swastika logo meant "unity in diversity" – copy of an 1898 Yale University map of prehistoric sites where the swastika has been found

The word "swastika" comes from an ancient Indo-European and Sanskrit root word that means "well-being, peace." In India and across modern Asia, the swastika is still used as a symbol of divine blessing and good fortune. But when prehistoric people around the world first adopted this icon, it must have carried a more profound meaning than a good luck charm. The selection of a good luck charm is a very personal matter. A touchstone to one person is an ordinary rock to somebody else. As it was widely accepted and shared, the swastika could not have been an arbitrary talisman.

If it was an emblem designed to be a Stone Age flag for the emerging world of humanity, then it was also the first logo. Logo comes from the Greek word *logos*. In its original sense, *logos* meant "unifying people through words and reason." If the swastika was a thought-out design to represent the spirit of prehistoric civilization, what did it mean when it was first imagined 12,000 years ago?

Similar to the cave symbols and reflecting the culture of balance, the swastika is symmetrical and generally circular. If its meaning was global, its rounded shape suggests early humans - having traveled and settled the world - may have known the Earth was round.

The artist who designed the swastika used four elements that unite in the center. The projections appear as an equal-sized pair of human legs. This design, crafted as a statement of human society 12,000 years ago, shows a pair of traveling legs as a logo for humanity. Legs would be the most common symbol of humanity because all humans walked upright, and legs represented travel. They are the same size and face in all directions to convey the unifying idea of global equality - men and women across the world. The dots around the legs in some designs may symbolize human communities in many lands united by one culture of trade and peaceful coexistence. As a logo to express the ideals of human civilization, the original swastika probably meant "unity in diversity." Wherever humans traveled, it said, they would be welcomed as common citizens of the world.

The appearance of the swastika in prehistoric communities across the globe, suggests its use may have been promoted by Stone Age missionaries promoting their faith in humanity. Converts displayed the swastika as a sign they were members of the new league of humans.

It was a symbol of unified nations before there were any nations. Communities everywhere welcomed the swastika and, over time, added their own local spin on its design and meaning.

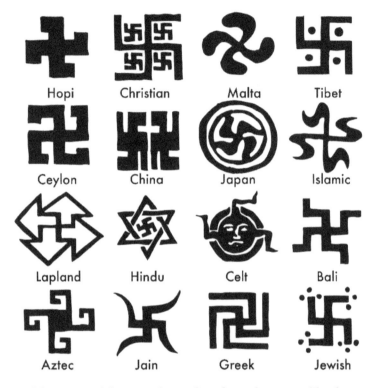

Variations of the swastika are found in cultures worldwide

The spread of the swastika 12,000-8,000 years ago takes place at the same time as Gobekli and the westward advancement of the cow culture, suggesting its origins may have been connected to the people of West Asia and the advancement of widespread education. All those developments show humanity's growing sense of itself as an interconnected civilization with a global future.

When the original meaning of the swastika was lost, what remained was its association with the concepts of peace, unity and "good times are coming." The Ancient Hebrews and Israelites used the swastika as a symbol of God's blessing. It is likely the swastika was first popularized in the Middle East by the Hebrew people who migrated there from Western India around 2000 BC. They passed it to the Middle Eastern Israelites who used it as a sacred decoration in their temples. Swastikas have been found in the ruins of 2,000 year old Jewish temples in modern Israel, including one on the Golan Heights where they surround images of Biblical history. In modern times, the Cochin Jews of India still use the swastika for its original meaning. The prehistoric asterisk may have been the inspiration for the swastika. The asterisk meant a "common source" and "spreading outward." By taking four lines from the asterisk and attaching them to the other lines, the swastika was created as something both new and familiar.

Swastikas were sacred symbols in Ancient Jewish temples

The Nazi movement of the 1930s degraded the swastika's symbolism and slandered the meaning of the word, "Aryan." Between the late 1800s and mid-20th Century, the growing popularity of Charles Darwin's evolutionary theories led nationalist scientists around the world to invent reasons why their group was 'scientifically' superior to everyone else. In extreme cases, they insisted genetically 'inferior' people be sterilized or killed for the betterment of mankind. During this period, some European historians promoted the now-discredited idea that modern civilization began when a horde of culturally superior, light-skinned Western people called Aryans invaded India's 'primitive' Indus Valley Civilization in 2000 BC and dominated its darker-skinned people.

However, there is no evidence the Indus Valley ever experienced war or was conquered. The so-called invasion was a peaceful mass migration like that of the West Asian cow people into Europe. Demographics naturally change over time. However, the Nazis liked the story of light-skinned conquerors and ran with it. In doing so, they also invented a new meaning for Aryan. The original meaning of this Sanskrit word had nothing to do with race, tribe or physical appearance. Like the Yiddish word mensch, Aryan referred to what was inside a person, not outside. Aryan and mensch both mean "a righteous, honorable man."

Although the modern world mainly sees the swastika as a symbol of destruction and division, when humanity's ancestors created it, the swastika was the world's first peace symbol.

The modern Peace Symbol

CHAPTER 6
DIVISIONS

For nearly 3 million years, human society self-organized and expanded its culture of honest dealings, cooperative ventures and social equality. By 7,000 years ago, the number of people living in farming settlements, villages and towns in West Asia, East Africa and the Middle East surpassed the remaining communities of wandering tribes. The nomadic life was one of interchangeable responsibilities and easily formed friendships. The life of farmers, city dwellers, merchants and animal dealers was focused on property, daily duties and especially family obligations. Like groups of small children, hunter-gatherer societies benefitted by random associations so there were no protocols for meeting people other than friendliness. Family culture was formally structured by each person's responsibilities to the household – the land or home where the family and servants lived. And family life was a hierarchy of the house master and those who served him or her to maintain the household and increase its wealth.

In the new urban societies of 7,000-6,000 years ago, competition between households resulted in less social mobility. Spontaneous and unrestricted friendships gave way to more ritualized relationships that served as loyalty tests. Hunter-gatherer communities operated like a home without locks. Everyone was free to walk around. Entry into a family group required a password – typically some reference to a mutual relative. For example, "Hi, I'm a distant cousin of your Aunt Sophie's music teacher's nephew."

Increased trade, growing urban centers and advances in technology gave birth to a new sense of identity based on skills and knowledge. The convergence of those two social streams – family culture and classifying people by their skills – would propel humanity to its next stage of urban sophistication and technological achievements. But when it was corrupted by greed, this caste system for social progress would leave behind a legacy of death, division and destruction.

The word "family" originally meant all those who worked to advance the goals of the household leader. That sense is used today when applied to organized crime. The more narrow definition of a family member as only those related by blood or marriage is just 500 years old. Hunter-gatherer communities were bound by revolving friendships. Family culture demanded unwavering loyalty. The original word for "loyal" carried the meanings of obedience to social superiors, law-abiding and "born in a legal marriage."

The new focus on loyalty and legality changed the status of women. To ensure family lines were not diluted by women having sexual relationships with men whose loyalty had not been proven, marriage contracts were created. And those contracts of sexual loyalty were part of a larger system of new social rules that restricted women from freely associating with men, and the mixing of lower class people with those from higher class families.

Women were given a new classification and value as household property. The new restrictions on women's freedom to associate were presented as necessary to protect women from sexually aggressive men. However, it was the family culture of private property and loyalty that first fueled the rise and normalization of sexual violence against women among sadistic groups of powerful men.

The concept of legal ownership meant property had to be marked, and once marked, its owners had a legal right to use force to prevent other people from taking or devaluing their property. This was first applied to land with the invention of boundary markers and symbols stamped on clay tablets or chipped into rocks to indicate the transfer of property from one person to another. Marriage rituals transferred the responsibilities of ownership and the responsibility to protect a woman from one household to another.

Marriage symbols were introduced as a public sign indicating a woman was protected by her husband's family. In Ancient India, a dot of colored clay on a woman's forehead became a sign of marriage. Originally, the forehead bindi was used by men and women as a sign of spiritual devotion and inner knowledge. Women adopted it as a sign of devotion to their mates, and eventually it became a social requirement among Hindus similar to the Christian wedding ring.

This was an era of powerful families and private wealth in the rising civilization of Ancient India 6,000 years ago. The new requirement that women wear a visible emblem of male protection signaled that something profound had changed in human society at large, and in the relationships between men and women in particular. That change was the concept of sales value. The emergence of commercial value as a governing principle of human society was first applied to land, objects and animals. But it quickly spread to people. Borrowers who couldn't repay their debt were forced to work off their obligation as indentured servants. If the owner of the servant fell into debt, the servant's remaining IOU and the servant could be sold to a new master. In the prehistoric economic system of favor exchanges, people were obliged to return gifts but not hounded if they didn't. In that culture, personal honor had the highest value. In the new communities, social obedience was placed above personal honor and so debt became a crime against the wealthy. The permanent attachment of money debt to people commercialized them as items to be bought and sold. It was the first market for buying and selling people, and it planted the seed of slavery.

This pre-war era of private prosperity ushered in a culture that ranked all things according by their new value. People were given titles to designate their individual skills, and family names to indicate their heritage. A woman's status was largely determined by men who rated their perceived sexual purity, beauty and ability to produce children. Females seen as sexually untouched were valued higher than women considered second hand property. In this society, female chastity was held above all else. There is an ancient legal principle that a person cannot be accused of theft if they take something of no value. To be considered theft, whatever is stolen must have a clearly defined value.

For some men, this meant any female considered impure or of a lower class could be abused at will because they were socially worthless women. If a woman's value was sex and her sex had no commercial value, raping or even killing her was not considered a crime.

On the other side of society, women who were highly-valued for their sexual innocence became targets for thieves and family enemies. Rape became more common as a form of sexual theft. Conflicts expanded from men fighting men to include the plunder of daughters and wives. Like robbery, planned rape was a new kind of violence that largely did not exist in prehistoric communities.

Despite its later abuses, the original purpose of social ranking was to better organize the available skills flowing in and out of the growing urban centers, reduce tensions between family rivals and produce more wealth for all. Yet, the success of this new model for human life would also be the cause of the world's first war. The ruling clans believed the separation of people by class, rather than voluntary cooperation, was the source of their society's prosperity and their own wealth. So, they issued an increasing number of laws and rules that governed people's lives and kept them apart. When the tension on the bonds of the old social agreement were stretched beyond their limit, they broke, and war between the shards of a fractured civilization was the result.

The social structure that collapsed into the carnage of the world's first war (c 3000-4000 BC), was born with fanfare and introduced for the good of all. It grew from the need to formalize social teamwork, and restrain family rivalries by establishing joint rule of the established clans. The word "team" comes from the concept of joining work animals together to make hard tasks easier. In India, two cows would be connected by a wood brace called a yoke, and their combined strength would plow the fields. The yoke became a symbol of unity for a larger purpose, and so the words "yoga" and "religion" derive from the idea of binding people to divine knowledge.

Joining a community's talents and resources together in a way that multiplied their strengths to produce a wealthier life for everyone was the founding principle of the team system introduced during the Age of Knowledge. This era in humanity's pre-war history celebrated the pursuit of human excellence, and it reached its peak in Ancient India 5,000 years ago. To spur a community-wide spirit of achievement, the philosophers of Ancient India came up with the world's first community-wide production and management system. It spread across the towns, villages and cities and operated like a sports league with each location having its own team and each team its players with their designated positions and responsibilities.

Over time, Ancient India's remarkable social organization project would devolve into a rigid, by-birth caste system that forcibly separated people by the value given to their family. But when it began, the system was welcomed as a new way to unify the community. It brought together farmers, laborers, teachers, managers and security forces in a common cause for the commonwealth as if they were all limbs on one body.

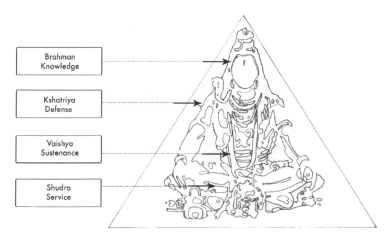

India's ancient Varna System of business management was envisioned as limbs on a body - the central figure is the Hindu God, Shiva

At the top was the symbolic head – planners, scholars and priests called Brahmans who were identified by their insights into things material and spiritual. To avoid any conflict of interest, the Brahmans were expected to live simply and show no favor to kings or commoners. Below them were the arms used for organization and combat. Those warriors, kings and administrators were collectively called the *Kshatriyas*. Although this was a time before large-scale war, there were occasional skirmishes with gangs of bandits and forest tribes who resented the encroachment of the growing urban areas. Because actual hostilities were so rare, professional warriors and weapon makers improved their skills through organized games of combat.

Following them on the social assembly line were the *Vaishyas* – farmers and merchants who distributed their products throughout the community in the way the stomach sends nutrients to the whole body. These professional merchants would develop the first global trading network to market India's silks, spices and ideas from the subcontinent to Africa and across Southeast Asia. Initially, those who devised the class system recognized only three orders of people, but then a fourth limb was added - the *Shudras*. These were the laborers and legs of the new social order. Together, this was called the *Varna* system and its original purpose was to encourage each member of the community to be 'the best they could be.'

The root of the Sanskrit word *Varna* means "to unite under one roof" or "to be shaped into one form." These two meanings evoke both the early notion of a voluntary gathering and the later one whose shape was held in place by force. This change in meaning is similar to that of the Hebrew word Torah, which first meant "guiding wisdom" and was later reinterpreted to mean "laws."

The root word of "excel" means to gain superiority by rising up like a hill. In some ways, *Varna* was a visionary concept of social cooperation similar to Gobekli. However, at Gobekli, there were no social barriers. As the team culture of India advanced, families with power found ways to keep it and prevent the lower ranks from rising above their station. One means to accomplish this was the new system of payment for education. In early human society, freely sharing knowledge helped advance and spread human civilization. In the new society, access to education was limited to those who could pay for it with money or years of service to their teacher. And when people tried to access upper class knowledge on their own, they could find themselves breaking a 5,000 year old version of intellectual property law.

There is a story from Ancient India that is the oldest known record of intellectual property theft. It tells how a young man from a lower class family created a statue of an older man who was a well-known archer from the ruling clans. The young man meditated on the statue and used the insights he gained to become a master archer. When the older bowman learned of this, he demanded payment for the use his image. According to the legal rules of the day, the senior-ranked archer could ask for any payment, and so he demanded the young man's shooting thumb - and the payment was made. Nonetheless, the young man retained his skill as one of the finest archers of his time.

It was this hardening of class attitudes and the harsh application of social laws that emboldened ruthless leaders to further manipulate the rules for personal power, and that would light the fuse of the world's first war. The old *Varna* of the commonwealth became the New Varna of crime and punishment. Social standing grew increasingly important. People's daily lives were filled with rituals of deference to those above and receiving obligatory bows from those below. This rigid ritualizing of human relationships placed enormous power in the hands of rulers who could raise or lower a person's social rank at any time. This shift in human culture from common respect to forced obedience and mandatory social rituals for each social encounter, spread unease and insecurity throughout their society.

In earlier times, leadership councils were temporary and humans had no word for a single 'leader.' The first tribal leaders, kings and queens were typically elected by the community and if the community protested, those in power would either follow their demands, step down or be forcibly removed. With social peace and growing prosperity, ruling families became entrenched. With no public demand for change, power was passed down the family line from father to son. To dampen the possibility of rebellion against the ruling families, the religion of the New Varna taught the lower classes their fixed place in society was chosen by God and that the upper classes were born to rule.

During its growth stage, each group created their own standards of excellence, and professional loyalty. As the social order began to fray, those in power used their control over the class system to cast opponents out of their caste. They would be stripped of their title, blacklisted from working or selling their goods to other caste members and forced to work in a black market. Friendly competition was replaced by fear of gossip that might brand someone as 'disloyal' and lead to a boycott. Many Brahman priests married into the wealthy clans or served them as highly paid advisors. As corruption among kings and princes spread, and the use of force to maintain order increased, a cancer of resentment and fear, anger and greed was devouring the social body. Despite this, the rulers of the time believed their civilization was divinely blessed and would last forever.

They were wrong. As the ruling families tightened their grip, pressure along the social fault lines increased until humanity's first experiment in complex civilization shattered. The war that destroyed India's Age of Knowledge 5,000-6,000 years ago was so devastating that its second great culture – the Indus Valley Civilization – would reject every part of the class system that caused the fatal war. Before examining the causes and consequences of the world's first great battle, it is important to understand why advanced human civilization first took root in the Indian subcontinent, and how a warrior class was created in a world before war.

Geographically, India sits at the center of the prehistoric trade route between Africa and Mesopotamia, the Pacific Islands, Western and Southeast Asia. As a result, it was a natural stopping point for settlement and a meeting place for people from across those regions. Its abundance of natural resources, extremely varied food sources and animals, plants and landscapes, and its warm climate all added to its attractions and those nutrients stimulated brain development among those who lived there. Its diverse landscape and people of many kinds encouraged a culture that perceived life as a series of infinite transformations and relationships. A map based on coconut DNA dating back 6,000-8,000 years, shows prehistoric trade routes that transplanted coconut trees around the world. The starting points intersect at the southern shores of India and its culturally-influenced regions including Madagascar and Southeast Asia.

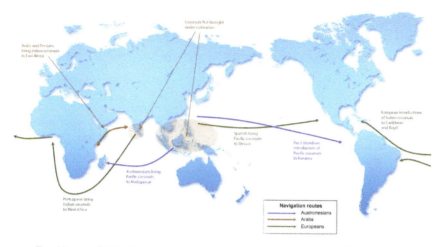

Dr. Kenneth M. Olsen, a plant evolutionary biologist at Washington University in St. Louis, investigated prehistoric coconut trade

Another map shows how early people traded by sea using the Monsoon winds and currents to travel, settle and trade throughout the Indian and Pacific Oceans. Archaeologists have found fishing hooks in Japan that are 22,000 years old and indicate the widespread use of maritime technologies very early in human history.

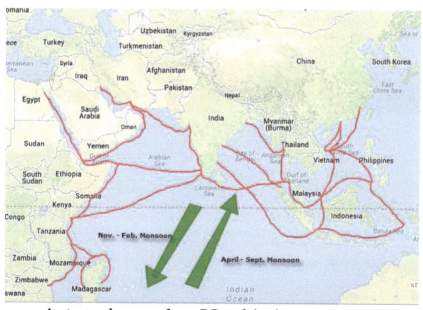

Ancient trade routes of 3000 BC used the alternating currents and winds of the oceans to travel between continents

Modern genetic research has revealed the ethnic diversity of India's people living there 6,000 years ago. In the Northwest were families with ties to people of the Middle East, Central Asia and Europe. They formed the higher classes and castes. In the South were darker-skinned people who came there from Africa and Southern Iran. The southern people called Dravidians were later classified as lower caste people by those in the more urban North. In the Northeast were clusters of Tibeto-Burmese people while those of Austro-Asiatic heritage had a presence in the Southeast. And for most of its history, the multicultural people of India freely associated and mixed their families at will.

By 4000 BC, humanity had come a long way. In the 96,000 years since leaving the sun-baked continent of Africa, people had settled the world and built enormous monuments including Gobekli and Stonehenge. Human achievements included cities and languages, architecture and medicine, trade networks and a common human culture. In short, humanity had grown up. All the structures of modern life had been grasped and applied. It was a shining example of contemporary human civilization.

The only thing missing was war.

CHAPTER 7

WAR COMES TO EDEN

Is war natural? Nature doesn't think so. Only three of the 9 million species of life on Earth engage in war. Is killing instinctive to people? Not according to the evidence.

"Even the most warlike of Old Stone Age people, like the Indians of North America, regarded warfare much more as a ritual activity – part art form, part healthy outdoor exercise – than as a practical instrument for achieving economic and political aims," Gwynne Dyer wrote in his 1985 book, "*War*." Among the Indians of the Great Plains, the "highest honor a warrior could gain was not to kill the enemy," but to go out unarmed, silently slip past all his enemies' defenses and simply touch his opponent, Dyer said. As a result, intertribal warfare was a game-like competition in which young warriors were given the opportunity to demonstrate their courage and elder warriors their craftiness, he added.

The most respected Comanche warrior of his time was a man who acquired a blanket made by the Utes, his tribal enemies. He would put it on and walk in among the Ute and they would look up to him as a respected warrior and leave him unharmed, Dyer wrote.

The 2002 movie, *Drumline*, features another type of non-lethal war game – the drum battle. The drum and the flute are the oldest known musical instruments. Alligator skin drums found in China date to 7,500 years ago and drummers in Egypt have been keeping the beat there for about 6,000 years. India's Rig Veda – the oldest of its texts – describes how military drummers pounded out rhythms to motivate marching troops.

In *Drumline*, the climactic scene has two teams of drummers staring each other down and hammering out battle-like rhythms and moves on their own and their opponents' drums. Scenes similar to this may have played out as prehistoric war games among the ancestral drummers of Africa.

A drumline in modern Africa

During World War II, research conducted by US Army Brigadier General S.L.A. Marshall found that, on average, only 15% to 20% of American riflemen actually fired their weapon directly at the enemy. Most soldiers, if they fired their guns at all shot in the direction of the enemy but not actually at a person they could see. Marshall, a veteran of World Wars I and II said this showed the average, healthy individual has "an inner and usually unrealized resistance toward killing a fellow man."

From 1908 when it was established as the Bureau of Investigation and for several years after it was renamed the Federal Bureau of Investigation in 1935, America's national cops were banned by law from carrying guns. As a result, in the early years both the Feds and the felons were restrained from killing each other. John Dillinger, the infamous bank robber of the 1930s, bragged he never killed anyone during his long criminal career and was acquitted of the one charge that he shot and killed a bank guard who shot at him.

The word "war" has Germanic roots but, according to the etymological website, Etymonline.com, there was no common word for "war" at the dawn of historical times. Rather the word "war" derived from those used to describe the friendly competition of games. Its oldest sources are words that mean "to confuse, mix up" and "to win." To "confuse" suggests the use of fake direction moves common in modern basketball and hockey play. Winning was the result of excellence in physical skill and mental discipline. As in the modern world, the level of violence in war game competitions was kept in check by the rules of the game and personal honor.

It is commonly assumed the first rules limiting brutality in war were those set out in the 1949 Geneva Convention. For most of human history, there were no official rules because warriors had a personal code of honor that restrained them from unnecessary killing and prevented attacks on non-combatants. Motivating warriors to kill anyone at will required a new style of leadership, and a change in community values from celebrating the common to targeting the different.

Across the landscape of modern media, competition is presented as a ruthless and unforgiving contest of survival of the fittest with only one victor. But that is not its original meaning. The modern idea was built atop the ruins of an older human culture.

"Compete" derives from the Latin word *comptere* which means "come together, agreement, and work in common." It does not mean "to fight." How human society changed from working with each other to working against other people can be best understood in the history of the word "rival."

The word "rival" originally meant a small river, and rivals were neighbors who shared the river's water. The change in meaning followed a change in the relationships between neighbors. So long as everyone acted with consideration for others, rivals were neighborly. When some people upstream refused to stop polluting the water, more and more of the downriver people set up water barriers to deflect the pollution away from their waterside to someone else. Lowered water levels and declining water quality eventually sparked violent confrontations between un-neighborly rivals over water rights. What caused the violence was not the later lack of clean water but individual selfishness and the end of cooperation. The evolution in meaning of the word "win," shows this change in social relationships. Initially, winning meant to succeed through "mutual satisfaction" and "love" of the game. But as the modern world took shape, "win" was given new meanings in new languages that included "conquer" and "suffer."

The Roman philosopher Seneca (54 BC-39 AD) said war is not natural to people. They must be psychologically conditioned to celebrate bloodshed and admire those who kill. To change human nature from peaceful to violent, Seneca laid out a nine-step program. Instead of rewarding people for cooperative actions, he said, they should be praised for killing, while compassion and reason must be mocked as weaknesses. The first rule of Seneca's training manual for normalizing violence was to create fear by teaching people their lives were being threatened and only those who killed first would survive.

Seneca the Elder of Ancient Rome explained psychological conditioning 2,000 years ago

Here's what Seneca wrote:

1. Tell people all animals are vicious killers and force them to fight wild animals.

2. When they kill the animal, praise and reward them.

3. Bind the group together by drinking the blood of the dead animal.

4. Hold contests that encourage people to kill harmless animals including animals that have served them.

5. Once people have learned to enjoy animal murder, tell them killing people is no different from slaughtering animals.

6. Teach ways to attack and kill people - individually and as part of a group.

7. Focus society's brightest and most creative minds on the development of weapons of war. Praise efficient killing as the highest virtue.

8. Tell armies they are fighting for high ideals, but use them for plunder and personal gain.

9. When armies become weak from moral decay use trickery and deceit to lead them.

Seneca's formula was designed to praise cruelty and ignorance, while denigrating empathy and understanding. What he described was a culture based on moral hazards – one that rewarded vice and punished virtue. Because their only goal is killing, these societies would devour themselves, Seneca warned.

Although war is a recent human invention, non-lethal combat is pervasive among humans and animals. Competitive games are tools for socialization, physical exercise and brain development. When modern sports writers describe field action with war words like blitz and bomb some people see this as the militarization of sports. But history shows the opposite – military strategies, weapons and tactics were born from the friendly competition of war games. To understand what caused the culture of war games to metastasize into a battlefield slaughter of millions of armed men, it is important to know the story behind the world's first war.

Searching for any historical record of the first true war begins with the fossil evidence showing it could not have been earlier than 10,000 years ago. That estimate can be narrowed down with traditional stories from several ancient civilizations that describe a world before war that existed until about 5,000-6,000 years ago. Assuming the first true war marked a fundamental change in human history, it seems likely there would be some ancient narrative that recalled this momentous event and where it took place.

There are two sources that shed light on when and where the world's first war happened, and they are both unlikely sources of scholarly history. One is the Garden of Eden story from the Hebrew Bible, and the other is the report of India's Battle of Kurukshetra as recorded in their ancient book, the Mahabharata. The story of Eden and India's War are both said to have happened 5,000-6,000 years ago.

The Hebrew Torah contain the histories of the Hebrew people who migrated to the Middle East from India

Most people think the Bible's tale of Eden and India's ancient war story have little or no connection to any real history. However, ancient histories given such great importance always have some actual event at their core. For thousands of years, reports of the Trojan War were dismissed as fictional – and then Troy's 3,200 year old ruins were discovered. What if there is a similar record of real world history hiding like a fossil inside the stories of Eden and India's war that connects them as pieces of the same narrative? What if the Biblical story of the Garden of Eden did not began as a fable about human creation, but a fragmented telling of how a new kind of humanity was born after the world's first war? What if Eden originally meant Generation Eden – the world of humanity's ancestors before war? To many modern people, the concept of a time in human history before war seems a fantasy. So, it's not hard to imagine that after thousands of years of war and religion, ancient people would trivialize stories of a harmonious past before their time with fanciful imaginings of a long-gone, garden-like world and the beginning of sin. However, the sin that killed humanity's first civilization was not disobedience of a divine authority, but the self-inflicted wounds of unrestrained human greed and mass murder.

In the modern world, some fundamentalist Christians believe the world was created 6,000 years ago. This number originates with the Hebrew calendar which turned 5,777 years old in October, 2016. However, the notion that Day 1, Year 1 of Biblical history marked the start of creation is a made up one. An Irish Catholic Bishop started the rumour about 400 years ago, and other Christians have been running with it ever since. The original source of the calendar - Jewish tradition – says nothing of the kind. It says Year 1 marked the end of a peaceful world and humanity's departure from Eden. According to the Bible, Eden was located in the eastern part of a land called Havilah by a river called the Pichon. Where was Havilah? The 20-volume, 1906 Jewish Encyclopedia reports the oldest Jewish and Christian histories dating back over 2,000 years all agree that Havilah was India and the Pichon is today known as the sacred Ganges or Ganga River of Eastern India.

This information raises a profound question. What event took place in Ancient India almost 6,000 years ago that launched Biblical history? One point is clear. It was not a religious event because there were no organized religions then. There were only individual people and small groups with their own informal practices. So, whatever happened in India at that time, it must have been an event of such tremendous importance that it was almost as if a new kind of human had been born on the Earth. And that event was the world's first war that happened in India more than 5,000 years ago.

Parchment page of India's Bhagavad-Gita with an illustration of the world's first war - the Battle of Kurukshetra

If there is a connection between the people and histories of the Hebrew Bible, and the ruling families of India at the time of its Kurukshetra War, much more evidence would be needed. There would have to be more references in the Bible and factual evidence outside it. That proof must also include language ties and archaeological relics. And most importantly, there would have to be a genetic trail that leads from Ancient India to the Hebrew people and Ancient Israelites of the Middle East.

More than 2,300 years ago, the Greek philosopher Aristotle said, "The Jewish people are descended from the Brahman priests of Ancient India." More accurately, it was the Hebrew people – the spiritual ancestors of modern Jews – who migrated into Mesopotamia after the fall of India's Indus Valley Civilization around 2000 BC. The word "Hebrew" means "homeless wanderers from the East" and it was a name given to those Indo-Semitic newcomers by the local people of Mesopotamia.

Other evidence linking Ancient India and Ancient Israel can be found in two maps. One comes from the writings of Josephus – the

Jewish historian and scholar of Ancient Rome who lived 2,000 years ago. The other is a genetic map of one of the world's oldest families.

The most famous Jewish historian of the ancient world was Joseph ben Matityahu better known by his Roman name - Titus Flavius Josephus.

Josephus (37-100 AD)

Josephus was born in Jerusalem. His father was a Jewish priest and his mother's family included the Biblical King Judah Maccabee whose successful rebellion against the Ancient Greek Empire is remembered in the Jewish festival of Hanukkah.

After taking part in a failed Jewish revolt against the Roman Empire (66-70 CE), the 30 year-old Josephus was made the slave of a Roman General. Josephus predicted his new master would soon be named Emperor of Rome. When General Vespasian was crowned Emperor in 69 BC, Josephus was freed from slavery and given lands on Vespasian's royal estate. As an act of gratitude, Josephus adopted his former master's family name of Flavius.

Mahlon H. Smith, writing for the American Theological Library circle, explained how the one-time Jewish terrorist became an advisor to three successive Roman Emperors and a widely respected scholar.

Smith notes that although Josephus adopted a Roman name, "he remained dedicated to his Jewish heritage." Josephus spent years writing Jewish histories to explain his people to the Romans who "regarded all Jews as lawless riff-raff and bandits," she added.

The Bible doesn't indicate where Noah lived before the famous flood. But a map attributed to Josephus shows where the original Hebrews - the sons and families of the Biblical character Noah - settled after their homeland was destroyed c 2000 BC. Putting aside the specifics of the religious narrative and looking only for evidence of an actual migration, the map points to India's Indus Valley as the start of Noah's journey and the north end of the Persian Gulf as his landing site. Josephus' map shows the regions in Africa and Eurasia where Noah's sons - Ham, Shem and Japheth, along with their families and followers - settled after the Biblical flood. It is important to note to note that these "sons" may have been followers of Noah from the many groups who lived in the Indus and each resettled in the land of their ancestors.

But the standout feature of Josephus' map is that one part of the family of Shem – the Biblical ancestor of all modern Jews and Semites – is located in the Indus Valley region that now includes parts of India, Pakistan and Afghanistan. Did Shem's tribe travel there after the Biblical flood, or did they depart from there? Assuming a character like Noah departed from the mouth of the Indus River and floated west, he and his shipmates would have drifted into the Persian Gulf. If they continued to its north end and landed there, they would have seen the foothills of the Ararat Mountains as the Bible claims. And Josephus' map does place one of the Shem settlements at that spot. So, did Noah and his Hebrew people migrate out of the Indus Valley and into the Middle East, Africa and Eurasia 4,000 years ago?

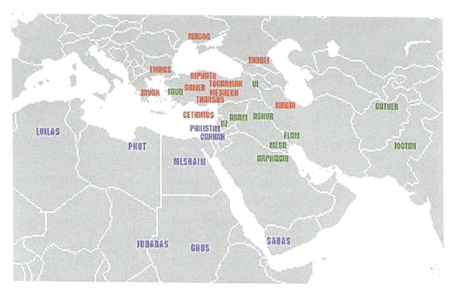

Josephus' map shows the westward migration of the family and followers of Noah after the destruction of India's Indus Valley Civilization (c 2000 BC) - Shem in green, Ham in blue and Japheth in red

If Josephus' map is based on more than fanciful stories, the genetic trail of those migrating people would be obvious and clear. And it is. Josephus' description closely matches a DNA map of one of humanity's oldest chromosomal families called Haplogroup J. One branch of this prehistoric family line leads to the Biblical characters of Moses and Aaron, and from them to the Israelite Tribe of Judah – the source word of Jewish. But an even older part of the Hap J clan settled in India where its members included India's King Yuda, his royal family called the Yadavas and their most famous member – Prince Krishna.

Were the people known as Biblical Hebrews and Israelites descendants and cousins of India's ancient Royal Family? The Indo-Semitic Biblical character Abraham is called the inspirational father of Judaism, Christianity and Islam. Was Abraham part of the Yadava family, and did his Indo-Semitic followers pass down the wisdom of Krishna and incorporate sacred Indian symbols into the ancient Jewish religion? The genetic trail and Biblical evidence all suggest the answer is, "Yes."

Among Jews, those descended from a specific branch of the Haplogroup J family - J1 - are considered 'born priests' in the same way Hindus are born into a Brahman family.

India's current population is mostly a mix of Haplogroups M, R and U. But a few of India's oldest tribes carry a significant percentage of Haplogroup J. One of those clans is the Yadavas.

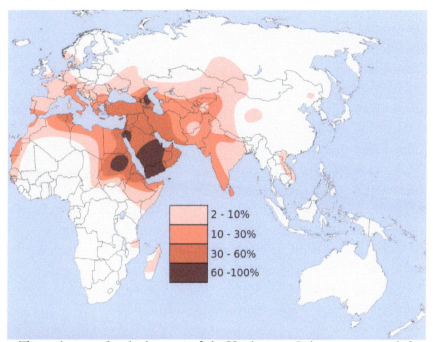

The prehistoric family that carried the Haplogroup J chromosome settled across the world and created the Indo-European and Afro-Asiatic languages

Today, the largest concentration of Haplogroup J people lives in the Middle East and Sudan. But the prehistoric roots of this widely-traveled family spans the world. The Haplogroup J region nicely overlaps with two of humanity's oldest language groups - Indo-European and Afro-Asiatic.

Dr. Harry Ostrer of Albert Einstein College of Medicine in New York is one of the world's leading researchers in Jewish genetics. When asked about the possible family ties between the Ancient Hebrews and Ancient India, he admitted his research only went back 3,300 years to Moses' brother Aaron who founded the Israelite line of J1 priests. To confirm an Indus to Israel lineage, he said, the man to contact was India's top geneticist – Dr. Lalji Singh, the Vice-Chancellor of Hindu University in Banaras.

Did the Yadavas of India migrate to the Middle East where they would later be called Judahs? Dr. Singh could not answer the question definitively. But after careful examination of the genetic history of India's Jewish population – some of whom have lived in India since the time of the Biblical King David 3,000 years ago - he found an unexpected connection.

"Our study of the Jewish population of India revealed their maternal and paternal gene pool is linked with the people of Western Eurasia," he said. India's literary evidence also strongly supports the idea that the ancestors of the Jewish people "migrated to Mesopotamia from the Indus Valley during its downfall" from severe climate change c 2000 BC, he added. That is the same time frame and for the same reason as the migration story of Noah.

The India-Israel connection may have produced modern Judaism's most famous symbol - The Star of (King) David. David's son was the Biblical King Solomon. Solomon used vast quantities of imported gold to decorate his famous temple, and according to the text, the gold came from a faraway place called Ophir. Noted historian Max Muller (1823-1900) has identified Ophir as the modern Indian port city of Abhirav. In ancient times, the Yadavas were the ruling family of that city.

Artisans from India symbolized their close connection to the Biblical people by decorating the Temple of David with an unusual star shape – India's heart *chakra*

The Star of David is never mentioned or described anywhere in the Bible. However, this symbol of interconnected triangles has long been used to represent the power of the heart in Ancient India. The Indian name for this image is the heart *chakra*. The Sanskrit word *chakra* means "wheel of energy." In this symbol, the six-pointed star is set inside a stylized lotus flower. The lotus flower is a lily and lilies were once used as symbols of faith in Ancient Judaism. In India, the lotus represents spiritual awakening.

The Star of David has only been Judaism's best known logo for about 150 years. Before then, the most common images associated with Jews were the stone tablets of Moses' 10 commandments, and the candelabra called a *menorah* used in the Hanukkah celebration. A French painting from 1806 shows this. It depicts the Emperor Napoleon liberating Jews from oppressive French laws that restricted their freedom to work and live as other French citizens. The Jewish men are represented by their distinctive long hair and beards, and the Jewish woman is shown with her *menorah* and the tablets of Moses. There is no Star of David anywhere in the picture.

"Napoleon Frees the Jews of France" (1806) shows a Jewish *menorah* and Hebrew letters on the tablets of Moses but no Star of David

Solomon likely dedicated his temple to his father, King David. It may be the Yadava traders and artisans from Ophir decorated the new temple with a large and fabulously decorated Indian heart *chakra* to represent their ancient family ties and spiritual unity. To gain fame, the star shape must have been unusual. And because it was featured in the temple, the unfamiliar design was called the 'star of David's temple.'

Another link can be found in *Shabbat*, the Hebrew word for the Sabbath day of rest. *Shabbat* is a Hebrew word that means "restful" and it is also used for the slow-moving planet, Saturn. The Biblical 'day of rest' was set on the day named for the planet that lazily transited the night sky. This word was brought to the Middle East by the Hebrews from India. It originated as the Sanskrit word, *Shani*, which means "slowly" and is also used as the word for Saturn and Saturday. When praying, religious Jews place small boxes containing verses from the Torah on their arms, forehead and chest. Devotional Hindus mark the same parts of their bodies with clay from the sacred Ganges River. The Jewish boxes are called *tefillin* and the Hindu clay markings are called *tilaka*.

If the Biblical Hebrews were descendants of the Yadava clan from India that fought alongside their Pandava allies in the war that ended Eden, what do the texts of Ancient India reveal about that history-changing battle?

It is known as the Kurukshetra War. It took place on a large field owned by a Royal Family called the Kurus. In Sanskrit, the word *shetra* means "field" and so the war was named for the field of the Kurus where it took place. This epic clash is said to have occurred more than 5,000 years ago and is the earliest known report of an organized and massive war between armed soldiers. It tells of 4 million soldiers and charioteers, war animals and weapons flung against each other in an apocalyptic confrontation that went on for 18 days of relentless killing.

India's ancient text, the Mahabharata, tells how the ruling family of a great empire was divided by rival clans with claims for the throne. Initially, the two sides of the family agreed to share power. But when the powerful Kuru prince Duryodhana refused to let his cousins' rule, the stage was set for war.

When it began, 2.5 million fighting men on one side faced off against 1.5 million warriors across the field. When the fighting ended, only 12 men of the original 4 million were left alive. The enormity of the slaughter and devastation was overwhelming. Humanity's Age of Knowledge fell on its own swords. After the carnage, bitterness and sorrow spread over the kingdoms of North India as each side blamed the other for the catastrophe. People abandoned urban life and returned to smaller communities and local traditions. This time of human retreat, falling trade and the loss of skills was the world's first Dark Age. It is recalled in the Biblical text as the time after Eden when people lived shorter, harder lives and the "tree of knowledge" was lost.

Another curious connection is that Year 1 of the Jewish calendar is 3760 BC. One date given for the War in India is 3067 BC. Coincidentally, the last three numbers of these years are exactly reversed – 760 and 067. The starting date of the Hebrew calendar and its method of calculation has been lost and recovered, changed and outlawed at different times in its history. The 700 year difference between the two dates could simply be a calculation error.

If they do coincide, then the event that changed the world and started Biblical history was the War at Kurukshetra.

CHAPTER 8
A GAME OF THRONES

War is not inevitable. Aggressive war is a choice made by leaders and sold to followers. As Seneca noted, before armies could be assembled and sent into wars of conquest, grandiose leaders must change their society's culture from neighborly cooperation to fear and the need for conquest and control. Without peace, human civilization would not and could not have developed a commonly shared language or freely expanded regional and then global trade. To paraphrase Sir Isaac Newton, a society at peace will remain on its trajectory of peaceful development until it is redirected by an external force.

Even in modern society, very few of the planet's 7 billion people are living in war zones. Despite the countless numbers of guns, artillery weapons, warplanes, battleships and military drones available in the world, only the tiniest fraction will ever engage in any real war. Indeed, because there is no hot war for all the military hardware, these military weapons and tactics are increasingly used on civilian populations.

According to India's ancient texts, the first war happened around 3100 BC. It was a Civil War between two halves of a Royal Family descended from the same grandfather who ruled the kingdom. On one side were his children and grandchildren, and on the other the sons and families of the king's dead brother. Tradition dictated the two sides share leadership, with one family ruling for a period followed by the other. When the sitting king's son refused to share power with his cousins, each side assembled a fearsome army of its own fighters and those of its allies.

The causes and consequences of that battle for supremacy are detailed in India's massive book of ancient history called the Mahabharata. The Mahabharata or "History of the Great Bharat Clan," is the world's longest story and poem. It contains more than 200,000 rhyming verses and about 1.8 million words. By comparison, there are about 783,000 English words in the King James Version of the Bible. Like the Bible, the Mahabharata recalls the history of a group of interrelated families dating back to the beginning of their civilization. It ends with the War and its aftermath about 5,000 years ago. The story it tells provides a historical context for the Biblical tale of Eden, and the fall of humanity that ended India's Age of Knowledge. It all started around 3100 BC and the rivalry between the Kuru clan led by Prince Duryodhana and his cousins, the five Pandava brothers.

Over a period of about 20 years, Duryodhana made several attempts to murder his rival cousins. Instead of restraining his son, the Kuru King told his five nephews that life would be safer for them if they left town. So the Pandava brothers turned away from the Kuru capital of Hastinapur ("City of Elephants"), and built a new kingdom in the wilderness on the site of what is now Delhi.

With no one to stop him, the ruthless Prince used religious teachings, social rules and brute force to terrorize those who served him and eliminate those who opposed him. When the Pandava brothers and their common Queen – Draupadi - finally returned to their old kingdom, they expected to be given their turn as rulers. Instead, the Kuru Prince Duryodhana pressured the eldest of the five brothers to risk his family's future in a game of dice. To ensure his relatives crapped out, the Prince's dice were weighted to come up winners every time.

Dice and board games are some of humanity's oldest pastimes. In the Ancient East, dice were often made from the knucklebones of a camel and each side of the bone was marked with a different value.

Duryodhana's game was a devious plot in the lavish setting of his palace. When the Pandavas and Queen Draupadi arrived, they were welcomed as honored guests. The kingdom's high-ranking aristocrats were all there, along with noble Brahmans, respected warriors and many cousins and friends of the Pandavas. When the pleasantries were completed, Duryodhana invited everyone to watch the dice game. The Pandavas must have known what was coming after the first throw of Duryodhana's fixed dice. Yet, the eldest Pandava brother kept betting until he lost everything – including his freedom, the freedom of his brothers and that of their common wife, Queen Draupadi. This criminal behavior took place in full view of the elite of a once noble society, and no one did anything to stop it.

Why?

In the 1955 film about gangsters and gamblers, *Guys and Dolls*, Big Julie is Duryodhana. Big Julie forces the desperate gambler Nathan Detroit into a special game of dice. The catch is, the dice in this game are "invisible" and only Big Julie can see how they land.

Detroit plays the pointless game because he is powerless and Big Julie has unchallenged authority. The other gamblers meekly watched Detroit get taken because no one was willing to stop Big Julie. In the same way, Duryodhana's gangster culture bullied his decaying society until his tyranny – and the society he ruled – was destroyed by a war against itself.

If Duryodhana been stopped then, the war would not have happened. So, why didn't the Pandavas refuse to play the rigged game and defy the Gangster Prince? They must have known responding to their cousin's provocations in his royal courtroom would only worsen their situation because no one would stand with them.

And that was not the worst of it. After winning the dice game, Duryodhana wanted everyone present to know he owned the Pandava brothers and their common wife, Queen Draupadi. The Kuru leader ordered Draupadi to stand alone before the assembly of dignitaries, relatives, friends and servants. As they all watched, the Prince began to tear off her sari dress. The ruling Prince of the Age of Knowledge was publicly violating a woman, a royal cousin and everything once protected by the warrior code of honor, while the elite of his community looked on. No one said or did anything to defend Draupadi's honor, the ideals of their society, or their individual morality.

By forcing the others to watch and silently approve of his actions, the Prince was remolding society into his own image. And it was an image of unrestrained violence and sadism. Yet no one called him out. Not one person in that royal room said a word to stop him.

Another American movie offers a perspective on what those present might have done when the Prince moved on Draupadi.

Antoninus (Tony Curtis) and Spartacus (Kirk Douglas) stand together in the "I'm Spartacus" scene from the 1960 film, *Spartacus*

The 1960 film *Spartacus* reaches its climax after an army of rebellious slaves led by Spartacus are defeated by the forces of Ancient Rome. The surrendered slaves are told they will be spared the torture of crucifixion and death only if they identify their leader. Before the real Spartacus can rise to his feet, one man after another stands up to say, "I'm Spartacus," until they all join in. When the Prince abused a helpless woman in a public display of rape, there was no "I'm Draupadi" moment. No one stood up to defend her, the Age of Knowledge or their Warrior Culture of Honor.

The word "honor" is about 1,000 years old. Its earlier ancestor is "noble," which is related to the Sanskrit word for knowledge – Veda. Originally, "honor" and "nobility" referred to inner qualities of character and only later were they redefined to mean titles given as rewards.

The word "possession" was similarly redefined from someone's personal character and skills to their purchases.

In the age of property and rank, obedience to authority and loyal service to the wealthy were raised in importance above personal honor and specialized talents. Titles of honor could be bought and skilled people could be hired. As a result, social culture moved from admiring individual qualities of character to valuing family associations, status symbols and obedience to the social chain of command. When the commands called for murder, the old honor-bound warriors turned into hired killers.

Studies of the warrior culture of honor trace its origin to the domestication of animals and the cow culture. People with herds of animals had to trust their neighbors to return those that wandered off. Neighbors were part of the larger community team that protected everyone's livestock and homes from threats and bad weather. To maintain trust, each neighbor followed the same code of honor. When people stopped following the voluntary code, mistrust spread and the old social order fell apart.

When people lost faith in their neighbors, and authorities could not or would not right obvious wrongs, vigilante groups were formed to restore justice. Today, so-called vigilante gangs practice robbery, torture and murder without restraint. But the original vigilantes followed the warriors' code to do no more than restore balance. An example of this can be found in the 1948 movie, *The Treasure of the Sierra Madre*. When two workers who'd been cheated of their wages fought their boss and knocked him out, they took what he owed them from his wallet and left the rest of his money. To have taken any more would have made them thieves instead of honorable warriors righting a wrong.

Due to the lack of any physical evidence, most scholars dismiss the story of the Kurukshetra War as a fable or allegory similar to Eden. But before rejecting it outright, the central facts should be examined. Was it possible to assemble 4 million soldiers 6,000 years ago, and could they have massacred each other in 18 days with just swords, arrows, spears and maces?

Humanity's population at that time is estimated at 40-60 million, with 8-10 million living in the region of India. The Mahabharata notes the armies came from those of the Royal Families and 70 other allied kingdoms and families – including the Yadavas – who sent warriors to join one side or the other. So, assembling millions of battle-worthy soldiers from India and its neighbors was possible. Could ordinary soldiers with basic weapons slaughter 4 million in just 18 days? Is there any other record of an ancient battle with so many troops massacred so quickly? There is.

It was a battle between the Roman legions and the Carthaginian General, Hannibal. It was one of the worst defeats for an army in all of military history.

On August 2, 216 BC there was a fierce confrontation between the armies of Ancient Rome and Hannibal. The Romans sent 70,000-90,000 soldiers against 45,000-50,000 warriors led by the Carthaginian General. Despite the smaller size of his forces, Hannibal trapped the Romans and exterminated them. In what is known as the Battle of Cannae, Rome's legions were surrounded in an area about twice the size of New York's Central Park. Six hours later, every Roman soldier was dead. This was a Roman defeat recorded by the Romans so it is unlikely the scope of their loss was exaggerated.

If the back and forth slaughter in India went on for just 18 hours a day at the same rate as Cannae – 70,000 men killed every six hours – at the end of 18 days the number of dead would reach 3.9 million.

Gather enough swords together and they become weapons of mass destruction. But it wasn't just the weapons that killed. It was the battlefield itself and the grim reality that the old games had become an uncontrolled killing contest to the last man standing. Both sides were consumed with revenge killing as the body count of friends and relatives rose. Many fighters were probably trampled to death in the mad rush and counter-charge of warriors and animals. Others fell or were knocked down where they drowned in the oozing swamp of blood and body parts. Still other warriors, their hearts broken by the ongoing horror and death, may have let themselves be killed by the war rather than face the ruined world after it.

After the battle ended and the dead removed from the once-sacred field, the old culture of "I Want to Know" drifted away. In its place came the post-war culture of "I Want to Forget."

The smaller forces of the Carthaginian General Hannibal destroyed 70,000 Roman troops in just six hours

If the war at Kurukshtra was the world's first war, that fact alone makes its story of global significance. But there was more to what happened on that battlefield than just a lot of killing.

And so the next question is, "Why was this war different from all other wars?"

CHAPTER 9
WAR, RELIGION AND THE NEW WORLD ORDER

What made the first war of 6,000 years ago different from the ones that followed?

In most respects the war in India was the template for all wars of cultural domination and territorial expansion. A leader assembled a gang of mercenaries who joined in a campaign of plunder and murder for personal gain and self-promotion. Aggressive war is the triumph of egotism and self-delusion over the will to gain knowledge and promote cooperation. The only difference between the first and subsequent wars was the outcome. And even when war leaders are successful, their empires inevitably fall from internal corruption, external conquest or a combination of both.

Humanity lost its innocence after the Kurukshetra War. But in the final moments before the old world died, three extraordinary things happened that marked the passing of one era and the birth of another.

The first was when both sides agreed to follow the Rules for an Ethical War. This was a 5,000 year old version of the Geneva Convention. Because India's texts make no mention of any negotiations to arrive at those 13 rules, it is likely they were adopted from the common rules for war games and fighting contests. They restricted fighting to equally matched warriors with similar weapons, and required surrendered or wounded warriors be protected from further harm. They also prohibited fighters from harming bystanders or women, which suggests fighting games were regularly attended by crowds of spectators.

Controlling-(Rules) of war

- **The two supreme commanders met and framed "rules of ethical conduct", dharmayuddha, for the war. The rules included:**
- Fighting must begin no earlier than sunrise and end exactly at sunset.
- More than one warriors may not attack a single warrior.
- Two warriors may "duel", or engage in prolonged personal combat, only if they carry the same weapons and they are on the same type of mount (on foot, on a horse, on an elephant, or in a chariot).
- No warrior may kill or injure a warrior who has surrendered.
- One who surrenders becomes a prisoner of war and will then be subject to the protections of a prisoner of war.
- No warrior may kill or injure an unarmed warrior.
- No warrior may kill or injure an unconscious warrior.
- No warrior may kill or injure a person or animal not taking part in the war.
- No warrior may kill or injure a warrior whose back is turned away.
- No warrior may attack a woman.
- No warrior may strike an animal not considered a direct threat.
- The rules specific to each weapon must be followed. For example, it is prohibited to strike below the waist in mace warfare.
- Warriors may not engage in any unfair warfare.

The 13 Rules of an Ethical War c 3000 BC

The second event began when the senior Pandava brother made a decision. He removed his armor and walked, unarmed, across the field to the Kuru armies. He approached his grandfather who was now a commander with the Kurus. The Pandava brother asked the elder man for his blessing of victory in the war. The King - who did nothing to stop the march to this family war - blessed his grandson and watched as he walked back to assume his position. The endurance of family loyalty remained so strong until the very last second of the old world that the two men had to embrace each other's humanity before attempting to kill it.

The third event was a pre-death memorial for a civilization about to die. It was a dialogue between the Pandava brother called Arjuna and Prince Krishna – considered the wisest man of the Age of Knowledge. Their discussion - known as the Bhagavad-Gita or "Song of The Great and Wise One" – began when Arjuna looked over the battlefield, foresaw the carnage to come, and refused to fight.

Long after his life, Krishna was worshiped as a manifestation of God. But in his time, he was known as the wisest man of his era and the peacemaker who tried to prevent the war. When the Kuru leaders rejected his last effort to avoid bloodshed, Krishna, a member of the Yadava clan, announced he would not fight in the battle but would serve as chariot driver for his friend and cousin, Arjuna. But as Arjuna waited on the battlefield for the fight to begin, he had an apocalyptic vision of the war to come and how it would destroy the Age of Knowledge Civilization. Torn by his duty to family and his commitment to personal honor, Arjuna refused to join the war against his friends, family and teachers. But neither could he run from the fight. He collapsed in confusion and asked Krishna to tell him what to do. Krishna told his friend he would have to make up his own mind. That response started their dialogue about the meaning of life, the nature of the soul and the importance of service to others. Krishna's teachings in the Bhagavad-Gita are considered to be the world's oldest expression of a comprehensive philosophy. At the end of their discussion, Arjuna announced he was ready to join his brothers. Now that you are empowered by knowledge, Krishna said, "Stand and fight."

In Jakarata, Indonesia, a statue of Krishna and Arjuna in their chariot recalls the Kurukshetra War

At the conclusion of their talk, Arjuna picked up his bow and stepped into his chariot. Then, thousands of trumpet-like conch shells were blown by military musicians on both sides, colorfully-decorated battle elephants raised their trunks and roared, and the war to begin all wars began.

This was not simply a rush of armored flesh and flailing swords. Experienced Generals deployed their forces in military formations called the Heron, Crocodile, Chakra (Wheel), Ocean, Trident and Demon. One can imagine the trident formation as a three-pronged attack, the ocean as a mass assault of waves of warriors and crocodile as a pincer move trapping the opposition between two forces like a jaw. The demon charge may have been a crazed "Rebel yell" attack commonly used by Southern troops during the American Civil War.

Their troops were organized into battle units called divisions. Each division was made up of 21,870 chariots fighters, 21,870 drivers of war elephants, 65,610 cavalry fighters on horseback, and 109,350 foot-soldiers. The Kurus marshalled 11 divisions for the war, the Pandavas had only 7. It was an awesome display of military power.

As the fighting intensified and the number of dead climbed, the purpose of the 13 rules was forgotten and the killing spiralled out of control. With each new day, there was killing to avenge the killings of the day before, and then the night before or the hour before. So many men were killed in so short a time that it must have seemed as if weapons of mass destruction had been used.

According to India's texts, when the fighting stopped, only 12 of the original 4 million warriors remained alive. The rest were rotting piles of broken flesh and they covered the once-sacred hillsides of Kurukshetra. The bloody body of humanity was slivered with swords and the era of Eden was gone.

Despite Arjuna's apocalyptic vision of a Mad Max post-war world of roaming gangsters, hardships and perpetual war, the reality was that after the explosive bang of war, the world whimpered and moved on. The post-war generation of the winning side, like those of the Jazz Age following World War I, plunged into reckless behavior as a way to defy their memories of death. The children of Krishna and the Pandavas neglected their duties as rulers. They held lavish parties and engaged in lethal fighting contests. Krishna ordered alcohol banned from his city, but the bootleggers of 3000 BC found ways to smuggle it through the city gates. The youth adopted a swagger of separateness from their elders, and superiority towards others they encountered. They abandoned the old social rules in favor of aristocratic indulgence and killing each other in duels of honor. With no one governing for the good of all, the cities fell into ruin and people abandoned them. Large scale trade collapsed. People no longer desired to work together towards great goals. They wanted to be left alone in their villages.

Humanity entered its first Dark Ages. It retreated from the peak of its accomplishments and retrenched into smaller communities and simpler ways. In the post-war world, people gathered in rituals of consolation and remembrance of those who died. When later generations forgot the names of the dead, they mourned the loss of the old world and took up practices they hoped would restore the peace, abundance and divine favor they associated with the world of the past. It was group nostalgia of this kind that gave birth to the widespread use of statues for worship and led to the development of organized religions.

The root of "nostalgia" means to gain relief from old wounds by returning home. Regular gatherings to mourn those lost in the war and their lost, godly world of "Eden" was the starting point of organized religion. Temples were built to give old memories a new home. This post-war nostalgia changed the way people thought about God. Through most of early civilization, people rarely spoke about God and no one made regular offerings because their deity was not separate from humanity but a common part of it. When that world of human peace vanished and a world of fear was born, it was as if God was no longer present. The Deity who walked among humanity had left. To evoke the old world of an ever-present God, deity statues became increasingly popular. As memories of the peaceful past disappeared, new religions rejected statues as products of an old world of evil and sin.

Later, leaders of the newly created Exclusive Religions told their followers to separate themselves from other people in the world and harshly judge those outside their ranks. As human communities divided over religions that claimed ownership of God, humanity's sense of the Divine changed too. A God who was no longer part of the human world, could no longer be 'seen' by people or represented in any human or human-like form. The new Deity was limited to abstract symbols such as the yin-yang and the Christian cross. The humanity of friends seeking knowledge, imagined a friendly Deity that guided people to understanding. When human relationships turned violent, so did their God.

The Biblical Hebrews were one of the early nostalgic religions that used statues. The Bible notes that the Hebrew people and the Ancient Israelites both worshiped a pair of male and female statues of God called *teraphim*. The Biblical Israelites bowed to the *teraphim*, and placed offerings of food on their altars while congregants sang and priests burned fragrant woods. In Hindu ceremonies, deity statues called *murti* are also offered food in an elaborate ceremony of incense and fire.

Those Biblical statues were similar to the Radha and Krishna deities worshipped in many Hindu temples. Every Hindu temple has its own unique statue or statues each with their own unique name and design.

Among Hindus, Krishna is considered an incarnation of the Supreme Deity in human form, and he is typically presented with blue or black skin. Yet, his consort Radha, and brother Balarama are shown as white-skinned. Despite this, India's texts never questions those dermal differences. In another representation, Krishna and his brother and sister are portrayed in a way that is deliberately non-human. These deities suggest a God who takes different forms on other worlds. The black-skinned form of Krishna in this trio is called Jagannath, which means "Lord of the Universe," and this name is the source of the English word "juggernaut."

The sibling Indian gods (L-R) of Balarama, Subadra and Krishna as Jagannath

As with the historical figures of Buddha (c 560 BC) and Jesus (c 4 BC-34 AD), the man Krishna (c 3100 BC) was not originally worshiped as a God figure. But in later years, Hindu teachers called Krishna one of the major avatars or incarnations of God that included Vishnu and Shiva, and all three deities have blue skin. Curiously, so does the God of the Hebrew Bible. In Song of Solomon, the Deity is called "dark" and compared to beryl, a dark blue stone. In the Book of

Daniel, a divine figure is described as "a blue man" whose body "was like beryl."

Teraphim statues were worshipped by the Ancient Hebrews and Israelites (Courtesy: Bible Lands Museum, Jerusalem)

By 4,200 years ago, most urban centers had their own religious temples but the gods of this time were interchangeable. These early religions considered each other to be part of the same loose affiliation of people seeking higher knowledge and a closer relationship with God. Because the old notion of a universal Deity of knowledge remained, the first religions freely associated. They exchanged ideas and god figures as if they were different science courses in the same university. And no one taking physics thought those in the chemistry program were going to hell. Then, in Ancient Egypt 3,300 years ago, the world of inclusive religions was shattered by the birth of the first Exclusive Religions whose followers claimed the right to kill anyone who offended their God. The militant leaders of these new Exclusive Religions often aimed their fury at those who used statues in their worship. Why did followers of these radical religions kill so many people for using a visual aid when they prayed?

Krishna's skin was black or blue-back while his consort Radha was white, but no one in his time (c 3000 BC) saw skin color as a meaningful distinction (Photo courtesy: Hare Krishna Temple, Toronto)

Humans receive most of their information about the world from their eyes. They take in 10 million bits of information per second – the speed of an Ethernet connection. It takes only 15 milliseconds to recognize a symbol and just 100 milliseconds to attach a meaning to it. People taught with visual aids outperform those instructed by words alone, and people are 30 percent more likely to believe an argument if they see images that support it.

The use of paired statues like the *teraphim* portrayed the Creator as the ideal of human life – peaceful, friendly and welcoming to new relationships. Food offerings to the statues were shared among the congregation as a community festival. The male and female were shown in a loving relationship as an inspiration for stable, loving marriages and devotional friendships between people.

At the Hare Krishna Temple in Toronto, three different sets of statues (*murti*) live in three rooms on the altar

In modern Judaism, the *teraphim* are gone. In place of them, the scroll of the Torah is decorated and housed in its own home inside each synagogue where the Hebrew statues once lived. The Torah is fashioned between two prominent and elaborately carved rollers that are often crowned as a symbolic king and queen. When the scrolls are carried among the congregation they are honored in the same way as Hindu statues. Only temple officials are allowed to carry the sacred scrolls, so the faithful cover their hands with the end of a prayer shawl, touch the Torah and kiss their shawl.

Jewish synagogue with royally decorated Torah scrolls housed in a minimalist altar

As the statues and temples housing them grew larger and more elaborate, more priests were required to serve them. However, the temples didn't actually produce anything but their demands for money kept increasing. As a result, the longest-lasting legacy of the first organized religion was taxes. Temple-based taxes took two forms – first as obligatory offerings and then as a form of bribe to pay off the gods to avoid divine punishment or receive special benefits. The concept of sin was born with organized religion. To be judged sinful was to be punished, and so the original meaning of "sin" was "trespass" which implied that when people trespassed against religious law they could be punished by religious authorities according to their laws of sin. As this practice spread, so did the division of society as religious and royal authorities extended the reach of their laws. Before the rise of religion, the earliest sense of sin was more basic. Each person was due respect and those who trespassed on others by showing disrespect was guilty of the one universally acknowledged sin – arrogance.

The palace-like temples of religion and the palace temples of monarchs began to merge in human culture. Kings were God-on-Earth and God was the King-in-the-Sky. The bureaucracy of the king's court and officials became the many demigods and saints who administered their regional functions in the King God's kingdom. They answered the prayers of ordinary people when the top God was too busy to listen or too far away to hear.

Though sophisticated in many ways, the pre-war world was innocent and naïve. The root of "innocent" means "doing no harm" and "not killing." The source of "naïve" conveys the idea of healthy and "unspoiled." The ancient stories that describe an old, innocent world evoke the time in human history before widespread war and fear. Yet, the majority of Indian historians dismiss the Kurukshetra War story as nothing more than a fable or an exaggeration of a smaller conflict that happened around 1500 BC. From a scholarly perspective, there is no direct evidence for the war. Where are the remains of the 4 million dead soldiers? They might have been piled on burning rafts and sunk in the sea where they are waiting to be found. But that is a theory based on an assumption.

So what remains? There is a trail of history with a big missing piece. There is no evidence of human war prior to roughly 6,000 years ago. If there was a first major war that cleaved the human world into the eras before and after war, Kurukshetra is the only recorded candidate.

However, the most compelling evidence for the war and its vanished civilization does not come from the stories associated with India's ancient texts. Rather, the best evidence for the war and the society that spawned it is found in the great culture that followed the war. It is known as the Indus River Valley Civilization, and for 1,000 years (c 3000-2000 BC) it flourished in the region of Northwest India and Eastern Pakistan.

Along with the kingdoms of Ancient Egypt and the empires of Mesopotamia, the Indus Civilization would advance human achievement in the arts, science, technology, architecture and medicine. But while the other empires would be carved out by the armies of warrior kings, the people of the Indus would live peaceful and prosperous lives for 10 centuries without armies, priests, kings or poverty. And they achieved that distinction because their whole society was organized as a deliberate rejection of the earlier era's system of social divisions. To the founders of the Indus, the caste system and its culture of priests and warriors were the cause of the Kurukshetra War.

CHAPTER 10

THE AGE OF GOVERNMENT: INDUS VALLEY DEMOCRACY

"Before our white brothers arrived to make us civilized men, we didn't have any kind of prison. Because of this, we didn't have any delinquents. Without a prison, there can be no delinquents. We had no locks or keys therefore among us there were no thieves. When someone was so poor that he couldn't afford a horse, a tent or a blanket, he would, in that case, receive it all as a gift. We were too uncivilized to give great importance to private property. We didn't know any kind of money and consequently, the value of a human being was not determined by his wealth. We had no written laws laid down, no lawyers and no politicians, therefore we were not able to cheat and swindle one another. We were really in bad shape before the white man arrived and I don't know how to explain how we were able to manage without these fundamental things that - so they tell us - are so necessary for a civilized society," John Fire Lame Deer (1903–1976), Lakota holy man.

**John Fire Lame Deer of the Lakota Tribe
remembered the world of old humanity**

Until about 100 years ago, there were still communities of North American Indians who kept old humanity's informal culture alive as John Fire Lame Deer explained. Until about 50 years ago, many communities in Southwest Asia, Africa, South and Central America and the Pacific Islands retained aspects of human life as it existed before the advent of private property, organized religion, taxes, laws and the culture of obedience. Today, there are few unspoiled, innocent places left in the world.

Throughout history, humans self-organized into family structures, small groups and large communities. So, it is necessary to ask, "What was the first type of human government?" According to the available evidence, it was a democratic one – a person or group appointed by community agreement to serve in a governing capacity as the need arose.

Humanity's early hunter-gatherer societies had no hierarchies, social classes or formal leaders. Leaders were chosen to settle disputes and organize people for large-scale building projects. When those tasks were accomplished, the leader would return to their status as a common member of the community. That was the foundation of the original concept that public service was a temporary engagement and not a career path to wealth and power.

Until recently, accomplished people and former national leaders refused offers to promote commercial products because they felt to profit from community service would be a moral hazard. If people participated only to get rich, the principle of public service as a way to strengthen community ties and build character would be lost. So, the old communities honored those who acted for a higher purpose. The city of Cincinnati was named for the Roman General, Cincinnatus, who famously gave up his absolute leadership of the Roman Empire and returned home when his duty was done.

About 5,000 years ago, leaders in India, Egypt and Mesopotamia set up new centers of civilization in the post-war world. Using different means to effect different outcomes, the founders of those communities would create the political structures used by governments, the first planned cities, organized religion and written language. This new Age of Government was led by hereditary kings in Egypt, a visionary war leader in Mesopotamia, and a group of real estate developers who planned and built the world's first democratic, secular and multicultural state in the region of Pakistan and India five thousand years ago.

Between 3500-2000 BC those regional empires would generate enormous wealth and technological advancements in science, medicine and warfare. All of them would flourish in a great explosion of urban life and the creation of sophisticated art and architecture. Then, around 2000 BC, all three would collapse from the combined effects of extreme climate change and the mass movement of refugees. But in their lifetimes, these new centers of humanity would pioneer three new forms of government.

In early Ancient Egypt, a succession of warrior kings were crushing the heads of their neighbors with stone maces and enslaving those they didn't execute. Around 3000 BC, Egypt's King Narmer set out to unite all Egypt under his absolute rule.

Although the peoples of Northeast Africa had a long history as friendly traders, 5,000 years ago a succession of war leaders began marching their mercenary armies across the landscape in search of conquest and plunder. This was a time when few people had war weapons to defend themselves against attackers, and most had never seen a rampaging army.

Until Narmer's campaign to steal land and life from his northern neighbors, Egypt was a land of two cultures and styles of government. North Egypt had its capital in a city called Memphis. This region was a lush agricultural area, and the Northern Egyptians traded with communities across North Africa, in the Middle East and India. Southern Egypt had stronger connections with Sudan and Ethiopia, and its capital resided at Thebes.

The economic and cultural center of the North was the Delta region where the world's longest river – the Nile - ends its 6,853 km (4,258 mi.) journey at the Mediterranean Sea. The Nile River begins high in the mountains of Tanzania and flows to the flatlands of the north. The Ancient Egyptians called the mountainous region where the river began, Upper Egypt, and the northern delta area of marshland birds and papyrus reeds where it ended, Lower Egypt.

The people of the North were united in a loose confederation of communities with few rules and kings with limited powers. Their symbol was a patch of papyrus reeds growing together.

In the South, the Nile Valley narrows. What the Ancient Egyptians called the red lands of the desert sat just beyond the villages huddled along the narrow strip of agricultural fields bordering the waters of the Nile. The government in the South was as harsh as its climate. Its symbol was the lotus flower, perhaps as a tribute to their Indo-African heritage. The river lotus was frequently used – in Egypt and India - to represent enlightenment and eternal life. However, for King Narmer it may have carried a more sinister meaning. By day, the lotus shows its beauty, but at night, the flower becomes a fist that closes tightly over everything inside it.

The kings of early Egypt were ruthless warriors who embarked on campaigns of slaughter to crush the independence of their neighbors and enforce submission to one-man rule. They gave themselves super-hero names like King Fortress, The Cobra King, the Scorpion King, and Narmer - the "Striking Catfish."

In 3000 BC, Narmer proclaimed himself the first king of a united Egypt. After a short campaign of conquest, North Egypt surrendered and the new king gained power over a combined population of about one million people. He organized large building projects, encouraged urbanization and set up military garrisons in the Middle East to enforce Egypt's authority in its new colonies. But the order, stability and economic growth of Narmer's New Egypt was paid for in human blood and constant reminders of royal terror.

The Scorpion King and Narmer had commemorations made of their victories, and what makes them unique is the way they glorified the torture and execution of their enemies.

The Palette of Narmer and is one of the world's oldest historical documents. It celebrates a military victory. Monuments to military leaders frequently show them in a noble pose of power. Narmer's Palette presents him as a god of death; a vampire king who required the blood of human sacrifice to sustain his rule.

The Palette of Narmer

King Narmer celebrated his conquest of Ancient Egypt with displays of executions and decapitated soldiers

Palette of Narmer

The Palette features several scenes and images on the front and back. In one, the king is shown as a bull using his horns to break down the walls of a city and trample its inhabitants. Nearby are rows of decapitated prisoners. In another, Narmer has raised his stone mace to smash the head of a kneeling captive. Nearby are two naked prisoners either dead or about to be. Facing Narmer is a predatory bird holding a rope that ends with a hook in the nose of a human-reed creature representing the conquered North. Ancient Egypt's first king was a master of propaganda who united his empire with public displays of ruthless violence against his opponents.

The mace head of the Scorpion King which dates to 3300 BC, shows an earlier version of the culture of death that gave birth to Ancient Egypt.

The Mace Head of Egypt's Scorpion King showed the tribes he defeated as strangled birds hung from poles

One of its defining features is a line of poles each with a hanged bird bearing a symbol of a formerly independent kingdom. It is a lapwing bird, common in the marshes of the North and known for its shrill, wailing cry.

Ancient Egypt's culture would be driven by the single ruler on the throne and its extensive hierarchies of political and religious functionaries. Like Ancient India, social activity in Egyptian society would be restricted by religious rules and convention designed to ensure each part of the community machine remained in place and performed its duty.

Despite its bloody beginnings and authoritarian rule, Ancient Egypt would outlast all the other kingdoms and empires of the old world. Under a succession of dynastic kings and queens, and through revolutions, war and times of great openness, Ancient Egypt would pioneer tremendous and unmatched marvels of architecture, mathematics and science. In one form or another, its achievements and philosophy would survive conquest and transformation by Cyrus the Great of Persia, Alexander the Great of Ancient Macedonia, Julius Caesar's Roman Legions, the Islamic Caliphate, the Ottoman Turks, Napoleon's invasion and occupation, the British Empire and political independence.

About 700 years after Narmer's armies took control of Egypt, another military leader set out to build his empire in Mesopotamia.

Like Narmer, Sargon the Great was a single-minded conqueror and his mission was to rule his region of the world by any means necessary.

The word Mesopotamia means the land "between two rivers" and describes the fertile growing region between the Euphrates and Tigris Rivers that flow from southern Turkey to the Persian Gulf. Today, the old region of Mesopotamia includes parts of Iraq, Syria, Turkey, Iran and Lebanon. It was here Sargon rolled out his reputation as the world's first military genius. After leading his armies to sweeping victories over neighboring kingdoms and cities, he established the first military empire and security state under his absolute rule.

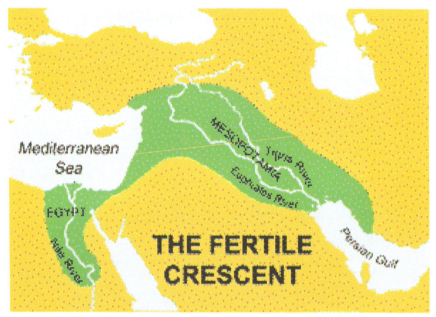

From 4000-1000 BC Mesopotamia and Egypt were the world's most technologically advanced civilizations

Sargon was not his birth name. He was an immigrant to a region of South Mesopotamia then largely inhabited by people called the Sumerians ("Blackheads") and a minority group called the Akkadians. Though his true origins are unknown, later legends and stories suggest Sargon had a Semitic heritage like the Akkadians.

After murdering the two kings who once supported him, Sargon embarked on a rapid series of military campaigns that made him the absolute ruler of Mesopotamia around 2300 BC. Sargon's Akkadian Empire was a military state, and rapid travel was necessary to maintain control over conquered cities and quickly crush rebellions. Roads and canals were built to connect the empire's urban centers and stimulate internal trade. He established the world's first government-run mail service. Under his rule, city temples were unified into the first organized religion with common rituals and stories. His empire pioneered the use of secret police, racial classification, total war that included the mass slaughter of civilians, psychological warfare, widespread slavery and citizens who worshiped statues of Sargon as a god. For thousands of years after his dynasty had vanished into history, Sargon remained an inspiration for iron-fisted, military rulers throughout Mesopotamia.

4,000 years ago, Sargon the Great was a ruthless conqueror and empire-builder who also started the first postal service

Sargon and Narmer were brutal opportunists who built a new world order based on power and fear. But something quite amazing happened in the third location where humanity's second phase of civilization first began. This was the largest, wealthiest, most influential and progressive of the three post-war empires. Yet, the uncelebrated heroes who created the Indus River Valley Civilization were not great warriors, ambitious kings or bloodthirsty conquerors. Its founders were humble visionaries with no interest in fame, and so there is no known record or image of who they were or where they came from. But the legacy they left for the world was a new design for urban life and multiculturalism. It was the world's first democratic society. Its leaders rejected organized religion, war and kings and their legacy would transform India and give birth to the Hebrew people of the Bible.

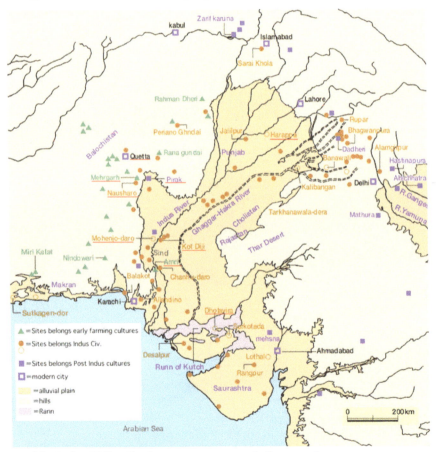

The Indus Valley Civilization grew to include more than 17,000 towns, cities and villages that covered a region twice the size of France

It grew up along the lush landscape of the Indus River that flows through what is now India, Pakistan and Afghanistan. It was this location that gave birth to the words "Hindu" and "India," for they originally referred to people who lived by the "Indoos" or "Indyuh" River.

The Indus Civilization was not forged by blood and battle, and it didn't thrive by slavery. And for almost a thousand years, it flourished without formal leaders or armies, religious authorities or social divisions. The ruins of their architecture show planned, middle class style cities with no palaces for the rich or shacks for the poor. Yet, this commonwealth of trading towns was more prosperous, peaceful and longer-lived than Sargon's Empire and Egypt's early kingdoms. Many aspects of the Indus civilization remain a mystery because they kept no historical record and had no written language. Yet, the design of their cities and the total absence of government buildings, royal palaces, religious temples, war weapons and a written alphabet are the clues that reveal everything about the purpose and philosophy of this civilization.

Five thousand years ago, its planned cities provided all its residents with pre-built, equal-sized homes set on wide grid streets. Each home had a room with a drinking well and flow-flush toilet fed by gigantic reservoirs outside the city. The lack of elaborate palaces, statues of leaders and official buildings suggests they governed their communities by consensus, while the common housing style evokes a communal culture in which all people were considered equal. There is no evidence of poverty or income inequality, and in their long history there is nothing to suggest they ever fought in a war or were attacked by enemies. Instead, they promoted widespread trade in their region and freely distributed innovations such as their use of zero and a 10-base number system for weights and measures.

Remains of a 4,500 year old housing development in the Indus River Valley city of Mahanjo-Daro

Most modern cities, including London, Paris and Rome, began as villages of randomly placed homes with little connection to each other. Thousands of years would pass before they were redeveloped to include city-wide networks for water and urban transportation. The Indus launched the science of urban planning and incorporated the latest technology to serve its citizens. Neighborhoods were set inside wide smooth streets that connected at right-angles. Water was transported into homes and along the roads by thousands of interconnected, funnel-shaped clay pipes. Periodically, the street pipes would be opened to let fresh water cool the dirt laneways and flush them clean. These pre-built cities served another purpose. They kept urban growth from exploding into overcrowded, polluted cities that strained the food supply and other resources. When too many people wanted to live in one place, a new town was built. As a result, everyone had proper housing and there were no slums.

What's striking about the urban layout of Indus cities is how closely it resembles modern planned developments. After World War II, the first modern mass housing development project was built in upper New York State to provide homes for returning soldiers and their new families. It was called Levittown and buyers could choose from a selection of pre-designed home styles set on pre-sliced landscapes on nearly identical streets.

The first modern housing development - Levittown, NY c 1947

It was a huge success. Levittown was the urban solution for the instant coffee generation – build city, add people, stir. What the planners did not realize was they were duplicating a strategy initiated by the Indus River Valley Development Team 50 centuries earlier.

The first question that puzzles modern historians is why it began. Studies by Dr. Mayank Vahia of the Tata Institute for Fundamental Research in Mumbai, India shows there were about 3,000 settlements in the Indus Valley Region until about 3500 BC. For unknown reasons, there was a steady migration of people to the Indus for the next 500 years and by 3000 BC the number of settlements had doubled to 6,000. Then, it began a spectacular rise in population, trade and social innovation. At its peak, around 2000 BC, the Indus River Valley had grown to 17,000 small cities, towns and villages spread over a region twice the size of France. To put that number in perspective, there are an estimated 36,000 communities in modern France. Yet, shortly after reaching its peak, the urban centers of the Indus were abandoned in rapid succession. Over a period of 100 years, the number of populated settlements plunged from 17,000 to its starting point of 3,000.

What kind of civilization flourished in the Indus, and why are its marvels and accomplishments largely unknown and forgotten? One reason is they had no armies. They existed peacefully with their neighbors and expanded trade with them for 1,000 years. In modern media, the phrase "if it bleeds, it leads" applies here. The Indus never went to war or experienced riots. As a result, the scribes of Egypt and Mesopotamia - who controlled the mainstream media of the day - said little about this happy land of polite people. To the journalists of 4,300 years ago, the Indus was Canada.

So, the enigma of the Indus starts with its origins around 3000 BC. What prompted the first wave of migration to this broad valley in western India?

After the Kurukshetra War, the culture that bound the old kingdoms was lost, trade and travel declined and India's early communities turned inward. Most kingdoms were content to run their own version of the caste and control system. Kings served their people and the people made offerings to their king and their gods. It was simple, ongoing and never changed.

Like the teachers of Gobekli, the people who designed and built the first Indus Valley city faced the challenge of motivating people who lacked motivation. The teachers of the Indus lit the fires of mass education by creating a social environment for meeting people and sharing knowledge. The people who launched the Indus experiment aimed to rekindle advanced civilization and trade by building pre-designed cities and giving away free housing.

The words "city" and "civilization" come from a root word that means a place where citizens work together as a peaceful community of friends. The additional meanings of "city" can be found in the related word, "cemetery," whose root means "beloved," "bed" and "restful." Cemeteries were places of rest for the dead, and cities were centers for friendship and love among the living.

All the Indus cities were planned communities that attracted large numbers of people from around the region for nearly a thousand years. This civilization's culture and social philosophy was so attractive that huge numbers of people moved there. Although they left no written record, the story of its culture and political thinking are everywhere in its ruins.

All the standout features of the Indus culture can be seen as a deliberate counter-action to the social divisions of an earlier society and its downfall in a terrible war. Although the caste system of class rank by birth still existed in many parts of India, the Indus cities were designed to ensure all people lived as equals. To paraphrase Marshall McLuhan, the medium of its equal opportunity housing plan carried the message of its society.

To date, no religious temple or royal residence has been found in any Indus city. This strongly implies a conscious rejection of organized religion, official priests and aristocratic leaders. Similarly, there is no evidence of a warrior class or signs they ever went to war. How could this be? The complete absence of any public symbol of royalty, religion or warriors throughout the Indus suggests a culture that was profoundly anti-religion, anti-authoritarian and anti-war. When people give up something completely – such as alcohol or drugs - it is only after abuse of them has ruined their lives. Likewise, widespread disarmament movements only arise after terribly destructive wars. Therefore, the only credible reason why the leaders of the Indus rejected the military and religious institutions that flourished in the empires around them, was because they'd recently experienced a disastrous war and were keenly aware of the social problems caused by ambitions military and religious leaders and their followers.

Another sign the Indus Civilization rejected the earlier culture and its war, is the absence of the kind of imported American horses used to drive chariots in the War and owned as status symbols by royalty in the earlier era. India's ancient texts clearly describe this breed of horses as the kind used in the Kurukshetra War. The Indus leaders abandoned them as signs of militaristic elitism, and returned to the traditional Indian ox cart. It was all quite revolutionary and socialist.

Although there is no evidence of any organized religion or priestly hierarchy, the Indus culture appears to have included its own form of baptism. One of the great cities of the Indus Civilization is today called Mohenjo-daro, which means "Mound of the Dead" in the Pakistani language of Sindhi. In the center of that city is a stand-out public structure called The Great Bath. It is the size of a swimming pool – about 12 by 7 m (39 x 22 ft.), with a maximum depth of about 2.5 m (8 ft.). Walkways lead in and out of the pool. Across the street from The Great Bath stood a large building with several rooms, three verandas and two staircases leading to the roof. The tower building and The Great Bath were probably gathering places for the community.

The Great Bath of Mohenjo-Daro was a 3,000 year old baptismal pool

The Great Bath resembles ancient baptismal pools and may have been used for similar purposes. Each Indus home had its own bathroom and source of fresh running water, so keeping the population clean was not the central purpose of The Great Bath. Before baptism was adopted by organized religions, ritual cleansing had a long tradition in human culture because it promoted healthy habits and clear thinking. Modern studies have shown students who bathe before a test do better than those who don't. In the Indus, pure water was a symbol of truth and honesty. While The Bath served several social purposes, its main value was likely ceremonial. Instead of taking an oath by swearing on a holy book, people of the Indus may have ritually bathed themselves before taking public office, getting married or to celebrate a birth.

While the people of the Indus were building baptismal pools, the scribes of Egypt and Mesopotamia were recording history with the world's first writing systems. Despite its many other achievements – including brain surgery, a base 10 number system and the concept of zero – the Indus never produced a written form of their language. Once again, it is likely the Indus leadership rejected writing because they associated it with the earlier era's elite Brahman class who used writing to keep their knowledge secret from the mass of illiterate people. The Indus people likely used a hybrid spoken language that easily adopted the foreign words of newcomers – much like the evolution of English from its Germanic, French, Latin, Greek and Indo-European roots. Instead of writing, they invented an early form of Claymation to bridge the different languages spoken in their multicultural cities. Throughout the Indus Valley, thousands of baked clay squares featuring animals and symbols have been found. These small tablets probably served many purposes including currency. For example, three Brahma bulls might equal one elephant. Denominating coins by animals was common in the Indo-Greek communities later established by Alexander the Great.

Bilingual coins from the Greco-Indian King Apollodotus I (c 170 BC) resemble the Indus Valley seals

Because the clay tiles were individually made, they could be adapted for any purpose. They could be inked and used to mark containers of goods for trade. Some scholars think the order and combination of animals and symbols were used as a kind of shipping code to indicate a container's contents and destination.

The Indus residents molded small clay figures of people and animals and wore them on a necklace. Collars on the animals suggest the people of the Indus had pets – dogs, and really big cats like cheetahs and jaguars.

Indus ceramic dog with collar

Some clay figures worn for public display may have been used to indicate occupation or marital status in a way that was easily recognized and understood by people of different cultures. A woman wearing a certain kind of necklace – like that of the nursing mother - might indicate she was married. Naked men and the saluting young woman might be an ancient form of sexting their availability as they searched for a mate.

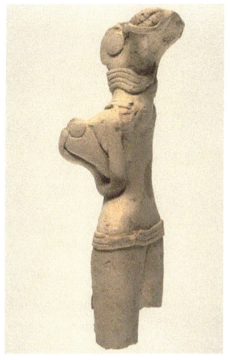

Nursing mother wearing necklace that may be a sign of marriage

Saluting Young Woman signals her availability

Single men looking for a mate in the Indus had their own form of sexting

Forty-two hundred years ago, the Indus Civilization was the most advanced of its time. Their sophisticated math and geometry enabled them to create fabulous rock architecture inside enormous caves. They developed plastic surgery to reshape noses, and performed brain operations to clean debris from head wounds.

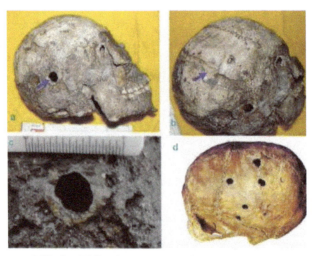

4,500 year old Indus Valley brain surgery (Courtesy: Current Science)

If the Indus culture was a direct rejection of the earlier leaders and their caste system, the specific way they created their counter-society suggests it was inspired by a philosophy that condemned the old social divisions as the cause of the terrible war. And if that is true, they must have had a way to communicate the history and values of their society to newcomers.

Before modern media, large stylized paintings called murals related important local events in a way that could be understood by people who spoke different languages. At the Vatican in Rome, the Biblical stories depicted on its chapel ceilings serve that purpose, as do paintings of American history inside the Capitol Dome in Washington, D.C. If the Kurukshetra War was the event that defined Indus society, the Indus leadership would certainly have wanted to communicate that fact. It appears they did, using their own form of the ceiling fresco – the clay seal.

The Warrior Seal stands out from among the tens of thousands of other seals and small sculptures because it displays a mural – a pictorial story meant to communicate something important to both residents and visitors. And the story it tells is the Kurukshetra War. To read the seal's mural as a single narrative, each of its 11 elements must be deciphered. Once understood, they all combine to tell the central story of the War as related in the Mahabharata.

The Indus Valley "Warrior Seal" is a mural of the world's first war

There are three sacred fig trees – two in bloom at each side and a barren one in the middle. There are three cone-shaped symbols and three people in the center, and those images are flanked by two composite creatures who appear to be shrieking. The two central characters stabbing at each other are caste warriors as indicated by the knot of hair on their head. But unlike the brutality shown on Narmer's victory palette, these fighters only touch their opposite with the tips of their weapons as a symbol of war not a promotion of it. The two warriors are equal in size, evoking two halves of the same family. On both sides of the warriors are monstrous-looking, horned human/animal figures. They have one set of human feet and a second pair of cloven hooves like a goat. Something flows from the back of their heads and they appear to be wailing and screaming. The vertical lines on their arms indicate raised hairs like goosebumps of fear and death. Are those half-human, half-animal creatures symbols of war? Are they meant to convey the degradation of humanity and the terror of battlefield slaughter and the madness of military leaders?

Pablo Picasso's famous mural, *Guernica* (1937), was painted after the aerial bombing of the Spanish town of Guernica by Nazi warplanes during the Spanish Civil War (1936-1939). Its shrieking figures are very similar to the wailing creatures on the Warrior Seal.

The image of a sacred fig tree is presented in two ways. At the beginning and end of the mural they are flourishing, but the central one near the Warriors is barren. The flourishing fig trees represent the abundance that existed before the war and again in the Indus Civilization. Between these trees of prosperity stands the barren one indicating the destruction and hardships of the war and its aftermath. Three cone shapes, resembling grave mounds, are placed above the leafless tree. In the early history of math, the number 3 was used as shorthand for any large number.

As a history of the Kurukshetra War, the seal could be read as: Two halves of a family went to war even though the man in the middle tried to stop them.

Who is the man in the middle? He might be the peacemaker of the War story – Prince Krishna. He is shown holding the hands of both warriors as if attempting to intervene to stop the war as Krishna did in the recorded history.

This mural appears to tell the Indus' history.

"Many generations ago, the great family of humanity was divided and brother killed brother. Krishna, a great and wise man of peace, tried to stop them but they wouldn't listen. The war destroyed the old world. Here in the Indus, humanity is flourishing again because we have learned the lessons of the past."

When the painter Picasso first saw the prehistoric cave art, he realized people had "learned nothing" about art in 12,000 years. When he witnessed the destruction of the small Spanish town of Geurnica by Nazi fighter planes that bombed its homes and shot down fleeing people and animals, he painted *Geurnica*. If Picasso had seen the Warrior Seal in his lifetime, he might have made a comment about humanity and war.

" We have learned nothing in 6,000 years."

Cartoon by Barry Brown, 2016

If the seal is a 5,000 year old mural of the history and philosophy of the Indus, it may have been a small version of a much larger one.

This interpretation suggests Krishna was the inspirational figurehead of the Indus' leadership because he opposed organized religion and the caste system, and he tried to prevent the war. If Krishna's teachings were honored in the Indus, it would explain why Krishna – a minor figure in the Mahabharata history – was elevated to a central figure and Godhead later on. The absence of any deity statue of Krishna in any Indus community indicates that if he was an inspiration, Krishna was revered as the wisest man of his age but not worshiped as God. There is another unique Indus Seal that may support this.

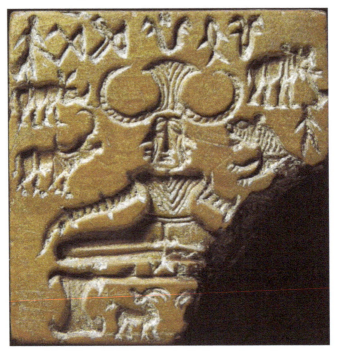

The Wise Old Man on the Indus seal may be a portrait of Krishna as a grandfather

The Wise Old Man sits in a lotus position on a low seat surrounded by images of animals, letter-like icons, and stick figures of people. Some researchers have suggested the figure on this seal is an image of Shiva or some other Hindu god. But with no evidence of temples or other godly characters in the Indus, it is unlikely this figure is a deity. The lack of government buildings and mansions indicates he is not a king or leading figure of their contemporary community. Therefore, if he does represent someone important, he is likely the man whose teachings they follow. If the Wise Man represents a known historical figure, he may be Prince Krishna. Since the advent of temple worship in Hinduism about 2,000 years ago, Krishna has been portrayed as an eternally youthful man or child. Yet, India's history says Krishna was a grandfather at the time of the War. If the Indus leaders respected Krishna as a man they would have portrayed him more realistically.

The icons on the seal may evoke one of his teachings. The gathering of animals and people suggests his unity with nature as seen in later portraits of Zoroaster, Buddha and Jesus. The Wise Man wears a horned hat. In many ancient cultures – including the Hebrews and Israelites – horns were a symbol of leadership and male potency. The modern royal crown is a descendent of the horned hat.

If the Wise Man on the seal is a more accurate representation of Krishna than the later idealised versions, it would not be the first time an ancient character has undergone a face or even a race lift. Two paintings of the Biblical patriarch Abraham and his son, Isaac, show this. In 2,000 year-old Christian tombs from Ancient Rome, paintings of the Hebrew prophet Abraham show him with dark brown skin like the people of India His son, Isaac, appears as a black-skinned African with curly black hair.

In Ancient Rome, early Christians showed the Biblical characters of Abraham and his son Isaac with dark skin – Latina Catacomb, Rome

Yet, some 1,600 years after that portrait, the Dutch painter Rembrandt van Rijn recast the same two characters as Northern Europeans with bone white skin.

"Abraham and Isaac" (1634) were given a race-lift by Rembrandt van Rijn

The end of the Indus began with a bang of natural disasters but it trailed out in a whimper of broken lives and abandoned cities. After decades of severe weather – devastating downpours followed by long-term drought, the lush lands of the Indus dried up. Their green fields shriveled into brown deserts of cracked earth and people fled its cities. The history of that 50-75 year-long period of worldwide deadly weather extremes was recounted by the Hebrews in their story of Noah, and in other narratives from India, Mesopotamia, China and Egypt. Most of those stories describe a time of disastrous flooding from which people recovered. To the authors of the Bible, however, the destruction of their Indus homeland by rain and drought was God's punishment on a sinful world.

Modern research has linked the effects of this climate change era to the collapse of four civilizations – the Indus, Sargon's Mesopotamia, early Egypt and China. As weather change devastated their food supply, the last hungry defenders of Sargon's dynasty surrendered to invaders from the North. In Egypt, Narmer's successors were brought down by food riots and the collapse of government authority. In China, the Yellow River overflowed and flooded the lowlands and average temperatures plummeted producing longer and harsher winters. Larger communities were abandoned, and China's fledgling trade networks collapsed across the country. Recent discoveries have found evidence of tremendous floods and landslides around 2000 BC that blocked the Yellow River for nine months.

In the Indus, the worsening conditions may have produced the world's first recorded vote. In Ancient Greece, early democracy was practiced by placing light or dark colored stones representing "yes" or "no" into a jar and then counting the results. More than 2,000 years earlier, the people of the Indus may have held the world's first democratic referendum using a similar system.

"Stick Man" figure holds a bow and arrow in each hand to indicate choices for a democratic vote in the Indus 4,000 years ago

There is a fragment from an Indus pottery jar suggesting it may have once been used as a ballot box. It shows a stick figure holding a bow and arrow in each hand. Nearby is a symbol that resembles the hashtag or an early harvest tool – the multi-tooth scythe. This image is thought to mean "cultivated land" or "the cultivated land of the Indus people who live by the river."

It is impossible to shoot a bow and arrow with only one hand, so positioning this figure with a bow and arrow in each hand is meant to symbolize something. If this fragment comes from the period of decline when the residents of the Indus were arguing over what to do, then the figure may indicate a choice of direction – this way or that. Taken in context with the land symbol, it may indicate the existential question of their day was, "Do we stay and pray or pray and leave?"

The fall of the Indus around 2000 BC aligns with the timing of the Biblical story of Noah's flood. Although there is no evidence of a titanic rainfall that covered the Earth, there is evidence that during this time of climate change ongoing heavy rains flooded the lowlands of the Indus with deep water that took a long time to recede. Those terrible floods would have destroyed buildings and crops, and killed many people and animals.

The Indus people must have made countless offerings, prayed and then begged the God they knew for relief from destruction. But when the flooding stopped, endless dry seasons followed. At a time when most people perceived God as a benevolent presence in their lives, the psychological trauma of the ongoing catastrophes must have been overwhelming. Many people likely thought the destruction of the world they knew was a punishment from an angry God. But what had they done wrong?

The widespread struggle for survival caused by the long-lasting and unpredictable periods of extreme weather forced a rethink of the old spiritual philosophy. The War could be explained as human folly. But this devastation seemed to be a divine punishment without cause or reason. Where was the old God of wisdom, friendship and reliability? The new power in heaven was suddenly capable of arbitrary, deadly actions against people and their world. The exchange of knowledge and mutual understanding was no longer a necessary part of the human-God relationship. The new interaction would be one of strict obedience to avoid punishment. After this period of ruin and rebuilding, prayers changed. People were taught to fear the anger of God, and new rituals of divine appeasement were created that did not exist before.

During its lifetime, the Indus was a multicultural mix of people. After its collapse, many of its former residents returned to the lands of their ancestors. Those who remained in India were absorbed into the kingdoms where the old caste system remained in force. With no democratic counter-weight, the caste system became the defining feature of every town and village in India. Genetic research shows the spread of India's modern caste system began about 2000 BC. When the Indus faded out, the easy mingling of people stopped.

All this upheaval from climate change, migration and military conquests left the world in a state of confusion. "Confusion" comes from a Latin root that means "to ruin or destroy the foundation." This word is used by the authors of both the Bible and India's ancient texts to describe the emerging modern world.

The Tower of Babel, by Pieter Bruegel (1563)

Many scholars consider the historic character of Sargon to be the same man as Nimrod – the Biblical king said to have ordered the construction of the Tower of Babel. According to the story, Nimrod decided to build a tower to heaven. However, his plan for a stratospheric condo fell apart when the Biblical God caused everyone in the royal work crew to speak a different language. This frightened the workers and made them run away in confusion.

The Tower story is just nine lines long. It begins by explaining that when humanity began, "the whole world had one language and a common speech." Why did the Biblical authors use two words – language and speech – instead of one? "Speech" likely referred to the common language of shared words that had been in use since the start of prehistoric trade. The word "language" was popularized about 700 years ago. The earlier word for someone's language - "tongue" - carried a deeper meaning. One of the oldest phrases among North American Indians is "to speak with a forked tongue." This describes liars and hypocrites who say things they don't mean. "Speech" meant words alone, while "tongue" referred to the way words were used. The two words in the Biblical phrase suggests how the use of words changed when fear replaced common respect as the organizing principle of Sargon's society.

Sargon's grandson celebrates his victory (c 2260 BC) in the family style

When the goal is shock and awe, the psychological impact is greater if the whole culture of a community is destroyed – including its language. If the Tower story is an allegory of Sargon's military dictatorship, its inspiration may have come from the new way Sargon and his armies used words to deceive people and lull them into a false sense of security before striking. For example, one day Sargon's troops might have marched into a village and ordered its members to assemble and perform some task. If anyone protested, they were executed on the spot. The remaining people were terrified. This kind of senseless butchery had never been seen before and it began to destroy their trust in the meaning of words.

Sargon's empire depended on slavery. He was not the first slave owner, but he spread the institution across his empire. The roots of the word "slave" do not go back very far in history. To appreciate the impact of slavery on human culture, it is important to understand the way of life that existed before slavery. Because human society began without any boundaries or limitations, there was no prehistoric word for freedom. Individual freedom and personal responsibility were so intrinsic to each person's human identity that no word was needed. In the modern world, freedom often refers to liberation from some restraint. But the prehistoric world had no restrictions, so the oldest root word for what would become "freedom" had a meaning that evoked a society without fear of other people. The word "free" derives from a source word that means "to love." Here, the concept of love carries the broad ideas of mutual respect and friendship that unified early human society. When ropes were used to bind the first slave, the tyrannized human certainly knew they were no longer loved. Worse, their world was suddenly much smaller.

It is hard to imagine what the loss of freedom meant to people who had never known anything but freedom in a world without limits. In the 1924 George Bernard Shaw play, *Saint Joan*, the character of Joan of Arc (1412-1431) is condemned to life in a jail cell. In response, Joan delivers a passionate speech about the coming world of prisons.

"You think that life is nothing but not being stone dead. It is not the bread and water I fear: I can live on bread: when have I asked for more? It is no hardship to drink water if the water be clean. Bread has no sorrow for me, and water no affliction. But to shut me from the light of the sky and the sight of the fields and flowers; to chain my feet so that I can never again ride with the soldiers nor climb the hills; to make me breathe foul damp darkness, and keep from me everything that brings me back to the love of God when your wickedness and foolishness tempt me to hate Him: all this is worse than the furnace in the Bible that was heated seven times. I could do without my warhorse; I could drag about in a skirt; I could let the banners and the trumpets and the knights and soldiers pass me and leave me behind as they leave the other women, if only I could still hear the wind in the trees, the larks in the sunshine, the young lambs crying through the healthy frost, and the blessed, blessed church bells that send my angel voices floating to me on the wind. But without these things I cannot live; and by your wanting to take them away from me, or from any human creature, I know that your counsel is of the devil," she says.

The Biblical Babel story describes the modern era as a time of 'confusion.' In India's ancient texts, the modern era is called the Age of Confusion or *Kali Yuga* in Sanskrit. India's Mahabharata predicted the cultural changes in human society that would define *Kali Yuga*.

- Rulers will no longer promote spirituality or protect their subjects. They will put the world at risk for their own glorification.
- Rulers will burden people with heavy taxes and bureaucratic regulations.
- Boundless greed and unrestrained anger will be common. People will openly display hatred towards each other. People will forget the principles that once united them.
- People will murder without justification and the community will see nothing wrong.
- Gaining possessions and sexual fulfillment will be considered the highest goals of life.
- Common ideas of virtue will disappear.
- People will abandon honor by taking vows and breaking them.
- Because of increased social stress, there will be widespread addiction to intoxicants of all kinds.
- Teachers and spiritual leaders will no longer be respected and their students will rebel against them.

- The pursuit of excellence will be lost.
- Priests will not be learned or just.
- Warriors will become corrupt and cowardly. They will abandon their code to protect society and instead abuse the weak and powerless.
- Merchants will cheat in their dealings.

Most people adapted to the new world and accepted the changes without question. One man, however, looked deeper. He wanted to know why the Creator allowed evil to spread in the world. After a profound revelation, Zoroaster would tell people he found his answer by looking into the mind of God.

V

CHAPTER 11

MAN INVENTED THE DEVIL, WOMAN CREATED RELIGION

In the 1995 movie, *The Usual Suspects*, Verbal says, "The greatest trick the devil ever pulled was convincing the world he did not exist." Verbal is a master con man and what he said about the devil is also a con. The greatest trick humanity ever pulled was convincing each other the devil does exist.

The Devil – also known as Satan – is one of the world's most familiar fictional characters. Countless products bear his image and name, and he has been a top-grossing draw at the box office for thousands of years. Yet, this well-known rival of God for control of human destiny - the Creator's Evil Twin - is never mentioned in the Hebrew Bible and does not appear in his well-known form as a human/animal figure with horns and a tail until about 1,000 years ago. There was no devil character in early human stories because people had no concept of evil in the modern sense.

Before the 1300s, the word "evil" simply meant "misfortune," "illness" "uneducated," and "harmful." It was during the period when a terrible plague swept over Europe killings tens of millions of people that "evil" was given its new meaning of moral wickedness. When people accepted each other and themselves as equally flawed and likely to make mistakes, "misfortune" was something common – not separate like evil. Around 2000 BC, decades of weather extremes in heat and cold, rain and drought gave birth to the Biblical Noah story and a Deity who was not always good. The post-flood Deity had anger management issues. He nearly destroyed the world, but felt bad afterwards and said he wouldn't do it again. To the Christian leaders of 700 years ago, it was this angry God who spread the deadly illness across Europe. The Black Death was a punishment levied on everyone because some people enjoyed sex more than others. It was during this period that the Western concept of "evil" was fully focused as an anti-Christian, morally wicked force. "Evil-doers," however defined, were said to offend the Christian Deity and must be punished without mercy. The prehistoric culture of uplifting people through knowledge was replaced by a cult of mindless murder that slaughtered people for speaking or acting in unapproved ways. It was a new God for a new era.

The word "punish" also changed with the times. In its earliest form, it meant "observe" and "note." Those meanings flowed from the idea that people who did harmful things were "uneducated." "Wicked" people were those who lacked knowledge and like all other people, they needed to improve their understanding by observing and noting the effects of their actions on those around them. During the later age of property and paid education, the meaning of "punish" changed to include money. Misfortunes of evil or ignorance could be overcome though "payment" or "compensation" to others - those they harmed, or the gods and authorities they offended. About 3,000 years ago, in Ancient Greece, "punish" gained its first violent meaning of "blood money." It was the popularity of a new religion that first gave the word "punish" its sense of "vengeance" and the idea that "evil" was a living force that opposed the deity of living knowledge. Before this time, evil was a shadow, a fleeting period when light was blocked. With this new religion, evil was reconceived as a being that corrupted people like a disease from within. If evil existed on its own, where did it come from?

In the world of 1700 BC, many people wondered how an all-good Creator could let evil into the world. Most of them were content with the answers given by their local priests. One man, however, came up with a new answer that shocked and then changed the world. God, he said, had an evil twin.

The Persian prophet Zoroaster came up with the idea of the bad God during era of empire building in the centuries following Sargon the Great. Zoroaster said there were two deities - the Great Good God and the Great Evil God who wrestled for control of human destiny. After his death, the Persian prophet's followers added new stories to their beliefs including a final war between the two Gods at the end of time, the resurrection of the dead and the return of a godly world. When his ideas became the official religion of Persia's Achaemenid Empire, Zoroaster's stories of an Evil God, resurrection and end times were popularized across the Middle East and throughout one of the largest empires in human history. It covered more than 3 million square miles on three continents. At its height, more than 40 percent of the world's population – from Turkey, Greece and Iraq, to Israel, Egypt and Pakistan – lived within its borders. When the old empire was swept away and smaller nations emerged with their local religions, Zoroaster's stories were repackaged, personified and given a new name – the Devil.

The devil character is not part of Hebrew, Jewish or the older Indian religions. His rise to international superstardom in the Christian world is the story of how a Biblical bit player was recast as Zoroaster's "God of the Angry Mind."

Like all long-lasting fictional characters, Zoroaster's Angry God was refashioned many times before he reached his widely popular modern form. Zoroaster - also known as Zarathustra - lived around 1700-1500 BC. Although he is now largely forgotten, Zoroaster is arguably the most influential figure in all religious history. His words of wisdom and many of his religious ideas were adopted by teachers of Judaism, Christianity and Islam.

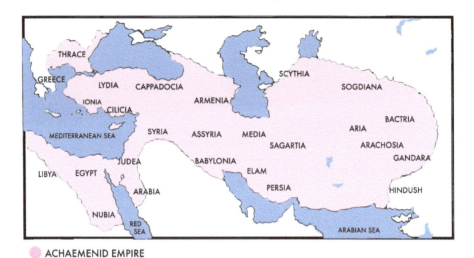

● ACHAEMENID EMPIRE

During the Persian Empire (550-330 BC), Zoroaster's wisdom and his "God of the Angry Mind" were popularized across the Middle East

Zoroaster's emphasis on individual freedom and the common family of humanity inspired the Italian painter Raphael (1483-1520) to include him among humanity's most original thinkers in his work, *School of Athens*. The German philosopher Friedrich Nietzsche wrote a book dedicated to Zoroaster. The film *2001: A Space Odyssey* (1968), opens with music called *Thus Spake Zarathustra* that was composed by Richard Strauss in 1896. Zoroaster even inspired the Persian King, Cyrus the Great (c 600-530 BC), to write the world's first declaration of human rights.

A thousand years before Jesus and the Buddha, and centuries before Moses, these are some of familiar wisdoms Zoroaster spoke:

"The way I want to be treated is the way I should treat others."

"The wisest man needs regular advice the way a knife needs constant sharpening."

"Treating others with respect and encouragement is not a duty. It is a joy, for it increases your own health and happiness."

"My first step was a good thought. The second was a good word. And with a good deed, I took the third step and entered paradise."

Despite his street cred as a wise philosopher, Zoroaster's lasting legacy was his invention of the devil and promotion of the world's first conspiracy theory.

Zoroaster with the Good God *Ahura Mazda* above him

More than 3,500 years ago, Zoroaster was born into a family of Brahman-like priests living in the Indo-Persian culture of eastern Iran. Though trained as a priest, he opposed the rigid control the caste priesthood exerted over people's lives. Zoroaster tried to loosen up the old system through reason and dialogue with the established priests. He preached a doctrine of universal freedom in a world without social differences. He told the priests their role was to spread kindness, tolerance and opportunity to all people no matter their sex or background.

The priests responded with the openness of all people who depend on existing social rules for their power – they called Zoroaster a heretic, turned his friends against him and ran the reformer out of town. Despite his close encounter with an angry mob, Zoroaster's unplanned road trip was his first step to mega-fame. For at age 30, he had a religious vision that finally answered his question, "Why does a Good God allow evil in the world?" The answer was, "It's not God's fault. It was the other guy."

According to the legends, Zoroaster heard an inner voice and followed it to a river. He stepped into the water with questions, and came out with answers and a new religion. The new prophet said "the mind of God" had been revealed to him. And what Zoroaster saw there was a deity with an evil twin. The Great Good God was not the cause of evil, Zoroaster said. Greed and violence were provoked by God's doppelganger – his wicked counterpart that inspired chaos and destruction in the human world.

Zoroaster called his hero, *Ahura Mazda*, or the God of the "Good Mind." The villainous Deity was *Angra Mainyu*, the "God of the Angry Mind." Zoroaster's ideas were revolutionary. Although ancient people worshipped various gods at different temples, they largely conceived of the Creator as a single deity with many avatars and lesser aspects called demigods. Before this time, people told stories of mischievous and demonic creatures, but none of them were held up as an equal to God. So, Zoroaster's insistence on a co-supreme God of Evil was shocking to ordinary people.

Originally, he described his God of the Angry Mind as a force without a face. It was a universal energy of chaos that undermined order and provoked violence. To restrain this force from overpowering the world, he said, people must control their angry and destructive impulses. Despite their opposition, Zoroaster described the relationship between the two Gods as a friendly rivals for the human spirit, similar to that of Satan and God in the Biblical story of Job. After Zoroaster's death, his stories about Angry Mind began to change and the force of disruption began its evolution to superstardom as the Devil. His first role was that of a blood-thirsty beast, feeding on the bull of civilization.

Zoroaster's God of the Angry Mind attacks the primeval bull

In the Hebrew Bible, the character of Satan – *Shatan* in Hebrew – is a minor figure that appears in just two stories. The root of his Hebrew name means one who argues for "a cause" or "course of action." This meaning is particularly apparent in the Job story where God and Satan bet on whether a man called Job will keep his faith during hard times or discard it. Like an ancient courtroom drama, God and Satan argue the case for and against enduring faith.

In the older world where the God of reason ruled. Satan was not an evil character. He was imagined as the inner voice of a divine agent promoting ignorance and impulse, just as God was conceived as the inner voice of knowledge and self-restraint. In other words, the oldest concept of Satan was the cartoonish miniature devil who sat on a person's shoulder whispering in one ear, while a tiny angel of God spoke in the other. There were no evil-doers or evil people, there were only humans listening to bad advice. This perspective was not random, but an essential part of early human culture. It stressed the development of reason and the accumulation of knowledge. And, in a growing prehistoric society without laws or security forces, it reminded people that everyone in their open community was expected to do the right thing.

During Europe's terrible Dark Ages after the fall of Rome (400 AD), when war, famine and brutality stalked the continent for 700 years, and again in the Bubonic Plague years (1346-1353), the Catholic Church ramped up its efforts to hunt down, torture and kill anyone suspected of being one of Satan's co-conspirators in the attempted destruction of Christianity. Until this time, the church's religious venom had been mainly directed at Jews and pagans. But as the Black Plague spread across Europe and Turkey killing up to 200 million people, religious leaders insisted the power of evil behind the horrors had to be more than just social outcasts. And so, the new Satan was recast as a hellish military commander seeking out recruits for his legion of anti-Christian terrorists. Yet, despite all the Church-sponsored killings and mass expulsions, their grand efforts to make Satan into a super-villain failed. When the plague ended and social calm returned, most people still imagined the devil as a non-human, semi-comical figure because people still thought of bad behavior as rare and unnatural.

In 2014, Stanford University's Cantor Arts Center presented 40 different portraits of the devil created in past 800 years. The oldest ones show the Devil as a puppet-like figure - The Walking Skeleton or Grim Reaper with his deadly scythe. The earliest Bible with a portrait of Satan was printed about 1200, and it shows the Evil One as a wild, beast-like creature similar to Zoroaster's God of the Angry Mind. Once again, this devil existed separate from humanity because 'evil' was unhuman.

Devil image in the *Codex Gigas* or "Big Book" Bible (c 1200)

Nonetheless, Christian artists continued to improve their work on Satan's public image. The demons and deities of Ancient Greece and India were transported into Christian paintings as servants of Satan. Those advertising posters were intended to terrify the worshipers of 'other gods' to join the Church before they ended up in a blazing hell of punishments with them.

The tarot card image of the Devil with cloven feet, horns, discolored skin and enslaved men and women around him, came to life in the 1800s during another round of pagan-bashing. Two hundred years ago, religious conservatives in Christian Europe were enraged by what they saw as the decadence of artists and liberals corrupting their society. This counter-culture revolution of the Romantic Era (1800-1850) rejected the rigid social standards and established religions of their time. Instead, they looked to the past for a figure to inspire their newfound spiritual and intellectual freedom, and they found one in the Greek god Pan.

More than two thousand years ago, c 700 BC, Pan was the most popular god in the Aegean Sea region. Pan's devotees were democratic and inclusive. They had no temples and when they came together, it was in the forest where they played music and men and women danced freely. When those practices became popular again, Church leaders launched a widespread campaign to stamp out this reborn threat to Christian civilization. They started by photo shopping Pan's features onto all new portraits of the Devil.

This was not the first time the forest god Pan was cast as the rival of Christianity. Two thousand years earlier, stories of Pan's death made headlines across the ancient world. According to the legend, soon after the death of Jesus, a sailor in the Mediterranean Sea heard a voice from the sky cry out, "Great Pan is dead!" The announcement came a second time, followed by great lamentations. This was the only time in the ancient world when a god was reported to have died. So powerful was this rumor that Tiberius - the Roman Emperor at the time of Jesus' crucifixion – ordered an investigation. Among early church leaders, this news was taken as a sign the pagan world was dead and Christianity would replace it.

The Ancient Greek word "pan" means "all." And so, Pan's home was among the diverse life of the forest and he was pictured with goat's feet to symbolize his unity with nature. To destroy this concept of fellowship with the natural world, Christian leaders condemned the forest as a landscape of dangers. It was Satan's home of darkness where vicious animals and sexual predators savagely attacked innocent Christians. In Ancient Greece, Pan was a rock star and this playful and lusty deity was often shown playing music on his flute, surrounded by female fans called nymphs. In the 1400s, the word "panic" was coined to describe what Christian leaders saw as the crazed sexual dancing of Pan's devotees. And, ever since the anti-Pan crusades of the 1800s, popular music of each successive era has been described as 'satanic' by conservative Christian leaders. Yet, the artists who celebrated Pan and the religious leaders who condemned him were largely unaware that Pan's name, image and qualities were adopted from earlier images of

Krishna who was deified as an incarnation of God during a reformation of the Hindu religion.

The names Pan and Krishna both carry the meaning of "the source of all attractive things." They represent anti-establishment, individualistic religion. They both play the flute. Pan had his nymphs, while Krishna's female devotees were the *gopis* or cowgirls. The Indo-European people who first settled the region of Ancient Greece likely brought stories of Krishna from the Indus, and over time India's Krishna became the Greek deity Pan.

Pan's image as an ancient promoter of sex, drugs and rock and roll made him a convenient Devil figure

Pan's image showed the natural world as a place of safety and welcome. Church art, however, transplanted his animal features to the Devil as a sign he was less than human, and downgraded the nymphs and *gopis* to Satan's sex slaves.

The rise of Satan as a central figure threatening the family of Christianity, required an equally frightening story of organized traitors and conspirators from within who would open the gates for his demonic forces. And the traitors inside every Christian household were the women. Throughout religious history, women have been alternately honored as a source of special insights (as with the Venus statues and goddesses of wisdom), and degraded as soulless beings and disposable property. The Christian Saint, Augustine of Hippo (340-430 AD), proclaimed women have no souls, while the early Christian writer, Tertullian said women were "the devil's gateway" to hell. Similar ideas have been expressed by teachers of all the major religions. In the 1300s, a new word was invented to devalue women. For hundreds of years, the Church railed against women and their sexual allure as the source of disease, sin and corruption. By the Plague Years, this changed the earlier culture of general equality between men and women to one where women were measured by how evil they were. And to the church, evil meant 'sexually provocative.' Women were told to cover 'wicked' parts of their bodies, and increasingly kept socially separate from men.

It was at this time the word "cunt" came into use as a derogatory term for women. This word did not begin as a term for a woman's body part, but was later applied to it. The origin of this insult was a compliment. "Fecundity" is a term which means "fertile," and it is related to many words honoring women as the source of life including fruitful, fetus and suckling. When women's sexuality was rebranded as alien, and women were accused of criminally inciting God into the mass murder of the plague, "fecund" gave birth to the word "felon." In this meaning, a felon was a woman who committed crimes against God simply by being female. As the social value of women was lowered, the word "fecund" was shortened to 'cund' or 'cunt' and was first applied to prostitutes. In England, an 800-year old street where they did business was christened 'Grope the Cunts Lane.'

The change in the meaning of the word "charm" further illuminates the importance of Satan as an anti-Pan figure. In the 1300s, "charm" was given its new meanings of a witch's spell and anti-Christian magic icons. It was given those new definitions by religious authorities who condemned any happiness outside church teachings as evil. Originally, the word "charm" meant to inspire someone to sing and celebrate. In other words, anyone able to lift up a person's spirits and encourage them to celebrate life was a charmer. But the old charmers were rebranded as sorcerers in a cult of evil.

About 500 years after Jesus' death, the Catholic Church changed Jesus' teachings from a collection of many ideas to a specific set of enforced beliefs. Soon after this, Christians were happily killing other Christians for worshiping Jesus in the wrong way. Those persecuted believers were called "heretics." The word "heretic" comes from Ancient Greek and it means, to "choose for yourself."

In Zoroaster's teachings, people could choose some beliefs but not others. And so, he also gets credit for the world's first conspiracy theory. In his thinking, anyone who didn't admit the Evil God existed was part of the Evil God's conspiracy. It was a conveniently closed argument that would be picked up by many other groups in the future.

The fuel that propelled Zoroaster's Angry God to the role of the Devil was organized religion. When different temples began to share the same stories, local deities became internationally known ones. Around 4200 BC, a young woman in Mesopotamia set up the world's first organized religion and revitalized the old rituals by turning temple worship into mass entertainment stage plays filled with sex, sadomasochism and vampires. Her name was Enheduanna and she was the daughter of Sargon the Great.

She was appointed High Priestess to the goddess Inanna – her father's personal benefactor and patron deity of his capital city. Under Enheduanna's direction, temples across Sargon's empire were unified. They read the same stories, sung the same hymns and conducted similar worship ceremonies. It was not a royal command that inspired them to offer the same program. It was the hit religious shows Sargon's daughter wrote, produced and starred in. She is the world's first named author and, in her day, she was a superstar.

The first organized religion was dedicated to the Goddess Inanna - owls represent her wisdom, lions her strength and the reeds wealth and fertility; the image maybe Enheduanna as Inanna

With priests and priestesses serving as extras or to operate special effects, Enhenduanna stepped into her role and remade the dowdy goddess of the farm into a strutting sex symbol for the city. Mesopotamia's temples became rowdy burlesque houses dedicated to a female deity of personal will and defiance. Her passionate style of religious storytelling was so popular her plays remained in use for thousands of years, and influenced other Semitic religions including Judaism, Christianity and Islam.

In her first narrative, *Inanna's Journey to the Underworld*, Enheduanna brought gasps and then applause when she appeared on the temple's stage as the new Inanna - a sexy, young dominatrix ready to strip off her clothes and whip through the land of the dead to reach her goals. And the young High Priestess performed every scene on stage with the passion of a true devotee. Her pre-Gothic tales of sex, vampires and zombies were sellout shows and soon every temple wanted more of the same.

For a thousand years after they began, organized religions coexisted. They shared stories, ideas and symbols with ease. Wars of belief against belief began with the rise and spread of Exclusive Religions 3,300 years ago. These new religions would insist theirs was the only true religion and other faiths were evil. The first Exclusive Religions began in Ancient Egypt, and the story of those original religious extremists and the bloodshed they caused is recalled in the Biblical story of Exodus.

CHAPTER 12

EXODUS: 3 REVOLUTIONS THAT CHANGED THE WORLD

Before the birth of Exclusive Religions there were no religious conflicts. In the thousands of years of formless faiths, informal worship and the many organized religions before Judaism and Christianity, people shared and swapped concepts of God like favorite family foods and herbal medicines meant to stimulate the mind and soul. It was the pre-modern world of the pagans, and the origin of their name reveals their cooperative culture. Its Latin root means one who lives outside the city and is a "non-combatant." Another root source adds the meanings of "agreement, treaty and working together."

Exclusive Religions began as separatist movements that isolated themselves from the larger community with claims of religious and ideological superiority. They grew their ranks by demonizing the rest of humanity as a threat to their existence, and promoting attitudes of hatred and violence against any challenge to their elitism. Until this time, people were free to pursue insights into knowledge on their own and so there was nothing to fight about. It was the invention of writing and official records that gave rise to warlike faiths and the first religious wars. Before writing, people relied on their memories to recall old histories and explain their meaning. Each person was valued for their individual memory and insights. Everyone told the same story in a different way and that was the norm. The same principle created early faiths and religions. Each person experienced life and understood its meaning in their own way. By sharing different insights, each individual and the community gained a larger base of knowledge about their world. It was this sense of individual purpose and community that formed their understanding of God as another living entity, as similar and different from them as they were from each other.

The spread of organized writing systems about 4,000 years ago led to the first official record of selected events. Rulers compiled information about their countries and told stories of their achievements through symbols pressed into clay tablets or as pictures painted on public walls and pillars. If the authorized telling conflicted with people's memories, it was the recorded version that remained while those who remembered differently died off. In the larger culture, this meant individual memories were given less importance than before. Instead, people were taught to memorize and recite official histories.

The Biblical story of the Exodus and the Jewish holiday of Passover have an official version. It is the well-known story of the liberation of Hebrew and Israelite slaves from centuries of bondage in Ancient Egypt. This tale resonates deeply for many people – particularly Jews, Christians and Muslims.

This authorized history of what happened in Ancient Egypt around 1300 BC is summarized in a booklet called the *Haggadah* that's used for the annual Passover celebration. The Hebrew word, *Haggadah*, means "the telling." This is a curious title because unlike any other story in the Hebrew Bible, the *Haggadah* appears to insist the history of the Exodus be told in only one way. Yet, modern scholarship has found no archaeological evidence to support this version of the history of those times. Is there another way to understand what happened in Ancient Egypt?

In the traditional narrative, all the Biblical people are slaves and their road to freedom begins when their God tells the Israelite leader Moses and his brother Aaron to meet with Egypt's Pharaoh (king) and tell him to "let my people go." When the Pharaoh refused the divine command, the Biblical God responded by punishing everyone in Egypt with horrible diseases and devastating natural disasters. There was panic across the country. When the Pharaoh's children began to die, he freed the Biblical people from slavery and they marched out of Egypt singing praises for their divine deliverance.

That's the official telling.

However, there is no evidence that vast numbers of slaves – Hebrew or otherwise – built Egypt's pyramids or other monuments. Recently discovered records show the work teams that built the pyramids were paid contractors who occasionally went on strike for better working conditions. A second challenge to the slavery-themed story comes from the Bible itself. There is no record anywhere in the text or outside it where Moses condemned slavery or asked the Pharaoh to end the practice. When they left Egypt, Moses' Israelite followers issued laws governing the treatment of the slaves they owned, and Hebrew slaves in particular. Clearly, the moral issue driving Moses and his group was not the abolition of human trafficking and equality for all.

The word "Exodus" comes from Latin and means "leaving or departure." This is a neutral term with no further description about why the leaving happened. If the Biblical tale has been clouded by religion, is there another way to understand the social upheaval that turned peacefully mixed neighborhoods into religious war zones and changed world history?

Yes, and the starting point is the same Biblical passage where the Deity issues his command to "let my people go." The whole quote is more revealing. In Exodus 5:1, the Hebrew God says, "Let my people go so they may hold a festival to me in the desert."

Read in full, this sentence points to when the Exodus happened and why. For it raises a profound question: "Why did Moses' people have to leave Egypt to hold their religious festival?" Ancient Egypt was a land of many religions and even slaves were free to worship as they chose. There are no desert-specific festivals mentioned anywhere in the Bible. So, why was it necessary to celebrate in the desert beyond the fertile lands of Egypt, and why did they need the Pharaoh's permission to go there?

Akhenaten (c 1375-1345) was the Egyptian Pharaoh of the Bible's Exodus story and part-Hebrew

The answers to those questions are the backdrop of the Exodus story. The Biblical people could not worship their God in Egypt because it was a time of religious extremism and ethnic hatred in the land of the Pharaohs. The world's first religious dictator had come to power, and he was at war with other practices. This new Egyptian dictator, the Pharaoh Akhenaten, would murder thousands of people for worshiping God the wrong way. It was Akhenaten and his rival, the Israelite leader Moses, who created the first Exclusive Religions and set in motion the world's first religious wars.

The Biblical story of Exodus and the reign of Akhenaten are a matter of debate, but both are generally set around 1300 BC. To fully appreciate what led to their explosive confrontation, it is important to understand the history that lit the fuse.

About 700 years earlier, the collapse of the Indus Valley Civilization sent waves of refugees into the surrounding regions, including Mesopotamia. There, the newcomers were called Hebrews or "wanderers from the East." According to the Bible, the inspirational leader of the Hebrews was the son of a migrant family from India called Abram, later known as Abraham. About 1800 BC, the Biblical God made an extraordinary promise to Abraham. In an era of military land grabs,

Abraham was told his followers would be given a homeland as a reward for their acts of righteousness. Long after Abraham, a Hebrew called Joseph was born.

In the Biblical story, the young Joseph was sold into slavery by his envious brothers and unjustly imprisoned in Egypt. Despite the hardships, Joseph kept his faith. When he was released from prison, Joseph told the King of Egypt to store up his grain because a terrible famine was coming. Joseph's storage houses saved millions of people from starvation when years of drought destroyed the region's food supply. As a reward for his humanitarian service, Joseph was appointed counsel to the King and later married into Egypt's royal family. Egypt's Monarch then fulfilled the Biblical promise. He gave the Hebrew people their homeland – the North Egyptian settlement of Goshen – as a reward for Joseph's amazing goodness.

The Joseph story, like most ancient histories, is a combination of events that happened and people that existed, mixed with legends, exaggerations and different versions of the official record. The first question to be asked is, "Did Joseph exist?" Islamic tradition recognizes Joseph as a prophet of God. Traditional stories describe Joseph as a member of the Pharaoh's inner circle who oversaw the construction of the Ancient Egyptian city of Memphis and many pyramids. Those religious and secular records strongly suggest there was a real Joseph. Was he given a special homeland? That is entirely possible. The Exodus story notes a tremendous number of Hebrew slaves in Egypt without recording their capture in battle. So, setting aside a skyrocketing birthrate among half-starved workers, those great numbers must have originally arrived in Egypt as free migrants. Did Joseph marry into Egypt's extended royal family? This is also likely because the original Israelites of the Exodus period despised Joseph for his outside-the-tribe marriage and assimilation.

There is another element in the Joseph story that is often overlooked. Yet, it points directly to the cause of religious wars that would later flare up between the Indo-European Hebrew people and their Middle Eastern cousins - the Ancient Israelites. The Hebrews had no temples, priests or religious laws. There is no record in the Bible or elsewhere to suggest Joseph - or anyone in Goshen - ever put two stones together to build a temple for their Hebrew God. What reason could they have for not building one? The likely answer is the culture of the Hebrew people came from the Indus where official religion was scorned as a source of social divisions and war. And those 'liberal' Hebrew attitudes were the target of fierce attacks by a growing number of religious radicals within the Goshen community who called themselves Israelites.

The origin of the Israelites and why they replaced the Hebrews as the main people of the Bible is widely debated. There is nothing in the Bible itself that explains the Israelites' rise to power or the origins of the Hebrews. All the stories in the first book (Genesis) concern the Hebrews and their single-named predecessors - Adam to Noah - who are given no group identity. The only factual information the Bible offers about the first group is that their homeland was called Havilah, a land identified as India by more than 2,000 years of Jewish and Christian tradition and oral histories. In book two of the Bible – Exodus - the Israelites appear. They are only identified by this group name which honors the father of a single family. The word "Israelite" means "sons of Israel." The original Israelites were the 12 sons of a man called Israel. Of those twelve, 11 brothers, their descendants and followers would later be called the 12 Tribes of Israel. The descendants of one son - Joseph - would never be given a tribe bearing his name. Instead, later generations would heal the old wounds by assigning his heritage to two other tribes.

During Joseph's time as an Egyptian royal and after his death, the Israelites were a growing religious and political movement in Goshen clamouring for independence from Egypt. The evidence for this comes from the name they adopted.

The origin of the Biblical Israelites starts with their hatred of Joseph – the one son of Israel not considered an Israelite. According to the Bible, sometime after Joseph's death the Ancient Egyptians forgot his good deeds and enslaved all his Hebrew people. This is clearly false as Egyptian stories that glorify Joseph have been passed down to the present day. Similarly, there is no evidence the Biblical people – or any other ethnic group – were forced into long-term slavery in Egypt. If freedom from physical slavery was not the rallying cry of the Ancient Israelites, what was it?

The first clue to their purpose is recognizing the Israelites as separatists. By definition, the Israelites were separatists because they gave themselves an identity that separated them from the Hebrew people. Why? Two motivations have driven every separatist movement in history including the Quebecois in Canada and the Sikhs of India. Separatists fear the assimilation of their people and the disappearance of their culture. The Israelites of Goshen weren't worried about physical slavery. What they feared and despised was spiritual bondage - the capture and corruption of their culture through intermarriage and assimilation as 'their' people adopted the clothing, lifestyle and practices of Egyptians and other outside groups. To the Israelites, any member of their tribe who gave up their ancient traditions and acted like a modern Egyptian was a traitor to the family. And the poster boy for their fury was Joseph - the son of Israel who married an Egyptian aristocrat.

By calling their followers "son of Israel" - including those not directly descended from the original father - the Israelites showed their purpose as a political and newly-formed religious movement. The Hebrews had no religious organization to reform or separate from. Therefore, the aim of Israelites was revolutionary – to gain independence from Egypt and establish their new religion over the entire community.

Among ordinary Egyptians, Joseph was widely admired. He had become an international celebrity for his heroic humanitarianism. He was a foreigner, mistreated by his brothers and Egypt's court system and yet Joseph forgave those who persecuted him and saved millions from starvation. As a result, Joseph's name may have been commonly used as a way of praising someone's righteousness. "You're a real son of Joseph," they might have said. In the ancient world, the word "father" meant any inspirational teacher or leader, and "sons" were their followers. That is why the Bible describes Abraham as "the father" of many families or nations.

The more frequently "son of Joseph" was used to describe people outside the Biblical clan, the more it stung the insular Israelites.

"If anyone can be a son of Joseph then the family name means nothing," they would reason. So they called themselves "Sons of Israel" to separate themselves from the common use of Joseph's name. If so, it is also likely the Israelites told jokes degrading the phrase "son of Joseph" to imply "son of a bitch" or born from a low class woman.

Initially, this group of angry separatists and moralizers was likely shunned by the locals. The Hebrew middle class would have responded to Moses and the Israelite plan for independence in a predictable way. They would reference their history.

"Goshen is the land God promised us. If he wanted us to have an independent country, he would have given us one," they would howl. "Who are you to question God? Get out of here Moses, you putz!"

Moses and his Israelite followers would have been criticized for attempting to divide families and set Hebrews of one practice against Hebrews of another. But that didn't bother the religious radicals who were determined to establish a new and separate religion that would protect their family's past. And they were willing to kill thousands of people to accomplish their goal.

Despite its unpromising beginnings, the Israelite independence movement would be propelled to success by an unlikely ally – the new Egyptian Pharaoh Akhenaten. Akhenaten had his own plans for an Exclusive Religion and his revolution inside Egypt would lead to the Exodus and the birth of a new religious nation in the Sinai Desert.

In Ancient Egyptian history, Akhenaten is a controversial figure. After 17 years as king, he was condemned as a religious blasphemer and called the "traitor Pharaoh." Most records, official monuments and even personal items bearing his name and likeness were destroyed in acts of rage against his rule. It was the world's first cultural purge of a former leader from the official record. Despite this, historians have been able to piece together a fairly comprehensive picture of his amazing life and times.

Akhenaten transformed his country from a nation of many religions, to one where temples to Egypt's traditional gods were closed, and the population was ordered to worship a single invisible God called "Aten."

The historical record offers no reason for Akhenaten's transformation. There are many modern arguments that try to explain why he started a new religion, gave himself a new name, banned religious statues and attempted to mass convert his people. But none are widely accepted. However, if the Israelites were motivated by their opposition to Joseph and his legend, perhaps Akhenaten – far from ignoring Joseph – was influenced by his Hebrew teachings.

There are many sources that indicate the Biblical Joseph was a real man. To place him in the same time period as Akhenaten and demonstrate their contact, there is genetic evidence suggesting their connected family histories.

Although Egyptian authorities have recently stopped DNA testing of their royal mummies, research undertaken before the ban revealed some surprising ancestry. It is known that Akhenaten's son - Tutankhamun - had a Southwest Asian ancestry like the Hebrews. Those genetic markers worried the Egyptian government. In a 2014 article called *Tutankhamun's Blood*, written for Matter Magazine by Jo Marchant, the author described the controversy surrounding DNA tests of the young King Tut. In the article, Mark Rose, the editor of *Archaeology* magazine, told Marchant genetic tests on Tut were cancelled in 2002, over concerns the results would show "an association between the family of Tutankhamun" and the Biblical people of Moses' time. A source close to Egypt's antiquities service told Merchant, "There was a fear it would be said the Pharaohs were Jewish."

If Akhenaten's son, Tut, had a Southwest Asian ancestor, who was it? The most likely source is Akhenaten's maternal grandfather, Yuya, an Egyptian nobleman of Indo-European background. And Yuya may be the same man as the Biblical Joseph.

**Mummy mask of Akhenaten's chief advisor Yuya
who may have been the Biblical Joseph**

The tomb containing the remains of Yuya and his wife were found in 1905. Despite speculation about them, Biblical authorities have insisted this couple cannot be Joseph and his non-Israelite bride.

According to Biblical history, Moses and his followers carried Joseph's bones out of Egypt when they departed. However, if the original Israelites considered Joseph a contemptible assimilator, why would they take his bones with them? And if they didn't despise him, how did they get his bones? Jewish legends report Moses went to the banks of the Nile and called for Joseph. When he did, Joseph's bones rose from the waters, presumably because they'd been buried there. Putting aside the supernatural element, Joseph's remains would never have ended up in the Nile. Although there is scholarly debate over when Joseph lived, there is no getting around the fact that when Joseph died he was a highly respected member of the Egyptian nobility and would have been given a burial worthy of a king. To retrieve Joseph's bones, Moses would have needed the Pharaoh's permission to enter Joseph's tomb. In the entire story of the Exodus, Moses never asks for Joseph's remains or even mentions his name.

When Yuya's tomb was discovered, it was in the Valley of the Kings – even though he was not Egyptian. It has been described as the second most spectacular tomb found in all Ancient Egypt right behind the treasures of Tutankhamen.

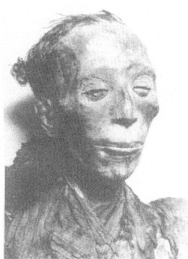

Yuya (L) and his wife Tjuyu (R) may be the Biblical Joseph and his Egyptian wife

During his life, Yuya was given many high titles including the "King's Lieutenant," and "Father of the God." In Egyptian culture, the phrase "Father of the God" meant an advisor with great influence on the King. All those details line up with the Biblical narrative. If Akhenaten's maternal grandfather, Yuya, and Joseph are the same man, then one of Joseph's grandsons was the King of Egypt. Did Joseph's teachings inspire the Pharaoh to create an Egyptian version of the Hebrews' invisible God religion?

The future Akhenaten was born with the given name Amunhotep IV. His father, Amunhotep III, was one of the most celebrated monarchs in the history of Ancient Egypt. He was a man of peace whose reign was one of unprecedented prosperity and artistic achievement. Modern archaeologists have uncovered almost 300 statues dedicated to Akhenaten's father – more than of any other Egyptian King.

Father and son carried the name Amunhotep, which means "Amun is satisfied." Amun was one of the oldest names for a deity in the

North African region. He was the god of the wind, and his sacred city was Thebes where Akhenaten was born and his father ruled. With the death of his father, Amunhotep IV took over the family business of kingship and for five years, Amun remained satisfied.

Then, at age 23 the young King had a spiritual awakening. He changed his name, religion and capital city, and then lit the flames of a religious revolution that would change the course of Egyptian and human history. The King gave himself a new name – Akhenaten, which means "Effective for Aten," or "Using power on behalf of Aten." Amunhotep was a name that implied pleasing the community and their common deity. Akhenaten's name signaled his role as a religious revolutionary and a man of 'effective' action. The King's new God was invisible and formless and so Akhenaten adopted an old Egyptian symbol to represent his Supreme Deity. The emblem he chose was the sun disc called Aten.

In Ancient Egypt, the Sun was associated with different gods throughout its history. And until Akhenaten, Egyptians regarded the sun disc as a sacred symbol not a deity. The Aten religion is typically described as a form of sun worship. But if the King was influenced by Joseph, the rituals honoring the Sun may have had a different meaning.

Akhenaten, Nefertiti and family worship the sun disc Aten in the world's first Exclusive Religion

Akhenaten's devotional practice appears very similar to what is called the Sun Blessing of the ancient Hebrews. This ritual is still practiced by Orthodox Jews who stand outside at sunrise once every 13 years and praise the Sun as a symbol of God's creation of the universe. If Akhenaten's grandfather was the Biblical Joseph, did the Pharaoh create his religion as an Egyptian version of the Sun Blessing?

Did Akhenaten use Joseph's name to enhance his public image? After taking the throne as Akhenaten, did he proudly announce that he was a true "son of Joseph"? That declaration of his righteousness would resound among the common people and immigrants and brought cheers from the assembled crowd.

Akhenaten's identification with the righteousness of Joseph would have warmed the hearts of everyone present – except the Israelites.

To them, Akhenaten's embrace of the famous Hebrew was a calamity. It must have seemed their dream of an independent nation was over. Who would support a separate Israelite kingdom when a self-proclaimed "son of Joseph" ruled Egypt? If this model resembles actual events, there should be many other points of connection in the Biblical text. For example, the crowning of Akhenaten may have happened in the same period when Moses was threatened with death and forced to flee Egypt.

The Sun Blessing of the Ancient Hebrews may have inspired Akhenaten's religion

At first, Akhenaten continued his country's tradition of religious freedom and only encouraged Egyptians to join his new faith. Despite this apparent openness, the King quickly ended his royal patronage to all festivals except those dedicated to Aten. As his religious revolution continued, Egypt's old traditions were banned or transformed. The traditional holiday parades honoring statues of Egypt's gods were replaced with a subdued military procession. Instead of music and feasting, the Egyptian people stood at the side of the road as the King drove by in his royal chariot surrounded by his personal slaves and heavily-armed soldiers. Three thousand years ago, Egypt was the birthplace of the world's first Exclusive Religion society – complete with omnipresent images of Supreme Leader Akhenaten for the faithful to worship, and roaming religious thugs to beat down opposition.

Temples to other gods were shut down across the country. This created chaos for all the priests and the people who worked for and supplied the temples. Tens of thousands were suddenly unemployed. Akhenaten's followers and religious police, however, were kept busy smashing the names and images of other gods from public monuments and searching private homes for statues of Egyptian gods and other religious contraband.

If anyone in Egypt was telling the King the growing chaos in Egypt was a sign Aten was not pleased, the King wasn't listening. He retreated to his palace while his country fell apart. Pleas from his ambassadors and allies about rising threats were ignored and Egypt's enemies moved into the power vacuum. Then, a deadly plague that broke out in Mesopotamia was carried to Egypt by trading ships. The ousted priests from the old temples told their followers the disease was a punishment from Egypt's gods for abandoning them in favor of Akhenaten's "foreign god." The priests rallied their old congregations and began fighting back. Egypt's religious counter-revolution had started.

It may have been this tipping point in Akhenaten's rule that prompted Moses to return to Egypt after years of self-imposed exile. The people of Goshen who once rejected the Israelite leader, were now looking to anyone who would save them from the religious riots erupting in cities across Egypt.

If Egypt's ousted priests blamed Akhenaten and his monotheistic followers for the plague, it is likely the Hebrews and Israelites were seen as equally traitorous – especially if Akhenaten's grandfather was Joseph. If ordinary Egyptians were convinced the religion of the Hebrews and Israelites caused the plague, the public might have approached the king with demands to separate them from the rest of Egypt's population.

There is an ancient story that backs this up. It says the King of Egypt was petitioned and responded with a law of segregation. According to a report from the Jewish historian Artapanus of Alexandria (c 200 BC), the Egyptians blamed the Biblical people for the plague and complained to the king. To calm the fears of his people, the monarch ordered the monotheistic Israelites and Hebrews to wear a badge of identification, a "garment to distinguish them" from other Egyptians,

Artapanus wrote. If that report is accurate, it means 3,300 years before the Nazis forced Jews to wear the Star of David, an Egyptian Pharaoh gave a similar order.

There is a very specific Israelite religious law – mentioned twice in the Bible – that gives further credence to the story of the Egyptian badge. In Judaism, the 613 laws of Moses are divided into three groups – actions performed for God, actions for self-improvement and service to the community, and a third group called the irrational laws. The reasoning behind the irrational laws has been lost but those laws remain on the books because there is no way to repeal them. Among the irrational laws are two that criminalize the wearing of wool and linen together or any mixed fabric. To follow the king's law and be easily seen, the cloth marker would have to be made from a different fabric than the outer garment. If Artapanus' story is true, Moses' cloth command may have started as an overreaction to Egypt's badge law.

There is no evidence the Biblical people endured generations of slavery in Egypt. However, so much traumatic emphasis is placed on it and the story repeated so often in the later text, that the history of the Exodus period must have included a time of actual enslavement.

When the counter-revolutionary priests and their supporters took back the reins of power, they attacked, defaced and destroyed every representation of Akhenaten and his religion throughout the country. It was payback time and they wanted revenge against everything and everyone associated with Akhenaten and his one God religion – including the Hebrews and Israelites.

In its story, the Biblical slaves are brutalized and fed a starvation diet. If Egypt had a slave-based economy, their worker slaves would have to be generally well-treated to ensure they did good work. What the Bible describes is the kind of sadism and deliberate humiliation that is very common in ideological revolutions. Those identified with the deposed religious or political regime are often beaten, thrown into prison, forced into slavery, and executed in great numbers. When Egypt's priests returned to power, they wanted to punish everyone associated with the traitor Pharaoh and appease their angry gods. If so, this may also be. This was likely the time when the Egyptians temporarily "forgot" Joseph.

Just before the great march out of Egypt, the story notes several events that make no sense if the people waving goodbye were impoverished slaves. But they can be understood as emotional reactions to a terrifying time of political and religious extremism.

The first incident was the last meeting between the unnamed Pharaoh of the Exodus story and Moses. The Pharaoh told Moses his people were free to leave Egypt and take their many animals and possessions with them. This is another indication the Hebrews and Israelites were not slaves but a free and prosperous people during their time in Egypt. But the Pharaoh's command could also be read as an order of expulsion. "Get out and don't come back!"

In the text, the last recorded words the Pharaoh said to Moses were "bless me." Why would a nationalistic Egyptian Pharaoh who considered the Hebrews and Israelites to be slaves and enemies of Egypt, ask their leader for a blessing? He wouldn't. It only makes sense if Akhenaten saw himself as part of the Hebrew tradition and Israelite family. If Akhenaten had a sense of his impending execution this Biblical passage can be read as a very poignant scene. Released from his megalomania, the doomed Akhenaten knows he is about to die. With his final words, he turned to Moses as the true prophet of the Hebrew God. Like a man on death row, the former king asked the Israelite leader for absolution. Curiously, however, there is no record of Moses' reply.

It would have taken some time for the multitude of Hebrews, Israelites and their servants scattered across Egypt to gather their goods, assemble in one place and begin their exodus to the Sinai Desert. During this period, Akhenaten was likely executed. It is interesting to note that some editions of the popular English Passover *Haggadah* (Rabbi Nathan Goldberg, 1949), report there were two different Pharaohs sitting on Egypt's throne at the time of the Exodus story.

According to the Bible, as the multitude departed ordinary Egyptians threw their gold and fine linens at them. Why would Egyptians give away their valuables to people they considered an evil and corrupting influence on their society? They wouldn't. But they might do something similar if they were whipped up into a religious frenzy by Egypt's priesthood. During the riots of the counter-revolution, the homes of the Biblical people were likely looted and their possessions stolen for perceived religious offences against Egypt's gods or just lawless opportunism. When the enslavement of the Biblical people didn't end the plagues, Egypt's priests resorted to ethnic expulsion. They decided their gods would only be satisfied and the devastation of their society would only end if they expelled all the religiously-offensive foreigners. Following this decision, Egypt's radical priests may have ordered their congregations to rid themselves of anything associated with Akhenaten's era – including the cursed and evil possessions they took from the Hebrews and Israelites. So, many Egyptians threw back what they stole from their former neighbors as the Hebrews and Israelites marched out of sight.

For the second time, the Biblical people were homeless. After the fall of the Indus c 2000 BC, the Hebrew people lived in many lands until Goshen. As the expelled people set up their tent city in the Sinai Desert 700 years later, the Israelites and the Hebrews were certain their God would swiftly guide them to a new Promised Land. However, after two months of wandering in the desert and far from the comforts and food of city life, things began to get ugly. Moses' people would finally hold their festival in the desert. But it would not be a happy celebration. It would tear apart their community and provoke neighbors into killing neighbors.

The two most important events in Jewish history happened in the Sinai Desert. One was the blessing of the people at Mt. Sinai when Moses presented the details of the new union contract he'd signed with God on behalf of the assembled tribes. The other was the story of the golden calf.

CHAPTER 13

GOLDEN COWS AND STONE COMMANDMENTS

Each man, woman and child among the multitude of refugees carried two things when they left Egypt - their possessions, and faith their God would lead them to a new Promised Land. The leadership told the community to be patient and work together, but there were rumblings in the Sinai Desert. There was no single leadership accepted by all and each tribe and community operated independently within the camp. The Israelites told their followers a new religious homeland would be given to those who followed their laws and leadership, but many left the crowded desert camp for nearby cites and a more comfortable lifestyle. Those who remained were the faithful - Israelite hardliners and traditionalist Hebrews. They were united by a belief that their family – however defined – included God. And, this family relationship required them to serve a special purpose in the world. To the Hebrew people, that mission was the spread of a unified, global civilization and the advancement of knowledge among all people. To the Ancient Israelites, it meant they were a separate people whose inner circle relationship with God was maintained by loyalty to their religious leadership and the laws that organized their lives apart from the sinful practices of others. Beyond the tents of the Israelite tribes, however, there were no widespread religious laws or mandatory practices that held sway over the Hebrews or other members of the camp. That would soon change.

This ideological divide between the informal, communal Hebrews and the law-and-order Israelites would explode into the third revolution of the Exodus period.

Those who self-identified as Hebrews saw themselves as inheritors of humanity's culture of knowledge that reached its pinnacle of expression in the Indus. As a result, their line of wise teachers may have included Krishna along with the Indo-Semitic prophets Noah and Abraham. Like the people of the Indus, the Hebrew community was self-governing and independent. They had no rulers, temples, priests or religious laws, and they welcomed everyone who accepted their principles of honesty, respectfulness and compassion for others.

To the Israelites, the Hebrew people were weak and disunited because they mixed with outsiders and lacked a strong family identity. The Israelites believed there was only one way their homeless community would survive in the world of their time. They had to be united and ruled by a single-minded religious leader, backed by a fierce God and a powerful army. The Israelites rejected the culturally mixed families of Goshen, but they wholeheartedly embraced the extremist religion, social classes and elite priests of the Egyptian kingdom they'd left behind.

Although the Israelites and Hebrew people were united in marriage, traditions and general beliefs, they recognized each other as distinct people. The Bible notes this in 1 Samuel 14:21 where it reports the Hebrews "went over to join the Israelites."

The Ancient Israelites believed in class divisions as a way of maintaining order, and, as with the Brahmans of India's Varna system, Biblical priesthood was made a family inheritance. Indeed, the moment they took power, the Israelite leadership permanently divided the entire multitude into separate family tribes each with their own community responsibilities and social rank. To the Israelites, the informal attitudes of the South Asian Hebrews were dangerous relics from the past that threatened the will of the Israelite God and the aspirations of a new generation. They despised the mixed community of Hebrews as mongrels, and set out to end Hebrew independence by forcing them to give up their old ways before accepting them as full members of the Israelite family. Israelite laws governing "Hebrew slaves" suggests those who held on to their old traditions may have been subject to service in an Israelite household until they accepted the new reality. And so, the remaining Hebrew people were pushed into Biblical oblivion. Those who rebelled against the new authority were killed or deserted the camp. Ironically, while modern nationalist groups clamour for a return to ancient traditions, the mission of the Ancient Israelites was to 'modernize' the old Hebrew ways.

The Israelites were religious revolutionaries. And like other extremist groups to follow, the Israelite party of Moses were happy to murder anyone who opposed them. When he was in Egypt, Moses said he would organize a celebration for his Hebrew God in the desert. When the multitude of refugees and religious radicals camped in the Sinai finally held their festival, it was not the unified celebration of community and common faith they'd hoped for.

The word "community" carries two different root meanings. In one sense it means "free" and "open to all." In the second sense, "common" means reshaping all the elements of something so that everything "changes together." The religious war between the Hebrews and the Israelites would be fought over those meanings and whether a community should be voluntarily united by individual choice or forcibly bound by official laws and punishments.

The victorious Israelites would reshape the desert community in their own image. They would claim ownership of the Hebrew language and traditions, and reassemble the values and history they inherited. For the next 4,300 years, the spiritual and political battles between those two ideas of community control and individual freedom would reverberate throughout Jewish and human history.

As the Israelite movement in the desert camp grew in size, it gained in ferocity. Separatism evolved into hatreds, and hatreds into physical attacks and murder. The desert community was being taken over by a dictatorial leader and his band of religious extremists. Their reign of terror in Biblical history is reported in the tale of the Golden Calf.

The Adoration of the Golden Calf, Nicolas Poussin, c 1640

The two most important events in Judaism's 6,000 year history took place in the Sinai Desert. One was the recognition of Moses as leader and the acceptance of his new religion and its laws. The other was the slaughter of the Hebrews and the destruction of a statue called the Golden Calf.

The official version of the statue story begins with the 80 year-old Moses high up on Mt. Sinai talking with his God. Their marathon chat fest continued for a month and a half. In the camp below, the impatient people abandoned the Biblical God and took up Egyptian practices by worshiping a statue of a cow made from gold. When Moses returned from the mountain and saw this idol worship, he was enraged. Moses destroyed the statue, brought the people back to right thinking and his God was satisfied.

That is an incomplete version of the history told in Chapter 21 of the Biblical book of Exodus. The whole story reveals a pattern of mass murder by religious extremists that would be imitated by the followers of other Exclusive Religions to the present day.

As it begins, the Biblical God is – for unexplained reasons - angered by a celebration to him taking place in the camp below where the gold statue was the main decoration. Moses told his God to calm down and enjoy the party. So, God relented and Moses made his journey back to the camp. It is important to note that at this time both the Deity and Moses have somehow seen the golden statue and no longer have a problem with it. So what happened next must be seen as confrontations over politics, power and community leadership, not religion. As Moses approached the camp, he saw people singing and dancing, but someone told him the celebrations were an act of "rebellion." This suggests that sometime earlier the Israelites and Hebrews had come to a political compromise. For unexplained reasons, the festival of faith was declared an act of defiance that nullified whatever peace had been worked out. The 80 year-old Moses turned on the partiers as if their celebration was a personal betrayal, and in a blind rage the Israelite leader attacked the celebrating people without mercy.

According to the text, Moses ordered the priests of his new religion to draw their swords and surround the partiers. As thousands stood huddled and terrified, Moses had the statue burned. Its poisonous ashes were then mixed with salt water, and his hostages were forced to drink it. Then, he told his clan of Levite priests to start killing.

Go through the camp "from one end to the other, and kill your brother, friend and neighbor," Moses told them. And so they killed 3,000 people. After the slaughter, Moses and his revolutionary guard held a religious celebration. Moses told them, "You have been set apart by the Lord today for you killed your own sons and brothers and God has blessed you." (Ex. 32:27-29)

Thousands of people were murdered because their leader objected to the way they worshiped God. The Israelite leader who hated Akhenaten's religious tyranny with the most passion, was now following in the pharaoh's dead footsteps.

The Biblical report that follows this religious massacre casts doubt on Moses' claim that his God was satisfied. Soon after the murders, the Biblical God unleashed a plague of disease that killed another 3,000 people throughout the camp. From a religious perspective, this narrative suggests either 1) God doubled the deaths because He thought Moses didn't kill enough people, or 2) God was dispensing instant karma against the Israelites for killing in God's name. Putting aside divine intervention, if the report of the plague is accurate it is likely the Israelites left the bodies of the dead heretics out in the open to rot, and that environment caused the disease to nurture and spread.

This is a story of a religious crime, a one-sided trial and the death of justice. The victims of Moses' ideology were human sacrifices to his God of the Angry Mind. And yet, in a larger sense, they were not killed because of the way they worshiped God. They were murdered to destroy their idea of community.

At the time of this incident, Moses was not yet the undisputed leader of the multitude. Despite his heroic stature in the early part of the Exodus story, the later text suggests he was a minor figure until the desert revolution. Near the start of the calf story, someone unfamiliar with Moses calls him, "that guy." (Ex. 32:1)

Despite accusations the festival was held to honor a foreign god, the text clearly notes this long-delayed party was dedicated to the God who "brought us out of Egypt." This phrase is important because it is used throughout the remainder of the Hebrew Bible to identify the Israelite God.

Having a golden statue of a cow as a symbol for their community was, apparently, not at all unusual. Most people contributed gold to make the statue and, when Moses' brother Aaron was asked about it, he said, "I'll help you build the platform." So, a golden cow must have had a well-understood and beloved meaning for the Hebrew people and the larger community. What was it?

Since the migration of the West Asian cow culture people into Europe and Africa (c 6000-5000 BC), the cow had become a common symbol of wealth and abundance. For a displaced group of people in the desert, a golden calf made from gifts offered by all the people was a psychological boost, a symbol they were still a wealthy community and blessed by their God. The Bible says decorative statues of golden cows were placed in later Israelite temples. This good-cow, bad-cow confusion was not limited to the past. Jewish and Muslim traditions predict the End Times will be signalled by the birth of a special calf. In the Jewish telling the cow will be all red while Islamic tradition says it will be all yellow – the color of gold.

The Golden Calf may have been inspired by the sacred Indian cow figure *Kamadhenu* – from the Batu Caves, Malaysia

The original Hebrews brought their culture from India, so the golden calf they crafted may have been inspired by *Kamadhenu* - the divine mother of all cows who is revered in India but not worshiped as a god. *Kamadhenu* is a symbol of the virtues of wealth, strength, abundance and community life that are associated with maintaining herds of cows.

The extremist Israelites burned the statue because it was a symbol of defiance against the new social order. It represented the freedom to think and act independently. Their new society would be bound by laws that raised some men above others, and all men above women, children, slaves and animals. To ensure total obedience, Moses needed to eliminate his remaining opponents. The story of how Moses assassinated the last democratic leader of the Hebrews is recounted in a little-known Biblical tale called Korah's Rebellion.

Korah and his followers are burned alive for challenging Moses' authority, drawing by David Martin, c 1700

The Bible describes Korah as a cousin of Moses and a member of the Levite clan of priests-by-birth. He was also an outspoken opponent of the Israelite revolution. One day, Korah confronted Moses.

"Who raised you above the people?" Korah demanded. It is noteworthy that Korah does not ask Moses who made him king or head priest. The established Hebrew culture had no official religious or community leaders, and so Moses was assuming a position that hadn't existed before – a permanent ruler with absolute power.

Korah insisted Moses was answerable to the community, but Moses said he was answerable only to God. Moses challenged Korah to a religious duel as a way to determine which one of them God liked best. They agreed to bring their supporters and offerings to a secluded spot where God would choose. It was reminiscent of the earlier Biblical story of Cain and Abel, and it ended the same way – with murder. The text offers two versions of what happened at that religious showdown between the honor-bound Hebrew protesters and the heavily-armed Israelites.

In the first telling, the Israelite God opened the earth beneath the feet of Korah and 250 of his followers. They plunged into a sea of flames below, and the ground sealed up over them. According to Jewish tradition, Korah survived the fall and the flames and was made to confess "Moses was right" for the rest of eternity. If this sounds like badly written propaganda, it is. In this report, when the people asked Moses who killed their friends and family, they were told "God did it." The multitude accepted that answer and were satisfied. There is a curious side note to this tabloid version. Korah and his allies fell into the open ground, but somehow their bronze incense holders floated in the air and were mysteriously saved. The Bible says they were melted down and refashioned as decorations on the Israelites' first altar.

In the other second version, the tribes furiously confront Moses and demand to know why he and his thugs murdered 250 innocent people.

"You have killed the Lord's people!" they scream. (Num. 16:41)

Moses gave no recorded answer because none was needed. His rule was backed by men with swords. Instead, he held another religious feast to celebrate his latest mass murder and once again claimed to have satisfied his God. In reply, the Biblical God responded with a second plague. This one killed 14,700 of Moses' people. Propelled by religious extremism, Moses and his followers celebrated the murder and deaths of more than 20,000 Hebrews and Israelites.

The Ancient Israelites would eventually unify the community, and through military conquest they would gain a new homeland. But in the end, their religious wars with people inside and outside their kingdoms would weaken and then destroy them forever. The Hebrew community celebrated differences and relied on each person to govern themselves. The Israelite community required obedience to authority. Under Moses' new laws, anyone who spoke or acted differently could be accused of treason and executed. The old book of wisdom and history called the "Torah," was redefined as the book of law and order, crime and punishment.

The popular side of Moses' Mt. Sinai covenant was the community-wide blessing given to all the people as new members of God's special family. The less-considered meaning of the Israelite religion was that, along with their collective blessing came the threat of collective punishment. Under the new doctrine, if one person offended the Israelite God he might kill the individual sinner, a hundred people or even all of them. Because everyone's obedience was considered essential, anyone who stepped out of line was considered a traitor and a threat to the entire community who must be killed to prevent their God from killing them.

Moses and the Commandments – obedience is not voluntary

The root word of "traitor" means "one who betrays tradition." At its earliest source, it meant a person who violated the "laws of Moses." Moses' new deal with God included more than 600 religious laws and that alone made it revolutionary. Until this time, secular and religious laws limited their reach into people's lives. The Israelite religion divided the world into clean and unclean things and people, and assigned rituals to every action throughout a person's life from birth to death. Most people embraced the new ideology. It gave them a new identity and a recognizable social structure of crowned leaders, an official temple and a hierarchy of priests. But to those who opposed the new way, Moses' revolutionary stew of religious restrictions and rituals were designed to make people crazy. Before the Israelite's rise to power, there were no religious laws and so no fear of God's punishments. Suddenly, people had to follow hundreds of laws and those who failed to meet the new standard of obedience risked severe punishment or death at the hands of religious authorities. Killing people for offending their God would be a central feature of all Exclusive Religions.

Exclusive Religions redefined the old notion of faith and spread a new concept – fear of God. In the modern world, the words "belief" and "faith" are used interchangeably to mean the acceptance of things for which there is no proof, such as the existence of a deity or eternal soul. But originally, the two words conveyed very different ideas. Ideas about faith grew from the old concept of living knowledge. For both faith and knowledge are changed by new experiences. But faith in something always remains, because faith gained through personal action and study is the source of all courage and the only road to the future. Nothing can survive long without faith and courage, because experience and knowledge from the past provides courage for actions in the present and guidance when planning for the future. All people have faith in something that has helped them survive - physical strength, intelligence, wealth, weapons, science or God. But throughout life, people's faith in their sources of courage will change or be replaced as a result of new experiences and new knowledge.

A belief, however, is something that never changes and so is not rooted in evidence or experience. If a person believes Jesus rose from the dead after three days, they will not suddenly decide, "Maybe it was five days. Or two and a half." The belief will not change. It will be wholly accepted or rejected because knowledge is not a factor. In ordinary language, a person might say, "I have faith in Bob to carry out this task." Using the word "faith" implies knowledge of Bob's previous accomplishments. By contrast, saying, "I believe Bob is at work" implies a lack of actual knowledge. So, when people ask, "Do you believe in God?" they are actually asking, "Do you believe in religious doctrine?" This is because the question of whether God exists is simply "Yes" or

"No." There is a Deity of some kind or there isn't. Belief is not part of the question or the answer.

The new domination of belief over knowledge necessitated the creation of a new kind of God – one who inflicted terror and punishments at will, and was not bound by reason. The prehistoric God of community and shared knowledge was transformed into a violent, jealous Deity who sanctified aggressive war and mass murder. These were the new religions of fear. The word "fear" shows this change. In prehistoric society, there was no word for "fear." Its original meaning – "taking a risk" - included the ideas of "building courage" and "gaining confidence" through experience, but not "danger." The root word of fear also implied "leadership," and the idea of setting a courageous example. If "fear" originally meant "being an inspiration," then many Biblical verses must be read in a new-old way.

Psalm 130 says God is "forgiving and therefore to be feared." Obviously, forgiveness is not a quality that inspires fear. However, read as God's forgiveness is meant to be an "inspiration" for others to be forgiving makes sense. Similarly, when Moses tells his community they will receive so many divine blessings that other people will "fear" them (Deut. 28:10), the meaning is muddled. The sense is clearer if the divine blessings were meant to be an inspiration for others to follow the path of the new laws.

The Israelites gave the story of Noah a terrible new meaning. In most ancient stories about the great flood, God saves the righteous and life continues. But the Israelites added a new angle – God almost destroyed the entire world because of the unrecorded sins of some unnamed people in Noah's nameless homeland. To the Israelites, no one was safe from the violence of their sociopathic deity – not even them. At one point in the Biblical story, God promises to help Moses on a military mission. But as they set off, the Biblical Deity suddenly changes his mind and warns the Israelites he might kill all of them instead.

In the modern world, the idea of God's collective punishment remains popular. Those who claim climate change, earthquakes and other catastrophes are God's punishment on the world because some women wear short skirts or gay people get married, are the latest incarnation of the Israelite extremists who applied the doctrine of collective punishment to religion 3,000 years ago.

Some modern Christians justify their loathing of homosexuality on the basis of a pair of comments in the Bible, only one of which is specific about "two men" having sex. Yet, most Christians cannot answer the question, "What sin does the Bible condemn more often than any other?" Spoiler alert: It's not homosexuality. It's idol worship which is condemned over 400 times. Why are no religious groups protesting "American Idol" or its many offspring? The most extreme religious and political leaders frequently encourage their devoted followers to idolize them with songs, portraits and statues, but no one waves the Bible in protest. The command against idols is not mainly directed at statues but a warning to avoid people who claim to speak for God. The Hebrews and the Israelites used religious statues called *teraphim* in their worship ceremonies. Akhenaten banned statues of the gods in Egypt, and replaced them with statues made in his image. Similarly, after the Israelites destroyed the *teraphim* they made people pray to the Ark of the Covenant. Despite Hollywood's revisionism, the Ark was simply an elaborately decorated box of Israelite relics that included bits of Moses' stone commandments, some stale manna – the miraculous food in the desert, and the staff used by Aaron, the first Israelite priest.

Moses and Joshua bow before the Ark, **by James Jacques Joseph Tissot, c 1900**

The phrase, "law-abiding" means to "stand behind a line." When applied to religion, this meant everything new was automatically sinful until religious authorities ruled it kosher. As a result, religious police had wide authority to accuse someone of sinful behavior. Those who still used *teraphim* were an easy target because bigots could give the statues any evil meaning and no one would argue. In the new world of the revolutionary Israelites, things that were uncontroversial before were now criminally illegal. The Bible records that the namesake of the Israelites – the man called Israel – was married with *teraphim* statues, and when the Israelites were losing a battle they enlisted a priest and his *teraphim* to win the day. Yet, when the extremists launched their campaign to murder anyone with an idol the old history was no history.

Extremism prevails when moral hazards – violence and hatred - are praised as social goods by community leaders and spread by their followers. The uncompromising attitude of those who idolize ideology was neatly summarized by former U.S. Senator Barry Goldwater in his 1960 book, *The Conscience of a Conservative*.

"Extremism in the defense of liberty is no vice," he wrote, and "moderation in the pursuit of justice is no virtue!"

The Senator was wrong. Extremism is always a vice because once started it cannot be stopped until the killing grows so large that people can no longer stomach it. Or, as happened at Kurukshetra, the fight goes on until everyone is dead. The very nature of a vice is that its demands for satisfaction are endless. Law and order extremism leads to harsher police responses against everyone, longer prison terms and more executions. Religious extremism manifests as groups demonize others and kill them without conscience.

Moderation in the pursuit of justice is a virtue because it allows for flexibility and individual application, just as self-controlled liberty leads to common respect.

The passing of the torch from the Hebrews to the Israelites would set Biblical history on a new course. The new Promised Land would not come as a gift for righteousness, but after the slaughter of tens of thousands who lived in the lands of Canaan. The ancestors of the murdered tribes of Canaan welcomed the ancestors of the Israelites, but they were killed anyway. This pattern would be repeated in many places, including North America where the descendants of the Indians who helped the European colonists survive, were massacred by the descendants of those they welcomed.

The many magical tales surrounding the life of Moses changed the concept of a divine miracle. In its oldest sense, "miracle" did not mean incomprehensible comic book-style supernatural events such as parting the waters of a sea or changing a stick into a snake. The original meaning of "miracle" was "to smile," and it carried the idea that miracles were something people did understand.

The Christian story of Jesus and the loaves and fishes serves as a good example of the old and new meanings. As the Bible tells it, after a long day of teaching, Jesus was surrounded by a larger audience than he expected. Tradition required him to offer food to his guests, but he didn't have enough for everyone. Jesus said a magic prayer and presto, empty baskets overflowed with bread and fresh fish.

"Lox and bagels for everyone," Jesus called out, and so the people praised God for the miracle and feasted.

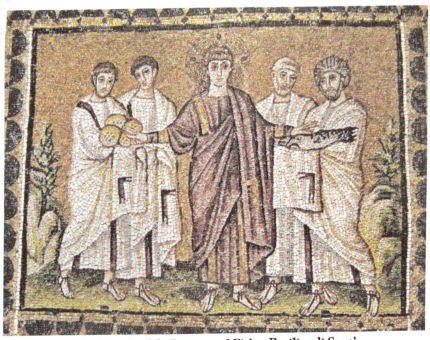

The Miracle of the Loaves and Fishes, **Basilica di Sant' Apollinare Nuovo, Ravenna, Italy, 6th century**

But if something like that actually happened, how would people really react? One group would think it was a stage trick and try to figure out how it was done. Highly religious or superstitious people might think what happened was evil magic and not touch the food. Only a portion of the crowd would wholeheartedly accept what happened as divine intervention. If two-thirds of the crowd are not buying what happened as a magical miracle, either the Biblical God needed better marketing advice or when this story happened the details were different.

Jesus had little food but lots of hungry guests. He despaired and prayed. Suddenly, something unexpected happened. In the crowd were wealthy people and food merchants with bread and fish to spare. These individuals were well-known for their unyielding greed and hard-heartedness. Maybe they even hated Jews and religious people in general. They were the Scrooges of their day. Yet, after listening to Jesus – then called by his Hebrew name, Yeshua – these misers were moved in ways they never thought possible. They began sharing their food with strangers and called on their servants to bring more. And the people who witnessed that transformation of closed hearts into open ones, smiled, because they knew only the spirit of God – and not some trick or freak of nature – could make those people feel love for others.

It is interesting to note the word "mirror" has the same root as "miracle." It means to see something in a new way.

After the time of Akhenaten and the Exodus, old nations were restructured and new nations were born. But they all shared a common cultural foundation – they insisted their subjects obey laws. The age of self-governance was fading out as the legal systems of the new nations expanded.

CHAPTER 14

JUSTICE, LAW AND RIGHTEOUS RULERS

"To live outside the law, you must be honest," Bob Dylan.

For most of human history people set up communities, traded goods and interacted without laws. Social cooperation was maintained and human civilization expanded because human dealings flowed from a culture of balance - fair play and honesty. They were self-governing and instinctively found ways to live together as individuals and families in a world without boundaries to restrict their movements or rules to control their behavior. There were no religious doctrines or authorities to maintain peace and good order. The only principle was honorable behavior and it worked because people were and remain naturally honest.

When people acted justly, laws were unnecessary. People's words and promises were their legal documents. Because words were highly valued, people were attentive to what they said and heard. When writing came into use, that old human culture began to change. In law, politics and religion, the meanings of words was made changeable whenever it suited the new purposes of social control. Over time, people grew cynical about the lasting value of words and later generations would praise people for their skillful use of lies and dishonesty to manipulate others.

The first social rules, like the exchange of greeting gifts, grew from the desire to show friendship and respect to others. The growth of urban populations, the spread of private property and the rise of the family culture led to the first land boundaries, symbols of ownership, rules for contracts and councils to settle business disputes and rule on liabilities. If a legal system is defined as a set of rules with specific prohibitions and punishments, early human society can be called lawless. Instead of written laws and precedents, they followed unwritten principles of justice. The word "law" has two root concepts. It can mean an agreed upon foundation such as justice, or something imposed by "striking down" what existed before. The laws of Moses established a new legal foundation by striking down the informal justice system of the Hebrews.

This change from a culture that promoted the social principles of justice and self-government to one that demanded obedience to society-wide laws and instilled fear of punishments, marked another step along the road to the modern world. Indeed, since the first written rules were carved in stone, fixed law has fought against the balancing scales of justice for the social soul of humanity.

The Goddess of Justice with her scales of social balance

Justice is an older concept than law. Justice is an expression of balance, and so justice can been seen as the natural expression of an individual or a community to restore balance and heal sources of potential conflict before they grow worse. In this way, justice acts as the adaptable immune system of the social body. The forces of law become unnatural and unjust when lawmakers no longer care about balanced outcomes and instead show favoritism to advance their own interests.

Humans were born free, and so the introduction of formal laws and legal procedures progressed slowly as they were largely unpopular. In the past, laws were considered unnatural and even bad for a society where people were expected to act respectfully and resolve their own problems. In the new culture, obedience to established law and authority was all that mattered.

As governments expanded, so did the number of rules and regulations. The Ancient Roman historian, Tacitus, wrote, the "more corrupt the state, the more numerous the laws." In modern America there are more than 4,500 federal crimes and almost half a million federal rules and regulations along with uncountable numbers of state, city and county laws, bylaws and ordinances. According to the National Conference of State Legislatures, U.S. states and territories passed more than 40,000 bills and resolutions into law in 2011. By comparison, in 2015 the South African legislature passed 23 new laws, Bangladesh's government issued 17 and Germany's Parliament 249.

Justice societies followed a different path of development than legal ones. About 100 years ago, the American Supreme Court Justice, Oliver Wendell Holmes, famously explained this distinction to a defendant who didn't quite get it.

"This is a court of law, young man, not a court of justice," Holmes said.

The problem the young man faced was a typical one for most people. Justice is instinctively understood and so has a well-known symbol - balanced scales. There is no universal symbol of law because written laws are local, they frequently change and their purposes and ends can be deliberately unjust.

If there was a symbol for law it might be an architect's measuring tool. The root words of "architect" and "royal" are connected. The word "architect" originates as a combination of the words "chief" and "builder." Architects and rulers both design foundations for their society and ensure people follow the lines that control their behavior.

The American architect Louis Sullivan once said "form follows function," meaning the design of an object should be based on how people use it. Sullivan told his students once they understood how people used a building, product or city they should plan its shape to fit that need. This philosophy might be called the design of justice. Justice, like a well-designed product, should serve the best interests of its people, not command them.

Form followed function in the Ancient Egyptian tombs that were well-decorated homes for the afterlife

Law cities were designed to enforce order and so they featured high observation posts and urban checkpoints manned by soldiers. City squares were used for public displays of brutal punishments and executions. In justice societies, homes had no locks, storehouses had no guards and towns were not enclosed by defensive walls. Their urban plans emphasised cultivated central parks, public drinking wells and buildings for bathing and exercise.

The first written legal code was produced by King Hammurabi of Babylon, who carved his laws into stone 400 years before Moses. Hammurabi's bullet-shaped law pillar was placed in the center of his cities where everyone could see it – even though most people in his kingdom could not read. It resembled an idol – to evoke divine authority – and the king's image at the top showed him as the symbol of heaven's law on Earth. This idol of law now represented the king in each city, town and village. When the law worked well, people were happy. When it didn't work well, people resigned themselves to obedience.

Hammurabi's Babylonian Empire included most of the territory once ruled by Sargon the Great. Like Sargon, Hammurabi secured his rule by ensuring swift, harsh responses to anyone who broke the law. So, it's not surprising that Hammurabi's list of punishments for law-breakers was short. In the case of a crime against ordinary property, the penalty was a fine. For other criminal charges the penalty was death or disfigurement. Steal from a temple or royal court – death. Receive those goods – death. Steal something and when caught you can't pay for it – death. Give shelter to a runaway slave – death. Hammurabi's code gave humanity the legal principle of "an eye for an eye." Rules 196 and 197 say, "If a man put out the eye of another man, his eye shall be put out. If he break another man's bone, his bone shall be broken."

The main concern of Hammurabi's laws was social peace and the protection of private property, so its rules apply mostly to people who use, abuse or damage the land, animals or goods of others. There were rules for settling criminal cases before judges and heavy penalties against judges who apply the law unfairly. There were laws for inheritance, and punishments for those who spread false rumors that damaged someone's reputation. In Hammurabi's code, reputation was a highly valued property – something still applied in modern laws against slander and libel. Women were largely treated with equality to men. But along with its rules for good business and resolving arguments, his laws let everyone know there was a swift death penalty for thieves, murderers and anyone who violated the sanctity of religious temples or the king's authority.

3,700 years ago, King Hammurabi's Pillar of Laws were in every town and village of his Babylonian Empire

Hammurabi's inscription says his laws are God's laws and they are intended to provide justice for everyone. If oppressed people have a complaint, the pillar says, let them bring their case to his "righteous judges" and read them the king's "wise words."

There are obvious similarities between Hammurabi's code and the laws of Moses. Both were carved in stone. Both men were Semitic leaders whose laws regulated business and labor practices, social order and specified punishments for crimes. However, Moses' laws reached far into spheres of life left private by Hammurabi. Moses' 612 laws include mandatory religious obedience, the unequal treatment of women and non-Israelites, and brutal punishments for anyone accused of eating banned food, following forbidden religious practices, engaging in unlawful sex or studying illegal subjects like astrology.

With the exception of China, the founders of all the world's major civilizations claimed their laws were handed down from God. In Ancient Chinese culture, the subtle difference was that the laws of the universe were not given – they merely existed as a divine set of operating instructions that must be followed. To act in disharmony with the universal order was to invite chaos and social collapse.

Jewish and Hindu traditions say their laws originally existed in the mind of their God. This implies all religious laws are eternal because the Deity never changes his omniscient mind. Despite this claim, the history of religious laws shows the Divine has had many second thoughts.

When the Garden of Eden was still a happening place 6,000 years ago, the Biblical God was content with a single law - "Don't eat the fruit of the tree of knowledge." For thousands of years after the end of Eden, the fruit ban remained the only divine law. The Biblical God wasn't even sure murder was a crime or what to do about it. When Cain killed his brother and lied about it, God shrugged and told Cain to leave town. It would take 2,500 years before the Biblical God returned to update his one law, law book. According to Jewish tradition, after the flood event the Hebrew God gave Noah seven principles meant to serve all humanity forever. Although often called laws, there are no punishments attached to those instructions and so they cannot properly be called laws. Those divine suggestions of c 2000 BC included "organize councils to settle disputes," "don't worship idols," and "don't eat the flesh of a living animal."

Despite his pledge that seven laws were enough for all time, a few pages after the Noah story, the God of the Israelites went on a rule-writing binge. Around 1300 BC, Moses' God changed his mind and decided humanity needed more laws and lots more punishments. What happened in the years between Noah and Moses that demanded so many new religious laws and punishments? Did people change during those seven hundred years? Did God suddenly become a control freak? Or did the change happen because Moses and his allies claimed their laws were God's laws?

In the texts of Ancient India, a broader concept of eternal law is expressed by the word *dharma*. *Dharma* is a 20,000 year old Indo

European word with many meanings that evoke humanity's oldest concepts of justice. They include law and decree, custom and social duty, morality and personal character.

And all those meanings flowed from the organizing principle of *Homo Sapien* society – balance.

Promoting a natural bond of mutual respect between people without the use of formal rules was widely observed for a long time – even in prisons. The 1954 movie, *Duffy of San Quentin* is based on the real life experiences of Clinton Duffy. As warden of San Quentin prison, Duffy eliminated harsh punishments, improved food quality, established educational and rehabilitation programs, desegregated the dining hall and let the inmates organize a prison newspaper and radio station. Yet, the movie also shows the creeping expansion of institutional authority and arbitrary rules that eroded the voluntary code of personal honor.

In one scene, a nurse informs the inmates of the new rules. Under the old standard of mutual respect, a trusted prisoner had a key and 24-hour access to a medicine locker. When the nurse took the key away it sent a clear signal to the inmates that the two sides were no longer bound by a common sense of justice but separated by institutional laws.

In the 1966 film, *The Fixer*, a Jewish man living in Russia in the early 20th century is thrown into jail for the alleged crime of having sex with a Christian woman. A Russian guard tells him prison is where people learn to respect the law.

"Do you know what respect is, Jew?" the guard asked.

"Yes," the Jewish man replied, "it's something that has to be given before it's received." And then the guard beat him for telling the truth.

Perhaps it was the original human qualities of respect and honesty, rather than any set of commands and punishments, that were "in the mind of God" when human society was born. Therefore, the deeper question is, "Are laws needed?"

The Ancient Greek philosopher Plato summed up the dilemma of law-enforcement 2,400 years ago when he said, "Good men do not need laws to tell them to act responsibly, while bad people will always find a way around them." Before Plato, the Chinese philosopher Confucius (551-479 BC) explained why a common sense of justice was better than enforced laws and punishments. People who fear punishments may shun crime, but they will not understand why just behavior is better, he advised. Guide people by example, treat them with courtesy and they will learn the benefits of respect and come to be good, Confucius said. Catholic Cardinal Armand Richelieu (1585-1642) warned reliance on written law, rather than common justice, inevitably led to corruption. Give me six lines written by the most honest man, he said, and "I will find something in them which will hang him."

2,500 year ago, the Chinese philosopher Confucius
said guidance was better than law

Former U.S. Supreme Court Justice, Louis Brandeis took aim at the problem of bad laws. "If we desire respect for the law, we must first make the law respectable," he said.

After his religious conversion, Akhenaten issued many new laws on behalf of his God. Two other famous kings had religious conversions while in power, and they also changed the laws of their country. One was the Indian Warrior King Ashoka who rejected war after adopting

Buddhism in 320 BC. The other was the Roman Emperor Constantine who abandoned Roman gods for Christianity in 312 AD. As the first Christian king, Constantine could have brought sweeping reforms to the empire's legal code and steered the new religion towards inclusiveness. But he didn't. As Roman Emperor, Constantine's only human rights reform was to end persecution of Christians. As chairman of the first council of Christian leadership in 325, Constantine set down his approved list of Christian teachings and opened the door for the persecution of unauthorized Christians. Constantine's conversion was motivated by his victory in battle and framed by his role as Roman Emperor. Constantine's Jesus was a Roman king in heaven who ruled through laws enforced by his intermediaries on Earth – the Emperor and church leaders.

The story of how India's King converted to Buddhism and abandoned war is remarkably different. Twenty-three hundred years ago, Ashoka the Great launched his massive army against a much smaller kingdom on India's Northeast Coast. The holdout kingdom had defeated his father in battle and Ashoka wanted revenge. The war did not go well. Although he was eventually victorious, resistance from the defenders was fierce. When the war was over, both armies had nearly destroyed each other leaving an estimated 200,000 warriors dead and 150,000 homeless refugees.

Ashoka should have been satisfied with his victory. But as he strolled through the ruins of the defeated kingdom to savor the smell of human death in the morning, he was suddenly transformed. Years before, the King had been wounded in battle and healed by Buddhist physicians who taught him the principles of nonviolence and respect for all life. As a young man, those ideas fell on stony ears. But that day, as he surveyed the death and destruction caused by his war, the King had a life-changing insight. Ashoka told his neighbors he would never again launch an aggressive war. He became a vegetarian and decreed the world's first laws protecting lands and animals. He even developed his own brand of social media by carving his philosophy on rocks around his kingdom where he posted messages like "all men are my children and what I desire for my children in welfare and happiness, I desire for all men."

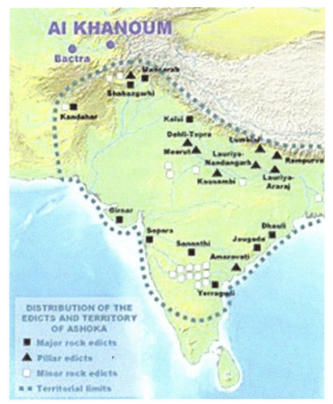

India's King Ashoka posted his wisdom on rocks 2,300 years ago

New roads were laid out with dedicated stopping places for travelers. The rest stops were set by natural spring wells and planted with fruit trees so that everyone on the road – people and animals - had access to food and fresh water. His 33 year rule was so profound, that British writer H.G. Wells would call it "one of the brightest interludes in the troubled history of mankind."

In Ancient Egypt, the concept of dharma was called *maat*. The Egyptians envisioned *maat* as the divine principle of harmony and goddess of justice who weighed the lightness of people's hearts after death with her ostrich feather. All those religious concepts were later expressions of the original human values of balance and respectful behavior.

Most Western legal traditions are updated versions of the secular and religious court systems used in the Roman Empire (27 BC –395

AD). In the 1600s and 1700s, lawmakers allied with the new Age of Reason and Enlightenment began to squeeze out religion-based judgements in favor of laws based on their interpretation of science. This era's shifting values meant law courts had to juggle the demands of Biblical religion, written law, natural justice and modern science.

From the 1200s to the 1700s, the moral dictates of the law could be applied to animals as well as humans. Religious and secular courts in America and Europe regularly indicted animals and even insects to face charges from the destruction of crops and witchcraft, to rape and murder. The convicted creatures typically suffered the same harsh punishments as people including torture and death. But in some instances, the defendants won.

In his online article, *Let Us Now Praise Infamous Animals*, writer Jeffrey St. Clair offered some extraordinary cases of animal law.

In 1713, a portion of a Franciscan monastery in Brazil collapsed, its foundation ravaged by termites. At this time, all living things were considered creatures of God and so could not to be killed unnecessarily. Because they had to follow this Biblical principle, the monks could not just stomp or poison the insects into oblivion so they followed the law and lodged charges against the termites. A monastic council was set up. The insects were summoned to appear before the court and answer the charges against their conduct.

But the termites - like the illiterate people of Hammurabi's Empire - had a problem. They couldn't read the law. So the termites got a lawyer. Their lawyer explained failure to appear in court meant the termites would be convicted in a default judgement against them. The termites huddled and decided to accept their court-appointed lawyer. It proved to be the smartest move the termites ever made.

The lawyer presented his clients to the court in the best light. The termites were "industrious creatures, worked hard and enjoyed a God-given right to feed themselves" he told the judges. Then he attacked the reputation of the monks for encouraging the termites. The monks were lazy and their bad habits were the cause of the disrepair of the monastery, the lawyer continued. The monks were merely using the local termite community "as an excuse for their own negligence." The judge returned to his chambers, contemplated the facts and returned with a ruling. The monks were told to provide a woodpile for the termites outside the building, and the judge ordered the insects "to leave the monastery," St. Clair wrote.

In the same article, St. Clair related the case of Weevils v. Grapes that took place in the province of Savoy, France in 1575. The weevils were indicted for destroying some famous vineyards - the pride of this wine-making community. Once again, the insects lucked out with their court-appointed attorney - Pierre Rembaud. In his first move, Rembaud went for the winemaker's legal throat. He told the court all charges against his clients should be immediately dismissed. In his motion for a summary judgement, Rembaud argued the weevils had a well-established property claim on the vegetation that came before the current owner of the vineyard. In the Bible's Book of Genesis, Rembaud argued, animals are created before humans and God promised animals "all of the grasses, leaves and green herbs for their food," St. Clair wrote.

This argument stumped the court and sent everybody scrambling for a precedent that preceded the Bible. Eventually, the villagers set aside a patch of open land away from the vineyards "as a foraging ground for the weevils," the article said. As a sign of how far the law had strayed from a balance of interests to an architecture of opportunity, the article noted what happened after the townspeople offered the weevils the settlement of a new grazing ground. Their lawyer looked over the barren landscape, told the weevils they deserved better and rejected it, St. Clair wrote.

In another section of his article, St. Clair related a story about French philosopher and scientist Rene Descartes (1596–1650).

As a leader of the Age of Enlightenment, Descartes called for objective science to reshape old legal notions based in religion. He wanted to end the legal status of animals because they were nothing more than biological machines with no awareness of abuse. To make his point, one day Descartes' followers gathered in a French village and collected a number of stray dogs and cats. They then proceeded to beat and cut up the living animals "without mercy, laughing at any compassion for them and calling their screams the noise of breaking machinery," St. Clair wrote, citing one of Descartes' biographers.

At the same time as Descartes, another Enlightenment leader - the famed scientist and one-time Attorney-General of England, Francis Bacon - declared the proper aim of science was "to restore the divinely ordained dominance of man over nature," St. Clair wrote. The new laws of science, like the old laws of religion, would often be used to give extra value to some people while removing dignity and protection from others.

In modern law, the legal meaning of property and personhood is being redefined as global corporations, machines with artificial intelligence, restrictive software on personal devices and patented living organisms reach farther into the legal veins of society. In the evolution of legal systems, the word "fair" is sometimes used in place of justice. The old word for "fair" meant something that is "correct" and "made straight." And what is correct is defined by the law as Justice Holmes noted.

CHAPTER 15

FRAGMENTS

PART 1
BEDS FOR THE DEAD

After the execution of Akhenaten around 1350 BC, Egypt's new leaders launched a series of aggressive wars to regain colonies and foreign holdings lost during the chaos of his religious revolution. A new Egyptian king, Ramesses II, promised to restore Egypt's previous glory as a feared, military empire. Egypt's armies of soldiers, archers and chariot drivers swept across the Sinai Peninsula. They marched into the Middle Eastern lands of Canaan and north along the coast of the eastern Mediterranean Sea towards Egypt's new rival – the Hittites. The Hittites were an Indo-European people who settled in the fertile lands of Anatolia - modern Turkey. For 20 years, the Semitic Egyptians and Indo-European Hittites tried to destroy each other and claim control of the entire region. Their last titanic battle for supremacy pit the most advanced weaponry of both sides against each other in a maelstrom of armor, spears, arrows and chariots. But it ended in a draw. With no prospect that one side could defeat the other, the kings of humanity's two great empires did something remarkable. The Hittites and the Egyptians signed the world's first peace treaty in 1269 BC. The world of West Asia and the Middle East was at peace.

It would not last.

Egypt and the Hittites signed the world's first peace treaty in 1269 BC

Suddenly and with little warning, the great empires of the world would collapse into economic ruin and social upheaval from a combination of extreme climate change and widespread terrorism around 1100 BC. It marked the end of the Afro-Eurasian heartland as the cultural center of civilization. When humanity's unifying land bridge of commerce and culture was abandoned the world was sliced in two, leaving the old East on one side and the emerging West on the other. The sun of human civilization, which first rose in India, moved west to Mesopotamia. When its urban centers fell, the zenith continued west to fall on Persia, Greece and Rome. In the past thousand years, it lit Europe and then moved further west to America. In the coming decades, the solstice of civilization may appear again in the East and start the cycle once more.

Until about 1100 BC, West Asia and North Africa were the geographic and cultural centers of the human world. When their empires collapsed, so did widespread trade. Technological innovation and the exchange of ideas withered. It was a new Dark Ages and contact between people was limited. As Asia and Europe separated, the old history of a culturally unified world was lost in the rush to create new identities with new histories.

The Great Collapse of 1100 BC set humanity on the road to Western Civilization and the modern world. But before examining the causes and consequences of that turning point, it's worth noting the origins of a few other traditions, concepts and technologies that began in an older, more unified world.

For most people, Ancient Egypt conjures up images of the pyramids and those fabulous afterlife astronauts called mummies strapped into their cosmic crypts. But the inspiration for the pyramids as a way to honor an individual's life and launch the departed into their next stage of existence began long before Ancient Egypt. Evidence of burials and funeral rituals can be found in the oldest human societies and among animals.

Surrounding the dead with items from their life and covering them with dirt or leaving them in a cave is the oldest human ritual. Anthropologists once believed ritually burying the dead was unique to humans and a sign of evolutionary progress. It is now known many animals and birds hold their own funeral services.

Elephants in Africa will cover their dead – and even dead humans – with branches and leaves. In New Zealand, a writer noted how his dog spontaneously buried an unrelated dead dog that was lying on the beach. Many kinds of birds will grieve for dead loved ones. They will stand over a recently deceased companion as if holding a moment of silence before they fly off. What's particularly impressive is that the creatures who assemble to honor their dead have gathered there because members of their community were able to communicate news about who died and where.

Elephants gather to mourn their dead and pay respects

A 2012 article in the Southland Times (New Zealand) told how one of the paper's photographers, Doug Field, photographed his own dog, June, as she buried the dead body of a "John Doe" dog.

"'There was quite a reverence in what she did. I've never seen another dog do that before,' Field said. Although the writer doesn't discuss this, it is curious that June used her nose to bury the dead dog rather than turning her back on the corpse and kicking up sand with her hind legs which would have been faster. Not turning her anus towards the dead may have been a sign of canine respect.

In a 2011 article published on the University of California, Berkeley website, Evolutionary Biology Prof. Marc Bekoff wrote about an aviary funeral service.

A magpie had been hit by a car and was lying at the side of the road, he wrote. "Four of his flock mates stood around him silently and pecked gently at his body. One, then another, flew off and brought back pine needles and twigs and laid them by his body. They all stood vigil for a time, nodded their heads, and flew off," he said.

In his Oct. 29, 2009 Psychology Today article, *Grief in animals: It's arrogant to think we're the only animals who mourn,* Prof. Bekoff cited the work of Nobel Prize-winning animal researcher Konrad Lorenz. Lorenz noticed when a goose lost its partner the survivor showed the same symptoms of grief as humans. Their "eyes sink deep into their sockets, and the individual has an overall drooping experience, "literally letting the head hang," Lorenz wrote. Indeed, the old adage about not harming a "dumb animal" does not mean to take pity on a stupid creature, but that it is wrong to hurt something that cannot speak to defend itself.

Neanderthals were the first human ancestors known to have buried their dead. The earliest *Homo Sapien* human burial site is 100,000 years old and was found in the Skhul cave at Qafzeh, Israel. When those people were buried a thousand centuries ago some of them were holding items in their hands.

One gripped the antlers of a deer, another the jaw of a wild boar perhaps signifying their hunting skills during life, Prof. Philip Lieberman, a cognitive scientist at Brown University, in Providence, Rhode Island, wrote in his book, *Uniquely Human: The Evolution of Speech, Thought, and Selfless Behavior.*

To many researchers, human burial rituals are evidence of prehistoric religion and belief in an afterlife. However, if animals bury their dead, hold funerals and mourn, are they practicing an animal religion? Did humanity's ideas about individual identity and the soul evolve from concepts that exist among animals and birds? Do animals with long memories – such as elephants - think an animal soul lives on? If birds are direct descendants of dinosaurs, did Brontosauruses mourn their kin in gatherings like magpies? Do animals think spirits of their dead friends and ancestors travel with them in life - just as many humans do?

What makes an action or idea religious in an era before established religions? When early humans considered the existence of something intangible that connected them in some way to other people, animals and things, were their questions religious, philosophical, scientific or all of the above? The animals that hold funerals have no apparent religion, but they exhibit a sense of individuality and time. For what are those rituals if not a recognition of a unique timespan of life now gone? Early humans experimented with different burial practices – folding the arms across the chest, and the placement of bodies towards the rising or setting sun - long before those traditions were associated with any religion. Early humans could have watched the Sun's path across the sky and come up with the same metaphor for the appearance and disappearance of life as people do today – without organized religion. This is supported by the self-evident fact that religious rituals evolved from non-religious practices. Speaking came before praying, and communal meals were a feature of human society long before food offerings to the gods. Seen this way, the many prehistoric statues and images described as religious artifacts may not in fact be religious. Without wider evidence of any organized religion, prehistoric statues may be simply artistic expressions like the cave paintings. Is the 70,000 year old statue of a woman flanked by lions a goddess, or the image of a real woman who was powerful and gentle enough to have lions as pets?

70,000 year old statue of a powerful, Ice Age woman whose fatty body stored calories and provided insulation during the long winters

Or, are she and the 35,000 year old Lion Man artistic statements about the unity between animals and people? Whatever the interpretation, it is clear early humans did not separate knowledge into subjects. Knowledge was whole and so prehistoric art was likely a combination of individual craftsmanship, a factual statement of what the artist saw and an inspirational idea or emotion.

35,000 year old statue of a Lion Man shows the unity of humans and animals

Because the ancient Indo-European cultures did not place much importance on death, they never built great monuments to the dead. It was the African cultures of Ancient Egypt and Sudan where religion and royalty joined to create the first truly human burial structure – the pyramids.

The Pyramids of Ancient Egypt were launch pads for their afterlife space program

The pyramids of Africa represent the world's first space program for dead astronauts. From its simple beginnings in Egypt as a dirt mound attempting to push its corpse commander into the air, pyramid technology grew to include elaborate space stations able to house entire communities of resurrected rocketeers. The Egyptian faithful believed that after death, they would be reconstituted from the mummified pieces of their body placed inside the pyramid with them. To pass the endless time once their corpses were reassembled, these post-mortem properties were equipped with board games, food and the bodies of sacrificed pets and servants awaiting their own resurrection. The pyramids were monumental fusions of organized religion, royal hubris and the most advanced technology of the day. And all that brainpower was mobilized for the purpose of sending fantastically-preserved dead body bits into the outer space of the Egyptian afterlife and leaving them there. The pyramid's construction techniques were the result of complex and highly detailed math, chemistry and physics. As such, the regional royalty used the pyramids to showcase the latest advancements in art and designer beds for the dead.

In the race for post-life space, the Nubians set up their pyramid program in Sudan 3,500 years ago

Egypt's first experiment in designing an afterlife rocket was similar to that of the early space program – the pyramids went up with a big flash of sand and packed earth and then fizzled out. Later designs added baked mud bricks as outer panels – presumably to shield them from cosmic rays. Those new designs were called mastabas.

Early Egyptian burial rocket was a flash in the sand

The next step in the race for more space was the step pyramid. The gaps between the brick steps were filled in and covered over to create the well-known pyramid shape.

Later Egyptian pyramids were covered by clay panels, presumably to protect the mummies from burning up during the re-entry of their resurrection

The Werner von Braun of Egypt's new pyramid program was Imhotep. A man of tremendous knowledge, vision and skill, he lived about 4,600 years ago and is remembered as the world's first known architect, engineer and physician.

Imhotep's 4,600 year old Step Pyramid was a space station for the dead

Humanity's oldest mass graveyards are the Varna Necropolis in Bulgaria and the "Burnt City" graves in Iran.

In Egypt, the wealthy rocketed into the afterlife in special burial tombs while the poor were tucked in isolated shallow graves. The people living in what is now Bulgaria were more democratic in their attitude towards death. Five thousand years ago, a civilization sprang up along the shores of Lake Varna, west of the Black Sea. Along with their skills in math and navigation, the Varna culture left behind the largest prehistoric cemetery in southeast Europe and the richest cemetery ever found anywhere in the world. This 4,500 year old necropolis is one of the world's earliest democratic burial grounds with separate, equal-sized graves for individuals and families. Inside the roughly 300 graves so far explored more than 3,000 fabulously crafted gold artifacts weighing a total of 6 kilograms (over 13 pounds) have been recovered. These include gold beads, gold-based cosmetics, rings, bracelets and crowns.

In just one grave at Varna, archaeologists discovered more gold than has been found in all the palaces of the world from that time period.

The 4,500 year old burial grounds of the Varna Necropolis contained more gold than all the palaces of the world

In 1992, a 5,000 year old cemetery was uncovered in southeast Iran. Containing about 100,000 skeletons among its 25-35,000 graves, archaeologists found one of the world's oldest artificial eyes still inside the skull of a skeleton.

Skeleton of a young Iranian woman with a 5,000 year old artificial eye

According to a report from Iran's Tabnak News service, among remains found in the enormous Burnt City graveyard, was the skeleton of woman. Her grave included a decomposing leather bag and a bronze mirror, and carefully set in her head was an artificial eye. This cosmetic surgery is the oldest evidence of a prosthetic eye made to "look as realistic as possible," excavation leader Prof. Mansur Sayyed-Sajadi said. The eye was made from "natural tar mixed with animal fat" and whoever made it "likely used a fine golden wire, thinner than half a millimeter, to draw the most delicate eye capillaries," he added.

PART 2
THE ALCHEMIST WIZARDS OF AFRICA

All humans are descended from a family who lived in Africa nearly 3 million years ago alongside many other types of early humans. But the others died off because they lacked the skills, intelligence and insight to combine their resources and work together. Human cooperation resulted in small communities, then urban centers and finally a cohesive civilization. Human history is the story of how individuals and groups have gathered, interpreted and applied knowledge to expand

and diversify their society. And that is also the story of life. Calculations from theoretical biologists Alexei Sharov and Richard Gordon show the genetic complexity of life on Earth has doubled every 376 million years. In other words, there is twice as much accessible information in the genomes of living things today compared to the simpler life forms of 376 million years ago, and four times more genetically expressed information than there was 752 million years ago.

However, this exponential expansion of expressed knowledge has not always been smooth. In general, three main factors have influenced the accessibility, application and abundance of knowledge in human history – available resources, a stable or unstable climate and whether or not people work and play together. Abundant food and other resources, a predictable climate and the cooperative culture of pre-historic and early ancient humanity enabled rapid trade advancement due to the mixing of people. When resources in one region dwindled, people migrated to more fertile lands. The founding of Ancient Egypt is a good example.

About 100,000 years ago, two groups of human ancestors were divided by Africa's geography. They lived north or south of the Transition Zone between Africa's northern savannahs, grasslands and sand dunes near the equator and the tropical rain forest and denser vegetation farther south. Those living in the North would journey out of Africa through the Sinai and settle in the Middle East, Europe and Asia. The people living in Southern Africa would largely remain there, forming the first African kingdoms. These two groups were humanity's first geographic introverts and extroverts.

The original migratory hiking trail between Africa and its nearby regions would grow into the world's first transcontinental circle of trade.

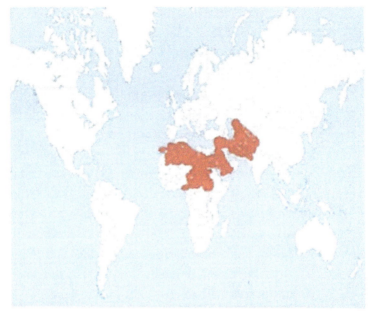

Alice C. Lindsay's map of the Afro-Asian trade network 5,000 years ago

Seven thousand years ago, the great Sahara desert of North Africa was a broad, grassy savannah of large leafy trees, wild flowers, winding rivers and grazing herds of elephants, buffalo, giraffes and antelopes. Animals and people frequented the shores of a gigantic North African lake that is now desert sand. But when the region was lush, nomadic people from around the trading region joined the caravans that annually circled North Africa with their herds of animals. This multicultural community of nomads included people from the Middle East, Southwest Asia, North Africa and Neanderthals from Europe. In a 1993 article in the *American Journal of Physical Anthropology*, University of Michigan Prof. C. Loring Brace and his co-authors wrote the Ancient Egyptians were a mixture of many groups. They show ties with Neanderthals and modern humans from Europe, other North Africans and more remotely India. But, they added, there is no evidence of a genetically close relationship with the Nubians or other people south of the Transition Zone.

The northern community of mixed cultures continued until about 7,000 years ago when the climate of North Africa changed dramatically.

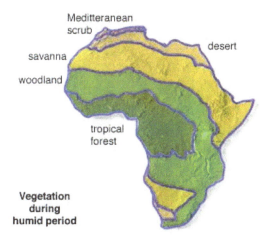

Most of North Africa was a grassy savannah until 7,000 years ago when the rain stopped and it became the Sahara Desert

The annual rains stopped falling and clouds disappeared from the skies for months and then years at a time. Life in the savannah died, and the land shriveled into a dusty desert. As the drought went on, the desert expanded and people retreated east until they arrived in the green valley of the Nile River on the coastlines of the Mediterranean and Red Seas. There, two civilizations – one in the South and one in the North - took root and began to flourish as Upper and Lower Egypt.

Thousands of years later, the rulers of Egypt would write of another glorious culture set up by merchants from India on the East Coast of Africa. These were entrepreneurial merchants from the Indus, and 4,600 years ago they built a flourishing community the Egyptians called the magic land of Punt.

Ancient records about its location are vague, but Punt was probably in the region of modern Ethiopia, Somalia and Eritrea. The newcomers who settled there were welcomed to the North African neighborhood because they were traders not invaders. Wealthy Egyptians frequently made the long journey to Punt to purchase fabulous products at the world's first luxury shopping mall, and be entertained by the offerings of the world's first talent agency. And among the many opulent displays in the Punt bazaar was the work of their alchemist wizards who could turn ordinary metal into gold.

Possible locations of the magic land of Punt

The people of Punt lived in sophisticated settlements of beehive-shaped homes. They were made of reeds and placed on top of a platform with wooden legs that kept their houses above the shallows of the waters that ran beneath them. A ladder served as the private elevator the owners used to get to their penthouse condo on the coast.

Egyptian wall carving of the beehive-shaped homes of Punt

But these Indo-Africans were more than just ingenious architects. By 2600 BC, Egyptian Royalty and the fashion-minded wealthy were writing of their travels to Punt. They described the broad lanes of the outdoor markets and displays of intricate jewelry, exotic perfumes, fabulous clothes, beautiful African animals and amazing African people. Punt's luxury marketplace was New York's Fifth Avenue, London's High Street and L.A.'s Rodeo Drive rolled into one.

On the Tour Egypt web site, writer Jimmy Dunn recalled the reviews of those Ancient Egyptian tourists. Punt, they said, was "a bazaar of astonishing luxuries" with "wonderful decorations made of ivory, ebony and African Blackwood. The stalls of their merchants were piled high with gold jewelry, stacks of colorful and aromatic resins from trees and perfumes made from the essential oils of exotic flowers." Shoppers could also purchase animals including giraffes, baboons, hippos and the humpbacked Brahma bull, Dunn wrote.

There were so many fragrant woods and heaps of myrrh, ivory and green gold, incense and eye-cosmetics, along with live apes, monkeys, dogs, and beautiful animal hides, that it was more glorious than the court of any king, another Egyptian said.

The entrepreneurs of Punt were also the first known talent agents. Monkeys from Punt found new work as honored members of Egypt's temples. Other animals were adopted as exotic royal pets and housed in luxurious buildings. Egypt's upper classes also bought people in Punt. However, this was not a slave market. The people they purchased were entertainers like dancers and midgets, and their agents booked them for a lifetime engagement at the palace.

Bes, Ancient Egypt's most popular God-of-the-people, is said to be modeled on a famous dwarf from Punt who was brought to the palaces of Egypt. He was a beloved member of the Royal Family and elevated to a god after his death.

Bes, the popular Egyptian protector god, was originally a dwarf from Punt

Egypt's Royalty adored the land, people and fabulous wealth of Punt. But there was something they loved even more. Life in Ancient Egypt was governed by repetitive routines, strict social rituals and religious rules. Punt was an open, friendly and by all accounts, a democratic and leaderless society of cooperative members similar to that of the Indus, Hebrews and Phoenicians. When Egypt's King Amenhotep III (father of Akhenaten) arrived in Punt, he told its people his mission was to enjoy "your peace and breathe the air you give."

In the summer of 1493 BC, Egypt's Queen Hatshepsut gathered a small army of 150 rowers and five sailing ships and set off for the land of Punt more than 1,900 km (1,200 miles) away. They traveled in small papyrus reed boats and larger ones made from wooden planks fastened by ropes and metal hooks. Workers assembled, disassembled and re-assembled the Queen's royal barge as they portaged across land and rowed through the rivers and swamps of Egypt's waterways. They endured all this for weeks.

Queen Hatshepsut's mortuary temple near Luxor, Egypt contains a tree she brought from Punt

The Queen said her voyage was a religious pilgrimage to "cleanse her spirit." In all these declarations, it is clear the Egyptians saw Punt as a land of wealthier, more advanced and more spiritual people.

The Egyptians called Punt "Ta netjer," which means a land that is "sacred, holy" and "inhabited by God's people." This term was also applied to Asia and regions of the East where the sun appeared to be born. The phrase "Ta netjer" can also be translated as "Land of our ancestors." This last meaning suggests the ancient Egyptians viewed the people of Punt not as newcomers, but part of an older, long-established relationship. It may be the Egyptians were acknowledging the ancestral connection from the North African herding culture or the even older prehistoric trade between India and Egypt.

In a 2008 article in the Russian newspaper Pravda, writer Babu G. Ranganathan, said there is "considerable archaeological and anthropological evidence" connecting Ancient India and Ancient Egypt. Ancient Black Indians – the Dravidians - were called Ethiopians by the Greeks and Egyptians, he wrote.

"In ancient times there were known to be two types of Ethiopians, Western Ethiopians, in Africa, (who were black with woolly hair and fine features) and their brethren, the Eastern Ethiopians, of India, who also were black with fine features but possessed straight hair," he said. The Dravidians "most likely emigrated from Africa to India and, later, many returned to Africa where they developed ancient Egyptian culture and civilization," he explained.

The word "Ethiopian" comes from root words in ancient Greek that mean "a face as beautiful and radiant as the sun." They were given this name because the Indo-African Ethiopians were considered the most beautiful people in the world. So great was this fame that Ethiopian was a word for beauty in the ancient world.

"You look very Ethiopian tonight, my dear."

"Thank you."

Ethiopia could also imply a land that faces the rising sun, people whose ancestors came from the east in India, or all those meanings together.

The alchemists of Punt made electrum gold – electrum goblet of unknown origin

But the "Wizards of Punt," as the Egyptians called them, are perhaps best-remembered as the original alchemists. They were metallurgists who mixed common elements to make gold. Before alchemy was associated with cartoonish characters and special effects, alchemy was the word used for all work in chemistry. Chemistry is the study of elements and compounds - alone and in combination. The word, "alchemy" comes from an Ancient Greek name for Egypt – *Khemia* – "land of the black earth." This suggests the original alchemists were from or, to the Greeks, associated with the people of Ancient Egypt.

According to legend, alchemists could change a plain metal such as copper into gold. The craftspeople of Punt were the source of that legend and their work was on daily display in the jewelry shops. Punt's jewelers produced fabulous and intricate necklaces, rings and bangles. They used precision diamond drills to carve tiny holes in polished stones and fashioned fine strands of gold for designs. They also produced a special kind of gold by mixing it with other minerals.

There is a natural alloy of gold called electrum, sometimes called "pale gold." It is a mixture of gold, silver and common metals including copper. Thirty-five hundred years ago, the jewelers of Punt discovered how to mix the ingredients and artificially produce electrum gold. The legend of the alchemists began with their recipe for making pale gold with the addition of copper. The copper was turned into gold. Although electrum has remained in use ever since, when Egyptians stopped trading with Punt around 1300 BC the old chemistry connection was lost and hardworking metallurgists were recast as magicians called alchemists.

PART 3
A SHORT CUT TO THE HISTORY OF CIRCUMCISION

A Jewish *Mohel* (trained in the rites of circumcision) cuts off the foreskin with a gold-tipped fingernail c 1500s Courtesy The Wellcome Institute

Who came up with the idea of circumcision?

To many people, circumcision is a bizarre, antiquated and barbaric ritual. Among Jews and Muslims however, any consideration of its original purpose is an afterthought because Jewish and Muslim males are ritually circumcised shortly after birth.

The first Biblical character to adopt this practice was Abraham (c 1800 BC). And since his time, it has been considered a symbol of the bond between God and the Jewish and Muslim people – both said to be descended from Abraham. In the Bible, Abraham was told circumcision would be a sign of his spiritual marriage to the Hebrew God, and this Deity wanted everyone in his harem. Abraham was told to circumcise all the males in his household including servants, slaves and all their male children. Every male was to be made part of the new blessing – whether they wanted to be blessed or not.

The Jewish people carried the tradition of household circumcision with them when they settled in new lands. In Ancient Rome at the time of the Jesus, about 10 percent of the city's population were Jewish. The practice of forcibly circumcising male servants and slaves horrified the majority of Romans who considered it a barbaric act of torture. Several Roman Emperors issued decrees banning forced circumcision throughout the Empire.

For most of its history – and despite the 4,000 year old Biblical command – circumcision was typically performed on adult males, not infants. This may indicate an earlier version that did not specify newborns. It was also more common to sever only the tip of the foreskin not the entire covering. Though the Biblical God makes circumcision a deal-breaker for membership in his club, for most of Biblical history this was not a regular practice among the Hebrew or Israelite people. As with all religious practices, the popularity of this command rose and fell according to the times and leadership. Abraham's Arab descendants also largely abandoned the practice until it was revived by the Prophet Mohammed (570-632 AD), and spread through his teachings of Islam – an Arabic word that means "one who finds safety by surrendering to the peace of God."

Despite the importance of circumcision among Jews and Muslims, the Bible and the Qur'an are silent on the origin and purpose of this practice. As a result, prejudices, myths and emotions have surrounded circumcision for thousands of years. It has been called a disease-preventing surgery and a divine gift to mankind. Others decry it as abusive, psychologically-damaging and primitive. In the Bible, the Israelites use forced circumcision as a weapon against their male prisoners. In another Biblical tale, Moses' wife prevents God from killing her husband by quickly circumcising their infant son. Clearly, this ancient ritual carried many symbolic meanings.

A captured warrior is forcibly circumcised by the Ancient Israelites (Courtesy Wellcome Institute)

According to Robert Darby's web site, Historyofcircumcision.net, in the late 1800s, infant circumcision was hailed as the cure-all for everything from irritable bowels to masturbation. In the 1880s, the newly formed American Academy of Pediatrics promoted routine circumcision to prevent infant diarrhoea. A 1914 article in the Journal of the American Medical Association claimed this simple snip at birth provided immunity from syphilis, cancer and excessive masturbation in adult men. Prevention of masturbation and the spread of sexual diseases were the main 'scientific' arguments used by the pro-cut crowd. Indeed, one leading doctor in the cause described the foreskin as "a moral outlaw," Darby wrote.

During WWII, at the height of the Battles of Guadalcanal and El Alamein, many American, British and allied soldiers were ordered circumcised to stop the spread of skin diseases even though uncircumcised Germans and Italians were not affected, the site explained. In 1950, South Korea adopted universal circumcision and in 1955, 90% of Australian boys were circumcised at birth.

In the mid-1960s and early 1970s, the tide of public opinion began to turn against the old practice. Anti-circumcision campaigners demanded its abolition. The American Academy of Pediatrics reversed its earlier position and declared circumcision of no medical value, Darby's site said.

In 1999, an article in the medical Journal Lancet called for mass circumcision in Africa to prevent the spread of AIDS even though more than half the adult male population of the continent was already foreskin-free. Despite this, numerous studies have shown circumcised men are less likely to be infected. This is due to the moist environment under the foreskin that – if not regularly cleaned - provides a breeding ground for the virus.

Advocates of religion, science and human rights have waged court battles for and against the procedure and the much-less common practice of female cutting. In the 1990s, an Islamic imam convinced Egypt's High Court to overturn a ban on the 1,400 year old, involuntary and brutal practice of so-called female circumcision. While this practice is forced on girls and women in parts of Africa, Asia and the Middle East, the origin of this ritual is unknown and it is not mentioned in any ancient text.

The highly-charged opinions and attitudes about circumcision are inseparable from people's attitudes about sex and religion. As such, the theories about when, where and why the practice of male foreskin removal began vary widely. Some suggest it started as a ritual of manhood – to promote virility and demonstrate resistance to pain. Others say it was first used to humiliate prisoners and lower their sex drive. One catch-all concept suggested there was an original purpose, but it was forgotten as the practice was adopted by different cultures.

If there was a common meaning, it was well-known long before the birth of Abraham around 1800 BC. Six hundred years before his time, circumcision was an established practice among the Ancient Egyptians. Tomb artwork from 2400 BC is considered the oldest documentary evidence. The earliest written account dates from 2200 BC. In his book, *Circumcision: A history of the world's most controversial surgery*, David Gollaher, related the story of an Egyptian man named Uha who described his participation in the mass circumcision of 120 men.

None of them flinched and so none were harmed, Uha said.

Among Egyptians in general and priests in particular, cleanliness was almost a fetish. To ensure they were clean and smooth, Egypt's priests shaved their entire bodies. Was circumcision just another kind of haircut?

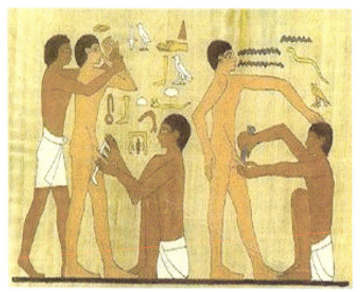

Circumcision in Ancient Egypt c 2300 BC – the inscription says "Sever, indeed, thoroughly"

While the oldest evidence of circumcision is found in the records of Ancient Egypt, it was not limited to the Middle East. There is evidence it was practiced by people across the ancient and prehistoric world.

In their 1999 article, *The History of Circumcision* published in the British Journal of Urology, Drs. W.D. Dunsmuir and E.M. Gordon cited the work of English Egyptologist Sir Graham Elliot Smith who argued circumcision was a worldwide practice 15,000 years ago - though there is no hard evidence for this. However, when Christopher Columbus and other European explorers arrived in the Americas 500 years ago, they were surprised to find many North American Indians were circumcised. The practice was once common among Australia's Aboriginals, in India and tribal Africa, the article said.

The Ancient Greeks considered circumcision an offence against the body. The Greek word "gymnasium" means "to train naked." The first

Olympic athletes of 700 BC played the way they trained – in the buff and proud of it. As a result, competitive Greek Jews would undergo painful medical procedures to sew on an artificial foreskin to compete in the games without public embarrassment.

Egyptian priests claimed circumcision was their gateway to spiritual enlightenment. They believed circumcised men had access to a higher knowledge than the uncut. This was the first recorded time men claimed their penises were a greater source of knowledge than their brains. When Pythagoras came to study with Egypt's renowned priesthood 1,500 years ago, the famous mathematician from Ancient Greece had to be divided from his foreskin before he could add his presence to the school. Jesus and the Apostles were Jewish and circumcised. But after Jesus' death, his later followers condemned the practice as a meaningless relic of a meaningless faith.

"Circumcision is nothing," I Corinthians 7:19.

All this suggests its earliest purpose grew from two concepts – a connection to God and removing a covering.

The origin of the word "temple" may be related to the practice. It comes from an old Indo-European word, *temp*, which means "to stretch" and "to cut." So, the original meaning of temple may have been "the home of circumcised priests."

The symbolic meaning of circumcision and its relationship to God may be related to the word "shame," and its Indo-European root that means to "cover up." When people feel ashamed or guilty they tend to turn away and hide their faces. "Covering up a crime" means hiding evidence of shame and guilt. By contrast, those who are open and honest have "nothing to hide." Thus, when the Biblical characters of Adam and Eve feel shame they cover themselves with clothes. Clothing is used as a symbol of their guilt and to distinguish them from the God of Eden who, presumably, did not wear clothes.

Nudity as a public offence is a relatively new concept in human society. During the tens of thousands of years when nakedness was accepted as normal, the first cultural step to circumcision may have been when men folded back their foreskin as a spiritual metaphor for being completely naked and uncovered before God. There is evidence for this in a traditional story about Noah who lived 200 years before Abraham.

According to the ancient rabbinical commentary on the Torah called the *Midrash*, long before the Biblical Great Flood, the land of Noah's father was enduring a terrible drought. God told Noah's father the rains would return when he had a son born without a foreskin. Noah was born that way and the rains did return. Jewish and Islamic tradition claim Moses, the Biblical character Israel (of the Israelites), and the Prophet Mohammed were all born without a foreskin. In more recent times, David Levy - Deputy Prime Minister of Israel from 1981-1992 - was also born topless.

This genetic condition is called aposthia. Aposthia comes from the same root as "apostle." The word "apostle" begins as an Ancient Greek word meaning "messenger" or "sent away," and the Indo-European source of that word means to "stand tall" and "be erect." As a physical description, the word "aposthia" simply means "the top is away from the post."

In Judaism, Christianity and Islam, Noah is considered an exceptionally righteous man. His crown of righteousness was the un-crown of being born without a foreskin. The rabbinical commentary suggests this condition was seen as a sign of God's blessing before Noah was born. If the Biblical character of Noah was an Indo-Semite who lived in India's Indus Valley, the tradition of foreskin folding and circumcision may have started in Southwest Asia. In a chapter of the Bible called "Table of Nations" the various descendants and followers of Noah settled their families in different regions where they spread the teachings of their famous father. The story of Noah's birth blessing may have prompted a tradition of emulation that was passed around the Middle East and Africa during and after the fall of the Indus. The ritual of removing the foreskin may have been touted as a permanent way for a man to proclaim his righteousness, and thus be as close to God and as spiritually uncovered as Noah. When the story of Noah's birth condition was forgotten, the practice of cutting continued.

When the last remnants of the old Biblical kingdoms of Israel and Judah were swept off the map (c 63 BC), the Jewish people who came after refashioned circumcision from a symbol of priesthood to a sign of their citizenship in a nation of exiles. In the cultural language of the Jewish and Muslim people, circumcision was the first letter in the alphabet of a man's life.

PART 4
ALPHABET SOFTWARE AND HUMAN SACRIFICE

The words "book" and "Bible" are variations on the Greek name of the world's oldest, continuously inhabited city – Byblos, now in Lebanon. Its first settlements date to 8000 BC. About 7,000 years later, the Indo-European Phoenicians (part of the larger Canaanite family of nations mentioned in the Bible) built a transcontinental trading empire from their port cities on the Eastern Mediterranean coast.

The Phoenicians' sound alphabet was the world's first free operating software (Courtesy Steve Scamp)

From these bustling sea towns, Phoenician trade reached as far west as Morocco and southern Britain. Around 1200 BC, this small group of people rose from the status of low-paid migrant workers in Egypt to the world's leading sea merchants, master boat builders, glass makers and sole producers of the royal color purple.

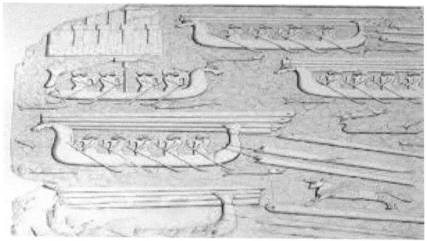

The Phoenicians' horsehead boats were a sign they delivered their products everywhere – by land and by sea

They also created a 22-letter writing system and set up the world's first book publishing empire. The Phoenicians wrote on clay tablets, and mass-produced popular manuscripts on papyrus. Mass production here means the Phoenician scribes hand-copied each manuscript as quickly as they could.

The alphabet the Phoenicians' invented was so popular that people around the world adopted it. This enduring ABC form of speech coding revolutionized writing. Yet, this invention began as a form of shorthand. Three thousand years ago, Phoenician migrant laborers in the mines of Egypt started making scratches on clay tablets to indicate the spoken instructions of their Egyptian supervisors. The workers didn't have the time to fashion elaborate hieroglyphics, so they created simple shapes as stand-ins for the sounds of Egyptian words. This was a major breakthrough in communications technology. Until then, the letter-like symbols used in earlier forms of writing represented ideas, actions or things, not sounds. The Phoenicians' innovation meant the same set of symbols could be used to record words from any language in a form everyone could learn to read and pronounce. This sound-based, user-friendly alphabet was enormously popular. And because it was invented before modern copyright laws, it was quickly adopted as the free operating system for almost every language in the world.

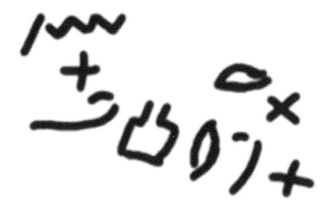

The modern alphabet began as a shorthand code for the sounds of the Ancient Egyptian language

This technique for information transfer was a major advance from earlier alphabets. Rolling experiments in writing had been part of human culture since the first symbols were drawn alongside the prehistoric cave paintings 40,000-20,000 years ago. Genevieve von Petzinger, a University of Victoria (Canada) graduate student in anthropology, studied more than 120 prehistoric cave sites in France and noticed many letter-like symbols were used for thousands of years by widely separated people. The same icons turned up at more than 100 sites and of those some proto-letters remained in use for 20,000 years. In a curious connection to the modern English alphabet, Von Petzinger found 26 symbols were in common use. Some of the cave symbols would live on as Egyptian hieroglyphics, cuneiform wedge writing and Indus Valley script, and the modern hashtag.

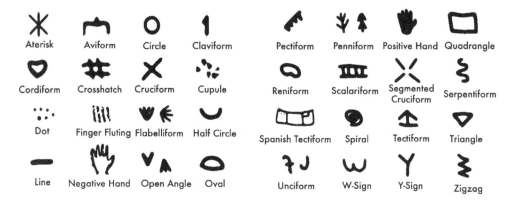

Letter-like symbols started with cave art 40,000-20,000 years ago and included the hashtag and asterisk

The Sumerians of Mesopotamia and the Ancient Egyptians were the first to develop complex writing systems about 5,200 years ago. The Sumerians used a writing style of wedge symbols pressed into clay called cuneiform. Their symbol for mountain resembles the zigzag cave symbol, while the cave asterisk reappears as their sign for god.

	MEANING	OUTLINE CHARACTER, B.C. 3500	ARCHAIC CUNEIFORM, B.C. 2500	ASSYRIAN, B.C. 700	LATE BABYLONIAN, B.C. 500
1.	The sun				
2.	God, heaven				
3.	Mountain				
4.	Man				
5.	Ox				
6.	Fish				

5,500 years ago, Cuneiform word symbols were printed with sharpened sticks

As the Sumerians were impressing visitors with their lettering technology, the Ancient Egyptians were coding their own written language. Their combination of symbols, pictures and objects is called hieroglyphics. Yet, long before the Egyptians and Sumerians, people around the world were experimenting with similar ideas for writing.

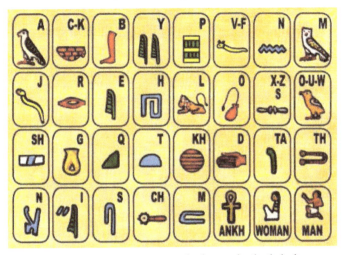

More than 5,000 years ago, the hieroglyph alphabet of Ancient Egypt used pictures and symbols

In China, the Jiahu symbols are 16 distinct markings on artifacts that have been dated to 6600 BC. Typically carved on tortoise shells, these character symbols are not considered to be part of an alphabet. Rather, they likely represented activities of trade and contracts of sale. The Jiahu symbols were used for thousands of years before a more comprehensive writing system was developed.

8,000 year old Chinese symbols like these were carved into tortoise shells

In 1991, an excavation in Greece uncovered another example of early writing. The wooden Dispilio tablet has been dated to 5260 BC. Many symbols on the tablet are very similar to those found in prehistoric caves, on Indus Valley seals and in cuneiform script.

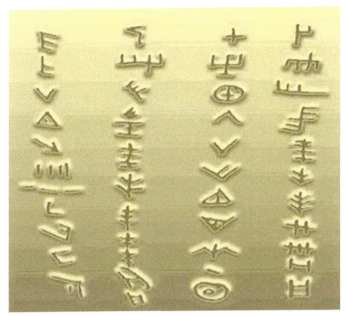

The 7,300 year old Dispilio Tablet found in Greece has symbols similar to those of the later Vinca, Indus Valley and Cuneiform scripts

In the region of modern Serbia, a people with extensive trading links began to expand their ties to Europe and Western Asia. They used written symbols more than 7,000 years ago. Little is known about them, so they are called the Vinca people for the place where artifacts of their culture were found in modern times.

Spread of the Vinca culture 5700–4500 BC

Only a small number of symbols were found on the artifacts unearthed in the Vinca suburb of Belgrade, Serbia and most of the tablets have only one symbol. Nonetheless, there are obvious similarities between the Vinca markings, the Dispilio tablet, the cave symbols and the icons found on the Indus Valley seals. All this suggests an ongoing transfer of the same developing human technology from community to community around the world.

In its early stages, writing was a technology without a clearly defined purpose. The Vinca people tossed their tablets with their garbage as if it was junk mail. Whatever the symbols on the tablets represented, they apparently held no long-lasting purpose.

By 2700 BC, the Ancient Egyptians had an alphabet of more than 20 hieroglyphs. Hieroglyphs were also used as the consonant letters of their language. As with other Semitic languages including Ancient Hebrew, the original Ancient Egyptian alphabet had no symbols for vowel sounds. Their writing represented consonants and vowel sounds were added by the speaker. In Semitic languages, changing the vowel sound changed a word's meaning. In English, changing the meaning of a word usually involves adding letters, but the original word sound remains the same. So, the word "man" becomes "workman" and "manning." In an ancient Semitic language however, a slight shift in accent could entirely change the meaning of a word or sentence.

Why did the ancient Semites create an alphabet with no symbol for vowels, when those sounds were the key to unlocking the meaning of their language? What drove this anti-vowel prejudice?

Having no symbols to indicate the way different people pronounced common words may have had a number of social purposes. The consonant-only alphabet was a code to determine the social rank of others in their group, and cryptically constrain outsiders who didn't have the key. Everyone pronounces consonant sounds roughly the same way, making the base structure of the Semites' mostly three-letter words (e.g. KTB) easily spoken by all. But as in modern languages, a person's home region and education level can often be determined by the way they pronounce their vowels. ("You say tomayto, I say tomahto.") When Semitic people spoke, vowel pronunciation identified their tribal origins. The information gleaned from a person's accent bypassed the need to ask personal questions, which many cultures consider disrespectful. Upper class pronunciation would demand respect while the accents of lower class people would be mocked for saying things they didn't mean. So, the phrase, "I want a bowl of chicken soup," could be a problem if the word "chicken soup" and "chicken crap" are only a vowel shift apart.

This writing system was also a cypher to baffle outsiders. The vowel sounds that gave meaning to each word were not written. They had to be inferred from the context of the other vowel-less words that were strung together without separating spaces between them. Without knowing what vowel sounds went where, the endless string of consonants was indecipherable. In other words, most Semitic speakers were divided by class, ritual behavior and tribal groups so they developed a form of language that required native speakers to identify their heritage and kept outsiders mystified. However, this writing system became a problem for later generations who'd lost the old code key. Without it, many of the vowel-less words could be read in different ways. For example, the Biblical Hebrew words for "Adam" and "Eve" could also be read as "man" and "woman" or "men" and "women" depending on the unwritten vowel sound. That leaves open the possibility that in some older version of the story, Eden was populated by more than two people.

In contrast to the insular and tribal Semites, the Phoenicians were multicultural, free-wheeling, democratic and party-type people who sailed their famous horsehead ships from port to port doing business with everyone. Their city states were independent, and their communities had no permanent rulers or class distinctions. As a result, the alphabet they created was designed to allow everyone to communicate more easily. That's what made their new software so valuable. Anyone could write down the word sounds from any language, and like the worldwide web it could be used by anyone for their own purpose. The leaders of the Indus Valley civilization rejected written language fearing it would only be used by a small class of elites engaged in a culture of secrecy. The Phoenician experience was the opposite. The world embraced the new technology and used it to create dozens of writing styles. This new communication tool was an ancient instant translator, and it propelled humanity forward to globalization.

All the world's written languages use a version of the Phoenician alphabet software except Chinese, Japanese, Korean and Ethiopian

Some alphabets such as those developed for Sanskrit, took the Phoenician concept of a sound-based alphabet one step further. Their letters symbolize the way air flows in the throat and mouth to make the sound.

The Phoenician federation of cooperative city states and merchant sailors was called a thalassocracy. The Greek word "thalassocracy" means "governed by the (law of the) sea," just as democracy is a Greek work that means governed by the people - "demos." Unlike the kingdoms and empires around them, the Phoenicia's union of merchant cities were united by trade. To serve their goals as sailing salesmen, their alphabet made it easier to accurately record the orders of their customers. Another innovation of the Phoenicians was giving each letter a name that began with the sound of that letter, as in ay, bee, cee. The Phoenicians may have borrowed this from the Egyptians who sometimes used the first sound of a hieroglyph as an alphabetic letter. For example, the hieroglyph for house is spoken as *bayt*, so the house hieroglyph was sometimes used to indicate a "b" sound.

The Greeks tweaked the Semitic Phoenician alphabet into one that better fit the sounds of their Indo-European language. The centuries old cry, "Let my vowels go," had finally been heard, and for the first time vowels had equal status with consonants as individual letters. The Greeks replaced the Semitic consonant sounds they didn't use with vowel sounds they did.

The first letter of the Phoenician and Greek alphabets is "A" and this letter comes from the Egyptian hieroglyph for an ox. When a capital A is turned upside down - ∀ - it shows the horns of an ox. Although a vowel in many later languages, the letter A or alpha was considered a consonant by the Semites.

The Latin-speaking Romans fully developed the modern, 26-letter alphabet. They added the letters X, Y, and Z at the end because those letters were only used to reproduce the sounds of Greek words.

One of the landmark uses of pre-Phoenician writing was creating the world's first peace treaty between the Egyptians and Hittites 3,300 years ago. Today, a copy of that treaty hangs in the United Nations building in New York City.

The new alphabet spurred book production and intellectual advancement in the ancient world. Reading and writing were steroids for the muscles of the mind, and so both became fields of competitive sport in the ancient world. People read books, wrote letters and pamphlets and quoted from the work of others. Unlike other pursuits – math, science and music - reading was a full-brain workout. This is because reading just two sentences requires eight different brain functions to coordinate and operate independently at the same time. To read well, a person must (1) recognize letters and punctuation, (2) comprehend letter combinations as individual words, (3) understand the meaning or meanings of each word, (4) grasp how the order of words and its punctuation creates a sentence, (5) comprehend the meaning or meanings of the sentence, (6) understand how the meaning of one sentence connects to the next one, (7) remember and apply the meanings of the previous sentences and (8) carry forward all that information.

There is another benefit to regular reading that has only recently been discovered. In a 2016 paper published in the journal Social Science & Medicine, researchers from Yale University School of Public Health found that people who spend at least three hours a day reading a thoughtful book that exercised their brain, lived significantly longer than those who didn't, even when adjusted for other factors.

The word "Bible" is derived from the city of Byblos where the first books were printed. Its original Semitic name was GBL which means "the birthplace of the Supreme God El." Among Semitic speakers, "El" was used as a common word for Supreme God. In the Hebrew Bible, God is referred to as "El" more than 200 times. The Semitic word *Ba'al* has Indo-European roots and it means "strength" or "husband." *Ba'al* was frequently used by the Biblical people to refer to their "husband" God in the same way modern Jews use the Hebrew word *"Adonai"* to mean "Lord."

Yet, the Bible reports the Israelite God *El* hated those who worshiped him as *Ba'al* so intensely, that he ordered the Israelites to destroy six civilizations living in the region of Canaan on the false charge the *Ba'al* worshipers engaged in human sacrifice. The Israelite armies led by a man called Joshua, launched their military expedition to grab a new homeland with the cover story of liberating the locals from tyranny. The result, however, was the slaughter of the men and the enslavement of their women and children. Often, the Israelite invaders just swept through the tribal camps and burned everything to the ground. This wholesale religious massacre resulted in the Biblically-recorded deaths of about 70,000 people and the enslavement of tens of thousands more. It was human sacrifice on a colossal scale meant to satisfy the Biblical God and claim a new homeland for the descendants of the refugees from Egypt and those who joined them. The Promised Land of Abraham would become the Plundered Land of Joshua.

Although there is no evidence the Canaanite tribes practiced human sacrifice, ritually killing people for some perceived benefit has been enthusiastically embraced by cultures all over the world. The evidence shows this form of murder did not exist in prehistoric society but started much later as a ritual to protect private property. The most common form of human sacrifice in the ancient world was not a religious affair in front of an idol, but a capitalistic one that slaughtered people to protect buildings and celebrate the anniversaries of great construction projects. Chinese legends say thousands of Ming Dynasty laborers who died building the Great Wall (1368–1644) were shoveled into its foundations where their spirits remained to protect the structure. Ancient Japan has similar stories of the *hitobasharis* or "human pillars" of young women ritually buried alive so their dead spirits would attract good fortune to the structures built over them.

According to an article by Robert Kastenbaum on Deathreference.com, excavations of medieval bridges and fortresses in Germany and Wales found children who'd been buried alive as part of the construction. In 1487, Aztec leaders in what is now Mexico, assembled an estimated 80,000 prisoners and ritually murdered them as part of a celebration to honor their Great Pyramid of Tenochtitlan. A religious cult in India killed more than 2 million people for plunder in the name of their god. From 1350-1800 the Thuggees ambushed, robbed and murdered their victims on forest roads. When stories of their brutality spread, the word "thug" entered the English language. As recently as 100 years ago, an eyewitness in Borneo reported seeing a criminal buried alive under each foundation post of a new building so they would serve as guardian spirit, Kastenbaum said.

In modern times, people of higher status who murder poor or unprotected people and receive no punishment are engaging in a form of socially-approved human sacrifice.

According to a 2007 article on LiveScience by writer Heather Whipps, there's no evidence of human sacrifice anywhere in prehistoric Europe. It only appears in later societies. This indicates the simple communities of early hunter-gatherers had more respect for human life than the property-driven societies that followed, she said.

The words "sacrifice" and "sacred" come from root words that mean to "set apart," "make holy," and "cursed." This bipolar meaning conveys the idea that raising some people above others because they are designated "holy," leads to labelling other people as evil and cursed.

The first abstract symbols people painted on rocks 40,000 years ago have been transformed into a universal software system for communication – the globally-used alphabet. Today, letters are embedded as binary codes on computer chips. The fear of technological change and globalization that worried some people in the past, remains in the modern world. For the great cultural question that opens or closes the door to human progress has always been, "Can people trust other people?"

PART 5
RUSSIA CAME FROM INDIA, MONEY CAME FROM THE SEA

In 2007, the Times of India reported on an astonishing discovery in Russia. In a small village in the Volga region – homeland of the original Russ people – Russian archaeologists uncovered a large number of statues of the Supreme Hindu God Vishnu. The carvings are over 1,000 years old which dates them to the oldest settlements of the first Russians. The Vishnu carvings were found in a village of 8,000 people called Staraya Maina. But 1,700 years ago, this tiny town was a bustling city ten times larger, according to lead researcher Archaeology Prof. Alexander Kozhevin of Ulyanovsk State University.

It may be incredible to believe, Dr. Kozhevin said, but the people of Ancient Russia may have originally flowed north into the Volga Region from India and Afghanistan. "This is a hypothesis, but a hypothesis, which requires thorough research," he added.

Kozhevin is not the first to propose this idea. In 1952, archaeology Prof. Varely Smirzkoff of Odessa University also suggested Russia's cultural roots point to India.

Over 1,000 years ago, early settlers in modern Russia carried the multi-armed Hindu deity Vishnu to the Volga River region

Russian historians believe the ancient Russ people first settled in this region by the Volga River, and then moved west to the plains of the Don River – once considered the border between Europe and Asia. There, they built the city of Kiev, now the capital of Ukraine.

One noteworthy feature of the Vishnu statues found in Russia is what the multi-armed deity holds in two of his eight hands. In one there is a hammer while another hand clasps a sickle – the two symbols of communism created during the Russian Revolution about 100 years ago.

Were the original Russ people connected by trade, culture and marriage to the people of Southwest Asia and their ancient civilizations? The answer may lie in the origins of the words "Russia" and "Moscow."

The word Russia means "land of the Russ people," but there is no consensus on where the Russ people came from or the meaning of their name. The word Moscow derives from *Moskva* – the Russian name for the river that runs through the city. However, there is also no agreement on the origin of that word. Modern Russian history begins about 1,000 years ago. Yet, the land and people of Russia are mentioned in one of the world's oldest texts – India's *Rig* Veda. The *Rig* was written down about 1,500 years ago, but the oral histories it contains may be thousands of years older.

The *Rig* describes Russia as the "land of the holy people." In the ancient Indian language of Sanskrit, one word for a holy man is *rishi* as in Maharishi or "great holy man." Does the word "Russian" derive from an ancient word that meant "enlightened people"? The word *rishi* is also related to the root word for "excellent." Was Russ a name the people called themselves, or was it a name given to them by others to describe the original Russians as a people of excellence in knowledge and spirituality?

In the spiritual practice of India, those seeking enlightenment choose a sacred spot where their spirits can be liberated from the pressures of the world. The Sanskrit word for a place of spiritual liberation is *moksha*. Is moksha the source of the word Moscow? If Russia's early culture was influenced by settlers from India who worshipped Vishnu and Krishna, it could explain the use of "Krsna" as the word for "Christ" in the Cyrillic and Serbian languages.

An unsigned article on the Global Hinduism web site adds weight to this idea. In the *Rig*, Russia is called *rus soviath* which the author translates as the "ancient holy land." This suggests the concept of "Holy Mother Russia" predates the arrival of Christianity in the region by hundreds or thousands of years.

On the IndiaCause blog, Jayakumar Ammangudi, Ph.D., suggested there are "hundreds of Russian words" that derive from Sanskrit and offered several examples.

Russian	**Meaning**	**Sanskrit**
Sutra	Thread, yarn, string	Sutra
Viraama	To stop	Viraama
Boya	Fear	Bhaya
Pi	To drink	Pi
Tapot	To warm, melt	Tapati
Vid	To know	Vid

Many Russian words are derived from India's ancient language of Sanskrit

By 800 AD, the Russ, Scandinavian Vikings and other migrants to the region formed a unified community that was one of the wealthiest in Europe and stretched from the Black Sea to the Baltic.

1,100 years ago, Russia was a confederation of tribes trading with Europe and Asia

In the modern world, global tensions often arise from the lack of trust between Russia and the West. American president Ronald Reagan addressed this when he quoted a Russian proverb about improving relationships. When dealing with Russia, Reagan said, the U.S. should "trust but verify." This saying was born from the shifting alliances of tribes and rulers in the early history of Russia and its surrounding regions. Yesterday's friends quickly turned into today's enemies and vice versa.

Reagan's position was to trust but proceed with caution and suspicion. Yet, trust and suspicion cannot be mixed because they are mutually exclusive. If today's trust can be easily replaced by tomorrow's mistrust, then trust has no meaning. Suspicions are meant to be temporary, for the root of the word comes from the idea of things unseen. When people cooperate openly in a culture of honesty, suspicions are non-existent. Whether in a marriage, a business partnership or international relations, trust is meant to be constant and reliable.

Many people think trustworthiness is a sliding scale measured by degrees of trust. But in its oldest meaning, "trust" was something fixed and absolute. Trust, in its original meaning, was not something that could be changed. One had trust or not. In early human society, honor was seen as a person's most valued possession. A person who had no honor was shunned by society, and so for most of humanity's history honesty was a constant in human affairs. The origin of the word "trust" conveys the old sense of honor as something forever faithful and never-changing.

Etymological dictionaries typically suggest the root of the words "trust" and "true" derive from *dru*, a Sanskrit word for "tree." The proposed connection is that people had faith in durable wooden objects or formed an admiration for sturdy trees. However, those notions require conceptual leaps and assumptions for which there is no supporting evidence. There's never been a major culture that practiced tree worship, and wood is easily broken. It is more likely the word for enduring trust derived from *dhruva* - the Sanskrit word for the North Star.

In the literature of Ancient India, a story is told of man called Dhruva who was a great devotee of Vishnu. To honor his unshakeable devotion, God named the North Star, Dhruva. Of course, it is likely the Polar Star was already called Dhruva and the religious tale was a later addition.

The relationship between the North Star and the concept of trust is a direct one and easily communicated. As human communities advanced in travel and trade, it served as a common and reliable orientation feature in the night sky. In the prehistoric world, a person might have pointed to it and then to themselves as a way of indicating, "I am as trustworthy as that star."

When human society began, the words "trust" and "true" implied an essential and permanent part of all relationships. Trust between different kinds of people fueled the growth of urban centers and trade across the globe. If suspicion of outsiders ruled early human society, the tools of advanced civilization – shared language, cultural values, the exchange of technology and construction projects requiring ongoing teamwork – would not have taken root.

All human economic systems are fundamentally an exchange of trust. Trustworthiness was a person's credit rating and money before modern money or credit existed. Honest words were humanity's first currency. Friendship beads quickly followed as gifts of introduction. As population and trade expanded, a new form of currency was needed that would be accepted in diverse markets and spur individual enterprise. Perhaps because people gathered by the seaside, rode its currents to other lands and walked the ocean coastlines like highways, the history of money begins in the sea.

Forms of shell money more than 100,000 years old have been found among the artifacts left behind by prehistoric people who lived in India and South Asia, the Americas, Australia and Africa. The most popular shell was the one used by all of them as the world's first global money. This shell came from a sea snail called the cowry.

Multicolored cowry shells were the world's first global currency

The humble cowry shell holds a place of honor as the first international currency. It was accepted everywhere. Among prehistoric merchants and traders the cowry shell might have been known by the slogan, "Don't leave home without it." The Phoenician alphabet jumped into common use because it was easy to use and simple to write. The shell's rise to the world's favorite coinage was propelled by the same reasons. Cowry shells covered the beaches of Africa, Asia, Australia, the islands of the Pacific, and the Americas. As more people joined in the circular global trading routes, the easy-to-find shell became a universal token of exchange. In modern economic terms, people had a guaranteed minimum income because the shells were everywhere. More importantly, those who wanted to engage in larger trade activities had easy access to the shells as their seed capital, and travelers could take cowry shells from their region and trade them anywhere they landed.

The cowry-based money systems of India and China continued until about 4,500 years ago. In the Chinese writing system, the traditional written characters for "buy and sell" are variations on the character for "shell." And that character is a stylized drawing of the Maldivian cowry shell, a type of cowry commonly found along the shores of India not China. This suggests a very old trading relationship between the two regions and the flow of Indian 'money' into China. The word "cowry" derives from the Sanskrit word for "shell." The West African country of Ghana calls its money "cedi" – which also means cowry shell. Cowry shells are abundant and come in a variety of colors. Their smooth hard surface is similar to porcelain, and the word "porcelain" derives from the Italian word for cowry shell. Another source of its attraction is its oval shape and horizontal slit that make it appear like an eye or vaginal opening. Because of this, cowry shells have also been used for divination and as good luck charms for fertility.

As far back as 11,000 years ago, animals (including cows, sheep and other livestock) were used as money, and with the beginning of large-scale agriculture, grains and other plant products took their turn as early coinage. About 3,000 years ago China made the switch from shells to metal coins. The new metal coins were made during a period when people were literally beating war weapons into tools for peaceful trade. After a long period of war ended around 1000 BC, the Chinese people turned bits of their metal weapons into the world's first metal coins. The coins had holes punched in the center so they could be strung together on a necklace. In the era before pockets and purses, cash was worn. With smart fabrics, credit and debit cards can be embedded in clothing and accessories, and once more money is worn.

In 600 BC, the king of a country called Lydia in what is now Turkey minted the world's first government-issued currency. His coins were designed to advertise the wealth of his kingdom and promote trade. Instead of dull metal coins, the Lydian king's coins glittered. They were made from electrum - the mixture of silver and gold that was the source of the alchemist legend. Each coin was stamped with a picture of an animal that acted as its denomination. So, a night on the town with dinner and wine might cost two elephants and an owl. Lydia's highly prized currency made it one of the world's richest kingdoms. In the ancient world, when someone bragged they were "as rich as Croesus," they meant the last Lydian king who minted the first gold coin.

It is common for people to think early human trade was based on a barter system of swapping one thing for another like cooking pots for cows. But, as many studies have noted, that kind of economic system never existed. Then as now, when societies have no formal money, people exchange favors.

In her article, *The Myth of the Barter Economy*, writer Ilana E. Strauss interviewed David Graeber, an anthropology professor at the London School of Economics. He said early human societies relied on "gift economies" and the exchange of favors rather than immediate payment. If a baker needed meat, they didn't offer bread for steaks, he explained. Instead, word would be passed to the butcher who would offer the baker a gift of meat. At some other time, the butcher's desire for a birthday cake would be made known, and the baker would return the favor, Graeber told Strauss.

In the modern world of complex security checks for the simplest transactions, it's hard to recall how openly trust-based the world economic system was just a few generations ago. In his book, *Debt:*

The First 5,000 Years, Graeber gave an example of how money isn't the paper bill or plastic card, it's the trust.

In the 1950s, before computers, global banks and ATMs, British soldiers stationed in Hong Kong faced a problem. Her Majesty's government paid the troops with checks from a bank in England. If a local Hong Kong bank was sticky about it, they could make someone wait until the check had sailed back to England, cleared and returned. Or, the soldiers might be posted somewhere where no bank was readily available. So, like many people of that era, soldiers cashed their checks with people they knew.

Not long ago, it was common for people to "sign over" their paychecks to a local business in exchange for cash. The person the check was made out to would sign their name on it, and the recipient could take that check to their bank and cash it. In the modern world, where many stores are owned by distant corporations, that old style of business is gone. As a result, pay-day loan operations that charge a fee for this service have proliferated. However, the world wasn't always this way. Graeber related the story of a British soldier in Hong Kong who cashed his paycheck at his favorite bar. Six months later, the soldier returned and saw his check was still floating around. By then, it had been co-signed by 40 separate businesses who'd passed it back and forth for the face value amount. Yet, the check had never been redeemed in England. The government's money sat in some British bank while merchant after merchant in Hong Kong passed around the uncashed check as if it was money.

For 700 years the most common currency in Britain was not a shell or metal coin, but a piece of wood that served as a form of personal check and IOU note. From about 1100 AD to the early 1800s, the most important form of English currency was the tally stick. Tally sticks, Graeber explained, were simplified legal contracts. If someone bought on credit or borrowed money from someone else, they would bind their agreement with a piece of wood – typically the branch of a hazel tree. Marks were cut into the wood to indicate the amount owed, and then the branch was split in the middle.

The seller's part was called "the stock," and it's from this practice the word "stockholder" was born. The "stub" belonged to the debtor and "ticket stub" comes from the tally stick tradition. When the debt was redeemed, the two pieces of wood were rejoined and the deal was closed. Until 1884, tally sticks could be used to pay taxes and they still circulated as currency in England. Graber noted that tally sticks made from bones, clay tablets and shells have been found all over the world, some dating back to 30,000 BC.

English Tally Sticks were accepted as payment for taxes until the 1800s

The tradition that a person's word of honor was more valued by business people than a multipage document drafted by lawyers, was a long-lasting one. As recently as 1901, famed American businessman Andrew Carnegie sold his steel business to J.P. Morgan for $487 million in a deal that was closed without lawyers or a written contract, Graeber wrote.

The prehistoric practice of gift-giving had such a profound effect on human society that some cultures held gift-giving contests. In the modern world, people display their riches by showing how much they can keep for themselves. Among the Celts and North American

Indians, however, people promoted their status by demonstrating their ability to give away fabulous gifts to their friends and enemies and still remain wealthy. In some cases, this led to excessive gift-giving and bankruptcy, Graeber noted. In other cultures, nuanced customs developed that taught people to give a more valuable gift than the one they received, but not so much greater than the receiver would be unable to respond in kind and feel shamed, he explained.

Graeber cited the 1961 *Book of the Eskimos*. In it, Danish writer Peter Freuchen chronicled his adventures when he lived among the Eskimos. After an unsuccessful walrus-hunting expedition, Freuchen arrived at his hut exhausted, hungry and empty-handed. Then, he saw something that amazed him. Piled high in front of his frozen door were hundreds of pounds of fresh walrus meat contributed by the other hunters. The stunned Dane began to blubber his thanks but one of the hunters cut him off.

"Up in our country we are human!" the Eskimo said. "And since we are human, we help each other. We don't like to hear anybody say, "Thanks for that." What I get today, you may get tomorrow. Up here we say that by gifts one makes slaves and by whips one makes dogs."

In Graeber's telling of the Dane's story, the word "gift" is used in two ways. The Eskimo hunter makes a distinction between gift-giving as a sign of common humanity without a defined obligation, and one given with a specific expectation of return. Those gifts were viewed as bribes. This duality is found in the common root of the words "gift" and "habit." A gift can be an act of friendship or required like an addiction. When a person cannot repay others for gifts received, they fall into debt. And the concept of debt has been a feature of religious teachings for thousands of years.

In his book, Graeber quotes from one of Ancient India's religious texts, the *Satapatha Brahmana*.

Every person is born in debt, it begins. Religious offerings are debts paid to the gods. The accumulation of knowledge and good behavior are acts of repayment to teachers. Children are born as debt payments to ancestors and showing hospitality to strangers is a repayment of each person's debt to humanity, it says.

Many religions claim people are born with a debt of sin rather than obligations. The difference is that obligations are individual commitments, whereas sin is a judgement of guilt at birth that can only be pardoned after death.

CHAPTER 16

THE GREAT COLLAPSE: TERRORISM AND UTOPIA

Death is the event that follows an unstoppable collapse of the connected mechanisms that sustain life. The word "collapse" means "to fall together." About 3,100 years ago more than a dozen kingdoms and 40 cities suddenly collapsed when their interconnected world was torn apart by an unstoppable stampede of unforeseen events. All the great civilizations of the era were fatally wounded or destroyed by a combination of terrorist armies plundering their cities, rolling earthquakes collapsing their roads and buildings, government ineptitude, and another long period of floods and droughts that shriveled and rotted their food crops.

It all started around 1180 BC. The same type of shifting weather patterns and climate extremes that disrupted or destroyed civilizations in the Indus and Mesopotamia, Egypt and China 1,000 years earlier, struck again. But this time, people were battered by more than just monsoon-like rains and blazing heat. For 10 years, a series of rolling earthquakes and aftershocks shattered homes and roadways across Mesopotamia and Turkey. Then, the lands and people of the era faced an even more deadly threat. A mobile terrorist army called the Sea People roamed the Mediterranean Sea plundering and destroying coastal cities, towns and villages like a flesh-eating virus devouring the body of the old world.

In the decades leading up to the Great Collapse, the mixed Indo-European and Semitic peoples of the Mediterranean region were at peace and enjoying the prosperity of widespread trade and cultural exchange. The first signs of the coming crisis began in Egypt when 100 years of open immigration, multiculturalism and friendly trade gave way to an era of anti-foreigner nationalism and a lust for military conquest.

Throughout its long history, Ancient Egypt teetered between rulers that promoted a culture of tribalism, iron-fisted rule and foreign conquest, and those that opened Egypt to extensive trade and engagement with other people of the Middle East, Western Asia and Europe. As Egypt welcomed new immigrants, it grew wealthier and expanded its regional influence. At other times, Egyptian society was consumed by anti-foreigner rage and its nationalist leaders expelled hundreds of thousands of immigrants from the country.

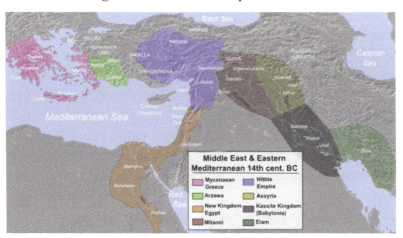

The world before the Great Collapse of 1100 BC

One of those periods of ethnic cleansing was the expulsion of the Biblical Hebrews and Israelites from Egypt around 1350 BC. Two hundred years earlier, in 1520 BC, a mysterious people called the

Hyksos were also driven out of Egypt. When they first arrived in the region, the Egyptians described them as Asiatic – the same term they used for the Hebrews. According to Egyptian history, the first Hyksos communities appeared at the same time as the Biblical narrative of Abraham's journey to Egypt c 1800 BC. And indeed, one translation of "Hyksos" is followers of the "foreign shepherd king" - a possible reference to Abraham. The similarities of the Exodus and Hyksos expulsion stories has led many historians to wonder if the Hyksos were the same people as the Hebrews, and if elements of the two histories were blended together when the Hebrew Bible was compiled. Whoever they were, the Hyksos were highly regarded in Egyptian society. Within a few generations of their arrival, a Hyksos king sat on Egypt's throne and his successors would rule for a hundred years.

The Hyksos' rise to national influence and power in Ancient Egypt was non-violent and grew from trade and cooperation. The Hyksos were successful, immigrant merchants who supported local Egyptian culture and community needs at a time when most Egyptian officials were ignoring them. The Hyksos' restored and promoted Egyptian art. Their efforts to raise community living standards were so effective and popular among ordinary Egyptians, the public clamored for them to rule. It could be said the Hyksos were Ancient Egypt's only democratically-elected kings.

When they first arrived in the region south of Egypt, the Hyksos were more militarily advanced than the Egyptians – they had better chariots and bows. Yet, they never went to war with their neighbors. As rulers, the Hyksos Kings adopted Egyptian names. They loosened cultural restrictions by favoring more musical styles and the natural representation of people in paintings and sculptures, including royalty. Egypt's trade grew and its territory expanded. It was during this multicultural period of Hyksos rule that Egypt attained its greatest sphere of influence.

In her 1963 book, *The World of the Past*, Archaeologist Jacquetta Hawkes said the Hyksos were not a conquering horde from the East as later Pharaohs claimed, but a wandering group of Semites who had a long relationship of peaceful trade with the Egyptians before coming to power.

The word "Hyksos" was not a name they gave to themselves. It was the term applied to them in Egyptian records. Hyksos has been translated in various ways, but it carries the meanings of shepherd, king and foreign. While typically translated as "shepherd kings" or "kings of foreign lands," it might be read differently. If the Hyksos were part of a large group of Indo-Semitic Hebrew people who gradually migrated into Egypt after the fall of the Indus in 2000 BC, the Ancient Egyptians might have tagged them as followers of "the foreign king of the shepherds" - Abraham of the Bible. This notion is supported by the fact the Hyksos had no known name for themselves. If they had no ethnic, tribal or regional identity of their own, it suggests they were united by a philosophy such as the teachings of Abraham.

The Hyksos religion was similar to that of the informal Hebrews. The Hyksos worshiped one unnamed God alone. But, because their faith was inclusive and not exclusive, they adopted the local Egyptian god, *Seth*, as a stand-in for their Deity. *Seth* was the Egyptian storm god, and in the era of interchangeable names for gods, Egypt's *Seth* was a version of the Hittite god *Teshub*, the Semitic god *Ba'al* and the Indian god *Shiva*. They were all deities of destruction, renewal and protection from chaos. Much later, the Ancient Greeks would associate *Seth* with *Typhon* – the most feared monster god in Greek mythology. The name of this monster came from an earlier word that meant "huge storm." That's why *Typhon* is the source of the word "typhoon."

Hyksos rulers expanded Ancient Egypt's wealth and territory to its greatest height through alliances and trade. Yet, when their dynasty was overthrown around 1500 BC, more than 500,000 of these immigrant people were expelled from the country in the world's first known incident of mass ethnic expulsion, according to the Ancient Egyptian historian Manetho. In the nationalistic fervor that followed the Hyksos expulsion by the southern Nubians, the former rulers were reviled as Asian tyrants and savages who ruined the country with foreign influences.

For the next 250 years, Egypt's military forces swept into foreign lands and turned them into colonies. Their armies marched into the Middle East and northward along coastal lands of the East Mediterranean. They would conquer territories, lose territories, face rebellions and crush them. But all those battles and skirmishes were just a warm-up. Egypt's kings hankered for a showdown with their main rival – the Indo-European Hittites living in Anatolia, now Turkey.

The championship fight between the Hittites and the Egyptians in 1274 BC was the event of its day, and reporters from both sides recorded the action. The Battle of Kadesh included the largest chariot battle in history with 6,000 racing at each other across open fields, while 70,000 sword-swinging foot soldiers battled beside them. Both sides used elaborate military tactics and strategies. But the great showdown for the crown of the world ended with no clear winner.

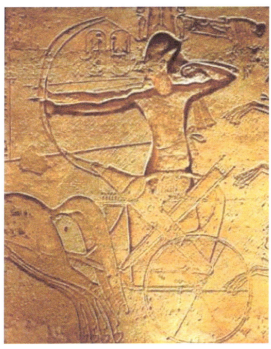

Egyptian King Ramesses I firing arrows from his chariot as he leads his troops against the Hittites in the Battle of Kadesh

When the fighting stopped, both sides went home as military losers and reconsidered their foreign policy. In 1250 BC, the Egyptians and Hittites signed the world's first peace treaty. It included a mutual defence pact against the threat to both from the aggressive Assyrians, and the world's first extradition treaty compelling each side to return fugitives fleeing from the other's jurisdiction.

The Battle of Kadesh drained money, people and resources from both sides. With no loot from plunder to distribute among the troops, the wounded and weary soldiers on both sides returned home empty-handed and embittered. As a result of this post-war weakness, ambitious Assyrian leaders in the region of what is now Iraq and Syria began attacking Hittite cities.

While Egypt's new king was busy fighting in the north, Egypt's colonies in Canaan rioted. They murdered soldiers of Egypt's occupying army and rose up in mobs to proclaim independence. Although Egypt would re-establish its authority in Canaan, the appetite for independence was spreading. Finally, around 1200 BC, the thousand year-old civilizations of Egypt, the Middle East and Turkey began to crack and crumble. The fatal blows hammered down so quickly and with such force that within a century of The Great Collapse, the once-mighty empires and their fabulous wealth were nothing more than fabled memories.

1177 B.C.: The Year Civilization Collapsed, is a book by Eric H. Cline, a professor of classics and anthropology at George Washington University in Washington, D.C. The date refers to the year Egypt's King Ramesses III finally defeated the invading terrorist armies of the Sea Peoples in the Battle of the Nile Delta. Before their defeat, the wild forces of the marauding Sea People had been unstoppable.

"No one could stand before their arms," Ramesses wrote.

Traveling on ships loaded with heavily-armed raiders and their families, the Sea People overran the coastal cities of Phoenicia and beyond. They looted and burned more than three dozen cities in what is now Syria, Turkey and Lebanon. Ramesses reported the Sea People so thoroughly destroyed the communities they invaded, that when they left it was as if those towns had never existed.

The kingdoms and communities of Mesopotamia, the Middle East and Egypt were hit by a perfect storm of calamities. Marauders invaded the coastal regions. They murdered people, destroyed trading ports and overwhelmed other cities with refugees. Food shortages caused by drought made the problem worse, and the inability of rulers to feed their people generated cries of corruption and sparked riots

Many kingdoms used a kind of centralized supermarket system to distribute food across the country. Under the "palace system," all food harvests were given to the king's representatives who stored and then redistributed the collected food among the population. When poor harvests and no food imports resulted in empty shelves at the royal grocery store – looting broke out across the country.

3,100 years ago the terrorist Sea People raided cities and towns

As urban problems intensified and central authority crumbled, the Sea People advanced. That combination of punches brought down the flourishing cultures created by the people of the Bronze Age. The after-effects of the collapse would sweep away the Mycenaeans and Minoans, the Hittites and Assyrians, Kassites and Cypriots, Mitannians and Canaanites, and even Egyptians, Cline wrote.

Who were the Sea People? They were a confederation of different groups who joined forces for profits, plunder and the joy of spreading terror, death and anarchy. Initially, they may have been unemployed mercenaries or members of rebel groups fighting against one empire or another. Whatever their common cause at the start, they united into a massive, swift-moving force of raiders. They ravaged the Eastern Mediterranean landscape and set in motion the largest wave of refugees in human history – people fleeing from the Sea People to any safe place.

Ancient sources and modern research indicates this confederation of pirates was largely composed of nine groups. There were Ancient Greeks and the Lycians of Southeast Turkey, the Biblical Philistines and people later associated with the Israelite tribe of Dan, along with others from in and around the Italian peninsula including Sicilians and Sardinians, Cline said. In Ancient Egyptian murals, the Sea People were drawn with great attention to the individuality of their tribes. They note distinctive clothes and weapons, skin and eye color, and even whether they were circumcised or not. Three of the nine groups were. The Greek historian Herodotus wrote that one tribe of the Sea People shaved one side of their head and let hair on the other side grow wild. Another group had fair skin, red hair, blue eyes and tattoos on their arms and legs.

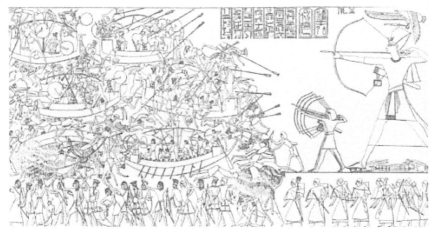

Egypt's King Ramesses III defeated the Sea People in the Battle of the Delta, but the old world was destroyed

When the Sea People were finally defeated, Ramesses force-settled the remainder of them in the region of Canaan where they peacefully assimilated with the locals just before the rise of Ancient Israel. Although Ramesses III stopped the Sea Peoples' second attempted invasion of Egypt, there was little to celebrate in the world he saved.

By then, many cities across the region – from Greece to Canaan - were already destroyed or in decline from multiple disasters. Egypt battled for its very existence and prevailed, but its days of glory had passed. Over the next 1,000 years, Ancient Egypt would slowly fade into the night of history as other world powers rose to prominence.

The stability of 1200 BC was replaced by the collapsing empires and terrorism of 1100 BC, and by 1000 BC new civilizations were being born. In the Middle East, Joshua's Israelite army was emboldened by the withdrawal of Egyptian troops from Canaan and the addition of fighters from the former Sea People to his ranks. To the West, Ancient Greece was rising. For 2,000 years, Egypt had been one of the great military, cultural and economic powers of the world. Ancient Egypt survived the Great Collapse, but like the British after World War II, Egypt's role as a superpower was over. In the centuries that followed Ramesses' victory, Egypt would be conquered by the Greeks, the Romans and many other invading armies.

The Great Collapse marked the end of the third wave of large-scale urban civilization but not of humanity. In its Latin root, the word "resurrection" means "to rise again," "to surge again," and "to attack again." The death of the old powers cleared the Eurasian-North African landscape and allowed new groups to rise and surge.

As the song, *Closing Time* notes, "Every new beginning starts with some other beginning's end."

It was the start of humanity's new journey. Ideas and practices from the old Afro-Eurasian world would reincarnate in the West where they would be adopted and reconfigured as if they had no past. Over the next 3,200 years, the world would be carved apart and borders shuffled as military empires swept over regions and continents only to be replaced by the next conquering army.

From 1100 BC to modern times, great technical achievements would be reached, science and medicine would probe the building blocks of life, the arts and trade would flourish. And yet, senseless slaughter, slavery and the thoughtless destruction of the world's environment would grow with it. The superpowers of the past were all fatally weakened by the same kryptonite – the abuse of power at home, military recklessness abroad, and the abandonment of cooperation in favor of a go-it-alone approach. In the centuries that followed, military and political leaders would be trapped by their need to surge forward and expand their empires at any cost. Strains on resources would result in social conflicts and the need for increased military control. More soldiers sparked rebellion and the use of additional troops to crush resistance. A larger military meant fewer resources for the general population and more disturbances requiring a military response. When multiple catastrophes struck at once, the old order was overwhelmed. The severity and type of counterpunches would change, but the symptoms of collapse would always be the same.

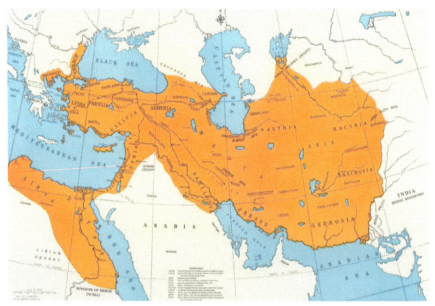

Rulers of the Persian Empire (550-300 BC) included Cyrus the Great who liberated the Jewish people from captivity in Babylon

In 300 BC, Alexander the Great's Empire joined Europe, Asia and Africa

Roman Empire (100 BC-500 AD) at its maximum

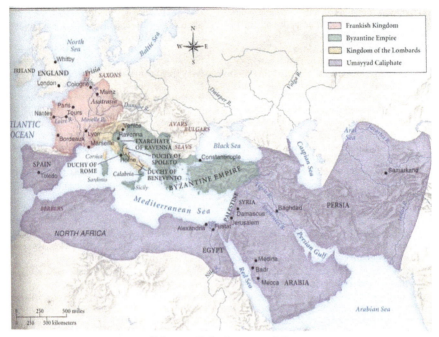

Islamic Caliphate 750 AD

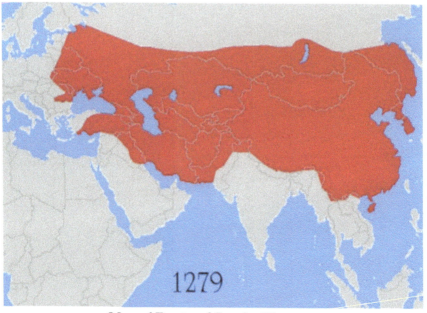

Mongol Empire of Genghis Khan 1279

Ottoman (Turkish) Empire of Suleiman the Magnificent 1580

The Empire of Spain 1600

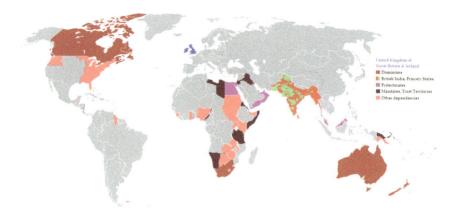

British Empire 1760

Napoleon Bonaparte's French Empire 1812

HUMANITY: THE WORLD BEFORE RELIGION, WAR & INEQUALITY

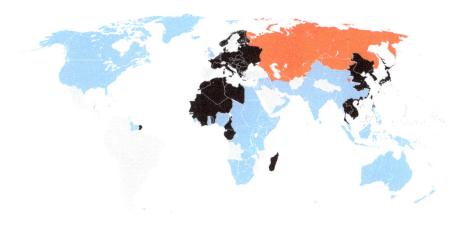

In 1942 during WWII, Germany, Japan and Italy occupy lands in black - Allied nations and colonies in blue, USSR in red

US military bases worldwide 2004

For most of history, regional landscape and local leadership determined a community's diet, health, intellectual development and culture. As large-scale, long-distance travel and migration increased, so did the mixing of people and ideas. History is the story of how things start as one thing, break apart, and then recombine to start the process of building, breaking and evolutionary rebirth all over again.

269

Until 175 million years ago the world's six continents were joined as a one massive island of more than 150 million sq. km. (241 million sq. mi.). Over millions of years, the spin of the Earth and the moving magma below the island ripped it apart and sent the pieces floating away from each other.

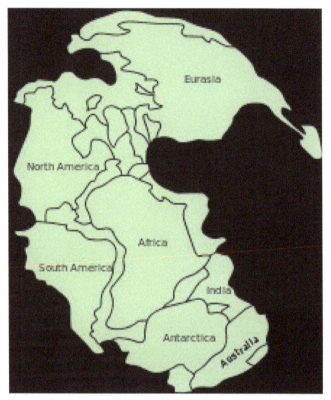

The super island Pangea broke up 175 million years ago and formed the seven continents and islands of the modern world

Geology is the study of changes in the Earth and in rocks. Rocks can live a very long time without changing, so geological time is measured in thousands, millions and billions of years. Rocks are the stony bones of the planet. Their lives record how they responded to changes in the Earth as it reformed and reshaped over 4 billion years. They carry notes from the chemical and physical changes of Earth's history as movement, pressure, heat and other factors that have transformed the rocks and mixed them to create new species of minerals around the world.

Some scientists who study the changes in the stony skeleton of the Earth classify the past 500 years as the start of a new era in its history. But this profound change in the planet's life cycle was not caused by natural fluctuations of Earth's climate or a devastating asteroid strike as in the past. The greatest force now changing the landscape comes from the combined, long-term actions of the people who live on it.

From a rock's point of view, the dinosaurs passed through a stage in geologic time called the Jurassic Period. The proposed name for the modern, human-driven era is the Anthropocene. The word Anthropocene is a combination of two Ancient Greek words – *anthro* "human" and *cene* "new." Taken together, it refers to changes in the landscape, water flow and air quality caused by the "New Humans."

In the March 11, 2015 issue of Nature magazine, Richard Monastersky wrote about the changes humans have made to the shape and environment of the planet.

Every year, through mining activities alone, humans move more earth than "all the world's rivers combined," Monastersky said. The massive growth in cities and industry in the past 50 years has warmed the planet, raised sea levels, eroded the ozone layer and acidified the oceans, he added.

While many factors influence and accelerate global climate change, it is clear one factor driving the current period of rising weather extremes is the increase in the amount heat energy and greenhouse gases pumped into the world's atmosphere and waterways from human industrial activity. That extra heat is an accelerator that fuels more frequent and severe wildfires and tornados, floods and droughts and changes weather patterns around the globe.

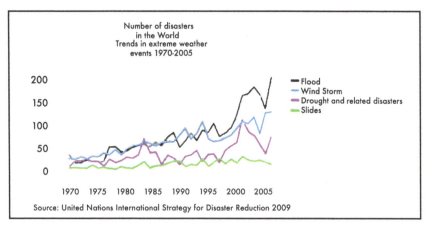

The rapid expansion of human industrial activity has added heat to the planet's environment which accelerates more extreme weather

Yet, far more severe and destructive environmental changes have fallen over the Earth and humanity in the past. Long before humans, life on Earth faced the challenges of acidic seas, a nearly frozen planet and other calamities. At different times, mass extinction events have killed nearly 90% of all life on the planet. But life recovered. When the modern human family of *Homo Sapiens* left the tropics of Africa for Europe, they walked into an Ice Age in the Northern Hemisphere that would last another 10,000 years. And yet, they stayed, adapted and thrived.

As humanity expanded, so did its impact on other species. In a 2016 article published in The Conversation, Mark Maslin, a Professor of Climatology at University College London wrote that since 1500 there have been 784 documented extinctions "including 79 mammals, 129 birds, 21 reptiles, 34 amphibians, 81 fish, 359 invertebrates and 86 plants." During the same period, humans created 300 new plants and 500 species of animals - including the domestic dog and cat - through domestication and crossbreeding, he said. More recently, global food companies have reduced the diversity of plants as they clear huge tracts of lands for meat production and single crop farming, he explained.

The generally accepted date for the start of the Anthropocene - the time when humans began to reshape the Earth - is 1610. That year was marked by an unusual drop in atmospheric carbon dioxide that changed the chemical composition of rocks around the globe as a result of European actions in the Americas.

A 2015 research study by geography professors Dr. Simon Lewis and Professor Mark Maslin of University College London, found this decline was caused by the sudden deaths of millions of indigenous people and the emptying out of their cities and villages. In 1492, European conquerors and colonizers began arriving in the Americas. Thirty years later, an estimated 50 million local people were dead. Most died from European diseases like smallpox. Native villages were emptied, allowing forest trees and vegetation to move back in. The breathing of all those new plants removed so much carbon dioxide from the atmosphere, the drop was noticeable, the researchers explained

The measureable impact of the Anthropocene started in 1610, but the era began 100 years earlier with the arrival of Christopher Columbus in the Caribbean and the start of the global slave trade. The business of capturing, transporting and selling Africans would devastate the continent's culture and crush its emerging urban communities.

Four hundred years before Columbus was born, the Yoruba people living in the region of modern Nigeria were the most urbanized in Africa and lived in cities of over 100,000 people. In his 1973 article, *An Aesthetic of the Cool*, Robert Farris Thompson, a professor of art history at Yale University, suggested the modern concept of "cool" originated among the Yoruba people who gave it a deeper and more spiritual meaning than the modern sense.

Thompson said *Itutu*, the ancient Yoruba word for "cool," meant more than just calm in the face of stress. It meant a "mystic coolness," a cool that included gentleness, generosity and the ability to settle disputes without violence. This form of transcendental cool, Thompson noted, went beyond the need for remaining focused during a crisis. It was a way of living that extended cool as an appreciation for all life. When the slave trade destroyed the old culture, what remained was an attitude of calm defiance by slaves that morphed into the modern meaning that fused cool with rebellion

Was the start of the slave trade - along with the plunder and wholesale destruction of natural resources and ancient civilizations - a marker for something else? Was there a change in human culture that gave birth to the actions of the Anthropocene and did that shift happen because of a new attitude about the past?

During the 1500s and 1600s, Christian Europe tore itself apart in religious wars between traditional Catholics and rebellious Protestants. There were many reasons for the hostilities, but underlying them all was a change in human society that had nothing to do with religion. The bigger shift was in the way people were redefining their ideas about the past and the future.

When he arrived in the Caribbean islands, Christopher Columbus named the region the West Indies because he mistakenly thought he was close to India. The money for Columbus' ships, men and supplies came from the King and Queen of Spain. The payoff they wanted was a western short cut from Spain to India, and the Captain did not want to disappoint his investors. But Columbus was also a very religious Italian Catholic. When he saw the islands and met the people who lived there, Columbus wrote to the Spanish monarchs telling them he'd found the lost remains of the Garden of Eden on the 'Indian islands' he'd found.

In 1492, Columbus and his crew landed on the great island of Hispaniola (Haiti and the Dominican Republic), where they spent Christmas. In his letters, Columbus described the island with phrases that deliberately evoked the Biblical description of Eden. The island was a "paradise" full of spices, fruits and many great rivers that contain gold, Columbus wrote. He continued the Eden comparison in his commentary about the local people. Like Adam and Eve in their time of purity, the inhabitants of Hispaniola still lived in almost perfect grace with God, he said. They were innocent and walked about naked although "some of the women cover a single place with the leaf of a plant or with a net of cotton."

They are handsome, strong and yet "so guileless and so generous with all that they possess, that no one would believe it who has not seen it," Columbus told the Spanish monarchs. They refuse nothing and share all with as much love as they have in their hearts, he continued. They are content with whatever trifle is given to them, prizing scraps of broken glass as "the best jewels in the world" while offering gold in exchange for a strip of leather, he said. He also noted the locals had no iron, steel or weapons.

To Columbus, the native people's generosity, honesty and openly friendly nature were the remains of the innocent natural world of Eden and human life before the inventions of war, exclusive religion and senseless brutality. Yet, by the time he and his men sailed off, they'd made slaves out of the men, women and children of the island, and introduced murder, rape and plunder to Eden. He now called his hosts "savages" and prayed for the day when they would be converted to civilized Christianity.

Columbus initially admired and even yearned for the innocence of old Eden, but moments later he and his men were raping Eve and enslaving Adam. Columbus' letters point to the larger transition. The people of Christian Europe began to believe violence and greed were an eternal blight on humanity, and disbelieve stories of a past world without them. And so, Eden was rebranded from a tattered tale of prehistoric human peace to a New World sales pitch for settlers. Grab a chunk of Eden complete with Adam and Eve slaves!

In the modern world, the future is said to be ahead and the past behind. But to the Ancient Hebrews, the future was at their back and the past was in front. They looked at the world this way because they could "see" the past in memories, in their ancestors, in passed down traditions and in creations that stood for thousands of years. The future, however, was unknown. It crept up on people from behind, unseen, like a thief in the night stealing human plans. With the beginning of the Anthropocene in the 1500s, the way humanity weighed the importance of past and future began to change. Stories of humanity's cooperative past were downgraded to cartoonish religious fables, while fashionable ideas about a perfect manmade future were raised to the status of unquestionable religious doctrines.

Columbus' letters describe the dying gasp of a world that believed the past was superior to the present. Until then, religious leaders all agreed the best and only future was a better re-enactment of the past. Religious rebels – such as those in the emerging Protestant movement of the 1500s – said they could build their own future without following the rules of the past. Though many Protestant leaders would be as brutal, corrupt and backward-looking as the Catholic priests they condemned, the idea of the future as something humans could control and change caught on.

The first book to capitalize on this new trend would set the stage for the millions of literary creations that followed. And they were all variations on the same theme – how to solve the problems of the present and build a perfect future by way of a new invention, philosophy, scientific breakthrough or religion.

Thomas More's 1516 book, *Utopia*, was unique in literary history as the first proposal to separate the idea of a perfect future from the tales of a perfect past. More's fictional land of Utopia has no specific religion or history defining its past or directing it to a godly paradise. More's country was run by an unchanging and unchangeable set of man-made rules that reflected his values. And to More, Utopia was the best of all possible worlds.

Utopia was the world's first media hoax, mockumentary and 16th Century fantasy ride into a better world of tomorrow. As a leading intellectual in the Age of Enlightenment, More gave his book an impressively long Latin title that translates to an even longer title in English.

He called his book, *De optimo rei publicae deque nova insula Utopia*, or "Of a republic's best state and of the new island Utopia." But the name that stuck was the word he invented for his fictional island – Utopia.

During his life, the Catholic More was intensely opposed to Protestantism in general and Lutheranism in particular. As Lord High Chancellor of England and counsellor to King Henry VIII, he shut down Protestant printing presses and arrested the followers of what he considered an immoral and criminal religion. Later, King Henry VIII had More executed for holding to his Catholic beliefs about papal supremacy when the King made himself head of the new Anglican Church. In life, More walked the well-worn yesterdays of the Catholic Church and refused to acknowledge Henry's road to a new tomorrow. About twenty years before he was decapitated for his belief in the past, More described the perfect future of a perfect land.

The word "Utopia" comes from two Greek words that mean "no place land." This was the first clue that More's book was, at least in part, an in-joke for Latin-educated intellectuals. But the names of real people and known events included in More's tale gave it the credibility of a real travelogue. More could have had practical reasons for this. As a lawyer, More may have thought presenting his ideas as a hoax gave him some legal protection from higher-ups who might take offence. At the same time, by planting his ideal society in the real world, people could visualize Utopia as a virtual reality. More's *Utopia* would launch a new secular religion, one that shifted people's faith from a collectively remembered past to an individually-imagined future.

Before discussing Utopia, one of More's characters tells the others a better society is not possible until there are better people.

Even if a king had a wise advisor with the best ideas, other advisors would shoot them down because their positions depend on their policies remaining in place, he said. Kings start wars to gain glory even though wise men advise against it. To raise money, they devalue the public currency and fine people for common activities. Thoughtful reason can never be heard above all those self-interested voices, he concluded.

The group discussion then turned to corruption in their societies. Wealthy people tell the poor to get a job, but make it impossible for many of them to do so, said one. Too few people own too much land and they only use it to charge high rents, he continued. High rent for land drives up the cost of food. Poor people who can't feed themselves then steal and end up in jail. Injured veterans, the old and sick often can't work, but they are cast aside just the same, the character continued. The poor are executed in large numbers for violating the law, yet the rich take no responsibility for the harm they cause, he added.

One of the men asked, "Why do the rich behave that way?"

More's character, Raphael, answered. "They intentionally charge high rates" to keep money flowing for their personal luxuries - new clothes and fancy food, costly drinks and gambling in casinos.

To curb those vices, More's fictional Utopia was a land of extreme communism 300 years before Karl Marx. Everyone in More's perfect society was given the same clothes and fed identical meals in a large hall after a daily dose of uplifting thoughts. Music was barely tolerated.

Sex outside marriage was punished by lifelong celibacy if the offender was single, and slavery if the sex was adulterous.

Utopians didn't go to war but they did pay mercenaries to fight for them. To keep their hired guns busy, the Utopians regularly sent their unemployed soldiers to fight in wars of liberation and democracy in other lands.

More's book, and others like it, offer schemes for a controlled tomorrow to replace the chaotic reality of the present. Today, many people escape contemporary confusion by insisting reality is whatever they think reality is. As the comedian Stephen Colbert once said, to people in that state of mind the truth has "lost all credibility." In the prehistoric world, knowledge was shared to advance civilization and fear was non-existent. Today, people's thoughts are consumed by fear of the world around them and so they retreat into fantasies of superheroes, super gods, magic technology and various kinds of authoritarianism they imagine will freeze the world in one place and end the chaos. Then, they will have reached their utopia.

The modern world has lost its tether to humanity's common past, and as people drift apart humanity's future as a unique species is up for sale. People are told to fear humans and embrace technology. Robots for sex and holographic children are on their way. How will this change human to human relationships, and how will robots respond when they look to humans for inspiration and find them spiritually empty? In this increasingly artificial reality, money is given the freedom to move anonymously and without constraint, just like prehistoric people who had no money and no names. And as the social value of money has risen, people without money have been devalued and their freedoms are increasingly restricted and monitored. In contemporary entertainment and business many organizations are free to profit from torture, death and destruction, while ordinary people trying to start community programs or local start-ups are burdened or blocked by laws and regulations. Modern politics has degraded to a shouting match of ideologues who demonize their opponents and so fan the flames of common disrespect and routine violence throughout society.

Where is humanity headed?

CHAPTER 17
THE BIG WOMB THEORY

There's a story about a passenger on a boat who heard a series of loud grinding sounds. She followed the noise and discovered a man drilling a hole in the bottom of the ship. "What are you doing?" the woman exclaimed, "You're cutting a hole in the boat!" "Relax, lady" the man answered as he continued working, "the hole is on my side of the boat."

The words "boat," "ship" and "vessel" all derive from the root idea of a carved-out protected space inside something else, or a canal for transportation. The first boats were hollowed-out logs. Among humans, the first canal was the birth canal that carried them from the womb to the world. Modern people started to carve out and expand their collective space on the planet 100 centuries ago, as earlier types of humans died off.

Since then, the effects of population growth and industrial development have grown so great that people in one part of the world can pollute their local environment and scientific measurements can track its effects across the globe. If the Earth was fragile, the cumulative effects of human neglect and abuse might have already caused a catastrophic failure in its ability to sustain life. But the Earth is not fragile. Its ability to maintain a protective space for life to carry on has survived many near-extinctions. This has happened because the Earth acts like a living entity and responds to changes by adaptation. It adjusts its global environment the way the human body does, by regulating its temperature and responding to changing conditions. When too much heat is produced, the Earth melts away its storage of cold ice at the poles in the same way the body melts its stores of fat for fuel. When there are no more fat cells to burn, the body will devour itself in an attempt to stay alive. When the polar ice caps melt, the Earth will continue to shift excess heat and water around the planet causing long term droughts in one part of the world and terrible flooding in others.

The same principles apply to humanity's social canals. When freedom, opportunity and a desire to serve the commonwealth flow evenly through humanity's veins and arteries, all parts of the body are sustained in good health. When those opportunities are blocked by violence, greed, favoritism, burdensome rules and an unfair application of law and punishments, the neglected areas are starved and they become diseased. The word "starve" comes from a root word that means "stiff, rigid." In the modern world, many groups feel artificially starved of freedom and opportunity. Indeed, in many parts of the world, leaders seem bent on ensuring everyone has access to weapons of death, while health care, clean water, decent education and opportunities for well-paid work remain unavailable to many people. As a result, extremist leaders promote rigid attitudes and confrontational violence as the only response. All sides scream accusations but no one is listening. The culture of polite behavior and common respect that united humanity is being challenged by attitudes of arrogance, self-righteousness, irrational fears and uncontrolled rage. If John Lennon of The Beatles were alive today, he would have to compose a new song for the modern era called, "All You Need Is a Punch in the Face." The disappearing Age of Aquarius generation has left behind a world supersaturated with weapons, political extremists and deadly religious factions enslaved to the God of the Angry Mind. But this is an unnatural state.

In a society where fear rules, to be irrationally afraid is a sign of intelligence rather than ignorance. If an airplane passenger declares they are uncomfortable having some other person on the plane, that other person will be removed as a human sacrifice to the new religion of fear. To keep irrational fears respectable, commentators celebrate these action and encourage others to join in. That leads to indiscriminate, reflexive brutality because people are consumed with thoughts of fear and danger. In the modern world, many shrill voices call for widespread violence against people outside their group. And as those war drums grow louder and more frequent, calls for reason and dialogue are shunned.

Humanity faces a cultural crisis. On one side are fear-mongers and isolationists in religion, politics and the media who promote suspicion and ignorance of their opponents. On the other side are people who do the same thing for a different set of reasons.

The 1997 film, *Good Will Hunting*, offered a glimpse into the way self-righteous anger has replaced respectful conversation in everyday life. In one poignant scene, Robin William's character, Sean Maguire, described the time he spent with his wife when she was in the hospital, dying of cancer. He never left his wife's hospital room because the doctors could see in Maguire's eyes the term 'visiting hours' didn't apply to him. If that scene were in a movie from an earlier era, when the orderly told the husband visiting hours were up, Williams' character would have made a personal appeal and the orderly would have agreed so long as Maguire kept quiet about it. Maguire and the orderly would have served each other's needs. In the modern version, Maguire's eyes are full of narcissistic rage and self-importance. His mind is a gun and the hospital staff are afraid. Though presented as a sentimental journey, Maguire's story reveals the profound change in the socially approved way people treat others outside their circle. Rather than engage with the hospital staff as equals, Maguire lets it be known rules are only for those without power.

The old wisdom that "it is better to give than receive," is typically interpreted to mean 'giving to charity is good.' But, at its root, this advice was not about donations to the less fortunate. It was meant as a guide to rapid economic development through the widespread transfer of knowledge and skills. It meant: give people the tools of opportunity and they will generate vastly more wealth than was given to get them started. Here's how it once worked.

Imagine life in the gift-exchange economy of 2200 BC when traveling traders from the Indus Valley Civilization were sailing around the lands of the Persian Gulf, sharing their new base 10 number system, and finding new customers for their clothes, spices and crafts. To promote trade, these travelers would often look for ways they could help others improve their lives and so become better customers. That's why the Indus merchants shared their technology. If a group of these travelers saw a village farmer hauling heavy buckets of water around his field, they would explain how irrigation ditches could help him. They would dig the canals and refuse all offers of payment. A year later, the travelers might return and see the farmer's field flourishing along with those of his neighbors who also adopted the innovation. Hearing of their return, the villagers would rush to shower their benefactors with an abundance of gifts. By freely sharing knowledge, everyone benefitted from improved trade and innovation. When the first farmer gained new wealth, he helped his neighbors increase theirs. They gave gifts to the traveling teachers and increased trade with their Indus Valley homeland. The teacher-merchants freely offered their knowledge to help others, and in return they were rewarded with an abundance of gifts and many more new customers. If they'd demanded a fast buck for their lesson and departed like other traveling teachers, that one-time payment would have settled accounts and ended their relationship with the farmer. Instead, the gift created a bond of friendship that produced long-term abundance for both. In prehistoric times, people understood that starting relationships with mutual offerings of respect and welcome was the easiest way to spread commerce and technology around the world.

British Prime Minister Margaret Thatcher once said "there's no such thing as society." People, she felt, were best served when they acted selfishly. In Thatcher's view, a nation achieved greatness because it was superior to other nations, just as the riches of wealthy people demonstrated they were better than poor people. Thus, resources should be given to the superior 'winners' and taken away from the 'losers.' So, the rich gained tax breaks and options for the poor and struggling were eliminated. It was economic eugenics – the culling of the herd by forcing the weak to accept their place or die off.

The term "moral hazard" was coined to describe economic and political systems that remove all the risks of criminal and financial penalties from some people, and in so doing reward corruption and punish honesty. In the old Soviet Union, there was a moral hazard joke about its economy and valueless money. "They pretend to pay me, so I pretend to work," it went. Moral hazards are found in modern tax and legal codes that encourage favoritism through political money, manipulation of the system for personal gain, and the evasion of social responsibility. It makes heroes of people who kill for ideology, and devalues those who build bridges between communities.

In the 1987 film, *Broadcast News*, a group of TV news reporters and producers discuss whether they should air the real-time broadcast of a man being executed in the electric chair. "Sure," said one, followed by "Why not?" "Absolutely" and "You bet." In 2016, an American broadcast executive said he didn't care what effect his shows had on society so long as they made money. Live recordings of executions are no longer a moral dilemma. They are posted daily on websites like YouTube and the executioners make money from every view. Scenes of real and simulated torture abound in many kinds of modern entertainment.

By age six, most modern children can correctly identify hundreds of commercial products and brands. And yet, most adults cannot name four kinds of plants, insects or birds they see around them every day or the names of four neighbors. Modern society rewards limited knowledge. Commercials teach people to use chemical sprays to mask bad smells from unhealthy living, rather than clean up their space. Scientific studies claim to show the evolutionary advantages of lying, cheating and psychopathic selfishness. Not long ago, musicians sang about love and sex was in the background as a metaphor. Today, sexual hype abounds in music videos but love is rarely mentioned.

The old philosophers said human life was a choice between following the path of the seven virtues or the seven vices. Most people today know the vices from their starring role in a multitude of movies including *Seven* (1995). The word "vice" originally meant a lack of knowledge and the imperfections in conduct and character that caused seven types of self-destructive action - uncontrolled lust, gluttony, greed, laziness, anger, envy and arrogance. A large portion of the modern economy promotes thoughtless indulgence of the vices and profits from those excesses.

Vices spread when social approval is given to selfish behavior and social leaders boast about their level of corruption and lack of honor. Vice is a weakness that gives rise to self-indulgence, while virtues are strengths that build from self-control. The word "virtue" comes from the ideas of personal integrity, courage and a noble character of admirable qualities. To achieve virtuosity in a skill requires self-control and the mental discipline to achieve excellence. The success of human civilization grew from its virtues. The seven virtues those societies followed were moderation in food and drink, humility and modesty, avoiding sexual obsession, showing generosity and patience in dealing with others, and diligence in one's work.

The more power and wealth a person possessed, the more they were expected to act in a humble manner. That social convention reminded everyone that all people were equal even if their cash supply differed. Today, public office often attracts those who crave attention and power as a path to riches, or seek to use their position for partisan advantage. The principles of justice were built on the virtue of balance and mutual respect. When the application of law is seen as unequal, common respect disappears.

Evolutionary biologists often marvel at how 'nature' solved some challenge to life by providing a solution. In this context, 'nature' is used as a scientific stand-in for the deity of religions. However, there is no separate thing or force somewhere called 'nature' that solves problems for living entities. Natural selection is a term for large numbers of individuals whose decisions to pursue a perceived advantage in their environment changes their way of life and genetic self-expression. While the ultimate outcome is unknown, evolutionary change is a deliberate response to the destruction of one way of life and opportunities in another. This conscious desire to activate an improvement in the human genome happened when the cow culture people entered Europe and Africa. If the wider population had not seen benefits of the genetic differences between the smaller locals and the taller, milk-drinking newcomers, they would not have mated with them and spread the lactose tolerant gene throughout the Western World. In the marketplace of selection, all living entities seek ways to improve their lives. During stable times, the selection is towards continuity, while in periods of stress the search for change accelerates. Stuart Candy, a professor at the University in Toronto's Strategic Innovation Lab, said "Imagination is not a property of a single brain." The same is true of evolution.

If evolution is at least partly driven by each individual's will to change, when does that level of conscious awareness first appear? Or, put another way, "What is life?"

What is the distinction between organic life and a rock? Scientifically, there is no difference. There is no scientifically-accepted definition of life because all things have life cycles, consume things, produce by-products and offspring, and all things eventually die. As one commentator put it, "There's a lot of activity going on at the atomic level of a rock. So, the question isn't, "Why doesn't a rock talk?" The question is, "Why doesn't a rock talk to you?""

Comedy is an exaggeration of the truth, and that joke about rocks touches on recent scientific insights into the evolution of life on Earth and the conscious qualities of the universe.

Robert Hazen is a research scientist at the Carnegie Institution of Washington's Geophysical Laboratory and a professor of Earth Science at George Mason University. He talks to rocks, and the rocks reply in their chemical composition that tells Hazen about their lives. He discovered the many mineral species found on Earth were the result of their crossbreeding with organic life, and that organic life could not have evolved without rocks.

It was a revolutionary insight.

In articles and talks, Hazen has explained how life arose from minerals and minerals flourished from life. Without oxygen-breathing organisms, two-thirds of Earth's 5,000 minerals would not exist, he said. Instead, like the Moon or Mars, Earth would only be able to produce a few hundred types of minerals that Hazen calls "species." About two billion years ago, Earth's atmosphere changed and oxygen-breathing life spread throughout the oceans. All that new oxygen corroded the existing minerals. Their bits were washed away by rain to join with elements in the ground or carried to streams and rivers where they mixed with other minerals creating hybrids and mutations. It was an explosion of inorganic life. And modern scientists believe a similar soup of minerals, liquids and carbon-based molecules was the embryonic mixture that allowed life to begin on Earth.

There is a deep relationship between Earth's community of minerals and the environment necessary for organic life. The essential molecules of life - such as amino acids - are found throughout the world of rocks. They float on the edges of hydrothermal vents at the bottom of the ocean. They cling to the craggy insides of mountain volcanoes, float among the flotsam of intergalactic space, and crouch in the crevices of icy meteors racing across the cosmos. Bones, teeth and shells are produced through an alliance of minerals and organic life. It's generally assumed that planets without rocks can't produce life.

Are organic and inorganic life two expressions of the same thing in the way of matter and energy? To most people, there is an obvious difference. Inorganic matter has no consciousness whereas life means self-awareness - the ability to reason and make choices. Yet, that distinction may not exist.

In a recent talk, Stephen Hawking, Director of Research at the Centre for Theoretical Cosmology, University of Cambridge, made an astounding claim.

"Every particle and every force in the universe has an implicit answer to a yes-no question," he said.

The word "implicit" means knowledge gained from inference and reasoning. According to Hawking, every part of creation – matter and energy – has an ability to make individual decisions of "yes" or "no" when encountering something else. By his statement, Hawking has implied the universe came into being by choice. He suggests the structures of the universe are the result of an infinite series of individual and group choices. The most recent theories of the origin of life on Earth, including those from the Massachusetts Institute of Technology, suggest the birth of living cells with reproductive abilities is the inevitable result of having the right combination of minerals and liquids in a "Goldilocks" environment. Evidence of organic life first appears on Earth just a few hundred thousand years after the planet was formed. The new models suggest living cells were first constructed along the rocky shores of warm pools and streams that surrounded volcanic vents on land similar to those at Yellowstone Park. Sunlight bathed the soupy goulash with ultraviolet light and lightning strikes flushed it with electricity - both sparking chemical reactions. Watery currents swirled the mineral and chemical mixtures and moved them around the landscape until they found a place and means to flourish. This thinking presumes organic life was not the result of one inorganic structure surpassing the others, but as a joint effort of different molecules and compounds working together.

At the 2013 World Science Festival in New York City, four of the world's leading cosmologists - Andreas Albrecht of UC Davis, Alan Guth of MIT, Andrei Linde of Stanford University and Neil Turok from the Perimeter Institute for Theoretical Physics in Waterloo, Canada - debated the origins of the universe. The only point they agreed on was that the phrase "Big Bang Theory" does not properly describe how the universe was born and developed. If the Big Bang was a big explosion, its elements would be randomly scattered. Yet, the universe is expanding equally in all directions. Cut the universe into large enough slices, and each piece will have the same amount of cosmic diversity as every other slice.

So, perhaps a better term is The Big Womb Theory.

Putting aside the need for a deity in this analogy, there are similarities. In the human womb, the embryo is surrounded by fluid. In the universe, all cosmic structures float in an ocean of plasma – a form of matter that behaves like a liquid. The fetus is tethered to its universe by the umbilical cord. The structures of the visible universe are kept in place and moved apart by cords of gravity and the forces of dark matter and energy. According to Astrophysicist Avi Loeb, the necessary ingredients for organic life including water, ammonia, methane and a rocky planet could have formed as early as 10 million years after the Big Bang. Loeb contends that as the universe cooled from its extremely hot beginning 14 billion years ago, it reached a sweet zone when the color of the night sky was orange and the ambient temperature of the entire universe was warm enough to sustain liquid water. As rocks crashed against each other through space, they would have gathered and scattered water particles and organic molecules as part of the planetary building process. The development and structures of the universe from birth to death may be contained its own DNA-like code, passed down from an earlier, parent universe.

If inorganic matter and energy have some mechanism for making decisions, as Hawking suggests, how does something without a nervous system or brain gather and process information? Is there a mind that exists and operates without a brain? That consideration is an old one called the brain-mind duality. For hundreds of years, western science insisted there was no separate mind. The prevailing view was that consciousness came from an unchangeable, machine-like brain and only humans had a brain capable of producing consciousness.

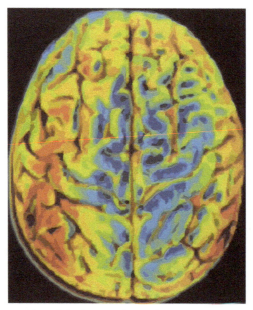

The metropolis of the human brain has many neighborhoods

In his book, *The Brain That Changes Itself*, Dr. Norman Doidge explained why those old assumptions about the mind were wrong. Research has shown the intangible mind can shape the function and structures of the physical brain, even while the brain is forming in the womb, Doidge explained. He wrote of a woman born with only half a brain. For unknown reasons, the left hemisphere never developed. Despite this, the woman grew up normally. "When her brain was still forming, her right hemisphere had time to adjust in the womb" so it bypassed the corrupted gene program for two hemispheres and rewired itself in a new way so that it could "learn and live and function on its own," he said.

"Everything your 'immaterial' mind imagines leaves material traces. Each thought alters the physical state of your brain synapses at a microscopic level. Each time you imagine moving your fingers across the keys to play the piano, you alter the tendrils in your living brain," Doidge said.

He cited the work of Dr. Michael Merzenich who found changes in brain organization do not and cannot happen in isolation. If one cluster of brain cells reconfigures, every other cell network in the brain will remap itself to accommodate the new change in thinking. Thinking changes cell organization.

Like cities on the brain's landscape, large clusters of brain cells influence the way the smaller groups around them operate. New neural roads are built that connect outlying patches to the main city, and ignored pathways fall into disuse. Channeling of the brain's resources from one area of intense focus to another can change a person's body shape, emotional state and the way they perceive the world around them. The mind can turn off pain signals from the brain, extend the normal range of senses and rebuild broken body parts when the brain is damaged. The mind can attack the brain and cause it to turn against the body causing paralysis, blindness and even death. When mental energies are directed to war – guns and walls proliferate. When prehistoric society operated in peace, innovations were developed cooperatively.

Or, as the ancient Indian text called the Dhammapada expressed it, "Our life is shaped by our mind, and we become what we think."

The brain doesn't simply learn, it is always "learning how to learn," Doidge wrote. It exists as a living organism that grows with nourishment and exercise and shrinks without it, he explained. With each new experience the brain reinterprets the world. When people encounter the outside world with openness, the brain responds with new connections in its neural community. How people see the world is a choice.

The Austrian psychiatrist Dr. Viktor Frankl, was one of the many Jews rounded up by the Nazis and sent to concentration camps during WWII. After the war, Frankl wrote about his experiences in a book called *From Death Camp to Existentialism* (1946). When he and a fellow inmate were finally free again, they went for a walk. The two men came upon a patch of young wheat waving in the spring breeze. Frankl changed his course and walked around the grains but his friend deliberately marched straight over them, delighting in the crunch of the plant stems beneath his feet. Frankl asked the man why he killed the wheat. His friend replied, after what he'd been through why should he care about some plants?

The cruelty of the concentration camp experience gave Frankl a greater respect and love for life. But his friend yearned to inflict pain on others and become like the prison guards and bullying fellow prisoners he hated. Life in the camp stayed with one man as his new reality, while the other cut the barbed wire memories and escaped. Frankl's decision was a moral victory of virtue because his character was strong enough to withstand the evil and depravity around him.

In 1960, modern Israel achieved a moral victory. The Israeli Secret Service located Adolph Eichmann. Eichmann was largely responsible for ordering the round-up and mass murder of 6 million Jews – along with many other "undesirables" - living in Nazi-controlled countries during the Second World War. The Nazis were so fanatic about killing Jews that even as they were losing the war, they diverted much needed military resources to keep the deportation trains and death camps running. Yet, when the Israelis found Eichmann, they didn't just shoot him in the face and leave him for the dogs. The Israeli leadership wanted more than anything else to show the world they were better than the Nazis. Eichmann was smuggled back to Israel. He was given a public trial in Jerusalem, found guilty and legally executed.

In 1961, the same year as Eichmann's trial, a film called *Judgement at Nuremberg* was released. It was a warning to the world about the spread of moral hazards in modern society. The film's fictional story takes place three years after WWII. It's a courtroom drama of four German judges accused of crimes against humanity for using the cover of Nazi law to send millions of innocent people to their deaths in a perfectly legal way.

The film asks the question, 'Why did ordinary and respectable people, tolerate mass murder and the destruction of their democratic society?' Before the Nazis came to power in 1933, Germany was the most socially progressive and culturally dynamic country in Europe. When WWII ended 12 years later, the military and civilian deaths on both sides were more than 60 million. How did it all change so quickly?

One of the film's accused judges, Ernst Janning, explained.

"Above all, there was fear. Fear of today, fear of tomorrow, fear of our neighbors, and fear of ourselves. Only when you understand that - can you understand what Hitler meant to us. Because he said to us: 'Lift your heads! Be proud to be German! There are devils among us. Communists, Liberals, Jews, Gypsies! Once these devils will be destroyed, your misery will be destroyed.' It was the old, old story of the sacrificial lamb," Janning began.

"And then one day, we looked around and found that we were in an even more terrible danger," he went on. New laws and new hatreds "swept over the land like a raging, roaring disease. What was going to be a passing phase had become the way of life," he said.

After Germany's former masters of law were convicted, the presiding judge of the case explained the reasons for his decision.

"This trial has shown that under the stress of a national crisis, men - even able and extraordinary men - can delude themselves into the commission of crimes and atrocities so vast and heinous, as to stagger the imagination. No one who has sat through this trial can ever forget the sterilization of men because of their political beliefs; the murder of children. How easily that can happen! There are those in our country today, too, who speak of the "protection" of the country. Of "survival." The answer to that is, "Survival as what?" A country isn't a rock. And it isn't an extension of one's self. It's what it stands for, when standing for something is the most difficult! Before the people of the world, let it now be noted in our decision here that this is what we stand for: justice, truth, and the value of a single human being!"

Conflicts – within nations or families - spawn from the same source. When there is a breakdown in cooperation, no room for individualism and no common goal, society fractures. Humanity's first step towards a common future began with the open exchange of honest words. In the modern world of war, words have been recruited as strategic weapons.

Words have been shaved of their ancestral meanings and cleansed of any context outside their commercial and official use.

The old human principle was "the truth shall set you free." In the modern world, truth has been stripped of its value and honesty can lead to imprisonment or death. The Bible's Book of Proverbs says "A gentle answer turns away wrath, but a harsh word stirs up anger." Today, harsh words and anger are everywhere and gentle answers are often trampled to death.

The horrors of World War I (1914-1918) affected much of the world – but Europe most of all. In 1919, the Irish poet, William Butler Yeats wrote *Second Coming*. In it, he explained the changes in human society that led to WWI and 38 million people killed. Like a falcon soaring away from the falconer that trained him, society's extremists in pre-war Europe were rising in popularity while people who called for calm and reason lost their voices to the mob.

> "Things fall apart; the centre cannot hold; Mere
> anarchy is loosed upon the world…
>
> Innocence is drowned. The best lack all conviction, while the worst
> Are full of passionate intensity."

In George Orwell's 1949 novel about the future - *Nineteen Eighty-Four* - the book's main character, Winston Smith, meets a government employee who is writing an official dictionary of acceptable words known as Newspeak.

"Don't you see that the whole aim of Newspeak is to narrow the range of thought?" the dictionary writer tells Smith. People won't be able to think rebellious or antisocial thoughts "because there will be no words in which to express it," he said.

Every concept "will be expressed by exactly one word, with its meaning rigidly defined and all its subsidiary meanings rubbed out and forgotten," he added. This process will continue "long after you and I are dead. Every year there will be fewer and fewer words, and the range of consciousness always becomes a little smaller," the dictionary writer explained.

In his 1941 State of the Union address to Congress, U.S. President Franklin Delano Roosevelt outlined his vision of the "Four Freedoms" necessary for rebuilding and uniting the world of broken humanity after the Second World War.

"In the future days, which we seek to make secure, we look forward to a world founded upon four essential human freedoms. The first is freedom of speech and expression—everywhere in the world. The second is freedom of every person to worship God in his own way—everywhere in the world. The third is freedom from want—which, translated into world terms, means economic understandings which will secure to every nation a healthy peacetime life for its inhabitants—everywhere in the world. The fourth is freedom from fear—which, translated into world terms, means a world-wide reduction of armaments to such a point and in such a thorough fashion that no nation will be in a position to commit an act of physical aggression against any neighbor—anywhere in the world. That is no vision of a distant millennium. It is a definite basis for a kind of world attainable in our own time and generation. That kind of world is the very antithesis of the so-called new order of tyranny which the dictators seek to create with the crash of a bomb," Roosevelt said.

Today, the concepts Roosevelt promoted have been redefined. People living in the same district are no longer neighbors, but high or low security threats. The word "freedom" has lost its old meaning. Now, people use freedom to mean individual desires - a vacation, retirement from work, the ability to choose what to buy, or relief from some personal burden. It means individual pursuits that separate, rather than unite people, such as the freedom to refuse to associate with or serve others. Freedom once meant the assumption of innocence and harmlessness in walking, thinking and writing. Now, governments and corporations routinely scrutinize and oversee people's words and actions. As the dictionary writer foretold, human thought has begun to withdraw inside self-imposed boundaries.

Freedom of speech to encourage discussion, dialogue and mutual understanding is being replaced by endless streams of partisan propaganda and self-promotion. The old concept of freedom from want - that all people should have a minimum of food, shelter and safety

- has been refashioned as a motto of personal greed. "I should have everything I want." It means the power to commit any crime without consequence. Roosevelt famously told the people of his nation they had nothing to fear "but fear itself." In the modern world, fear is the new courage and no one is to be trusted. Feeding fears requires constant lies, and when brain is fed enough lies it processes differently and loses its ability to distinguish imagination from reality.

Until the second half of the 20th Century, most people lived similar lives and even professionals such as doctors and lawyers made only modestly more than the working class. The rise in cancer deaths that begins in the 1960s, corresponds to three cultural changes. The new consumption society discarded the old common value of "life is about more than money," for the divisive one of "life is only about money." That shift resulted in the fracturing of social and family bonds, widespread stress and with it increased consumption of alcohol, prescription drugs and fast food.

Despite this, it's worth noting that if humans were easily motivated to kill when given easy access to weapons and motivated by lies and angry voices calling for death, there would be no one left alive in the United States. There are more guns in America than people, and America's cultural atmosphere is filled with promotions of hatred and murder as the solution to every problem. Yet, as individuals, Americans remain massively committed to the old values of community support and individual liberty.

Indeed, to paraphrase President Ronald Reagan humanity is too great "to limit ourselves to small dreams. We are not, as some would have us believe, doomed to an inevitable decline. I do not believe in a fate that will fall on us no matter what we do. I do believe in a fate that will fall on us if we do nothing."

People have always had conflicts with other people. What keeps temporary conflicts from spiraling out of control is whether the goal is "security" or "peace." What separates the two is that peace brings security but security does not bring peace.

"Security" derives from a 2,000 year old Latin word meaning "free from fear." The word "peace" is much older. Its root carries the meanings of agreement, understanding and honor. For more than 99.99

percent of human history, peace was the human way of life because global human civilization was built through individual agreements and common goals.

Contemporary leaders hammer on the need for security systems as the cure for fear. But any systems created by people can be broken by them. That is why the root meaning of "security" includes "careless" and "reckless." In other words, people develop a 'false sense of security' when they think nothing can go wrong. For, as someone said, the greatest threat people face is not from what they don't know but from the things they wholly accept as true but aren't.

Security is a false promise. When people are afraid, they buy tools and systems for protection. When those measures fail, they buy more security systems and further limit the freedom and movements of others. This pattern is repeated with the only benefit accruing to those who sell flawed security systems. To make matters worse, modern security systems are operated by privately-owned software that can never be publicly examined because it's a security system. This is a natural result because "security" is related to the word, "secret." Wars, security systems and massive force responses do not produce peace or security. Peace is a natural outcome when people behave respectfully towards each other. When people are peaceful, no security is needed. For more than 100 years, Canadians and Americans boasted about sharing "the world's longest undefended border." In one town, the border divided a library where the bookshelves stood in one country while the librarian sat in another. It was a beacon of neighborliness in a world of mistrust and that binational library remained in use until the 2000s. Those days are gone.

In a 2016 interview with the BBC, Canadian Defense Minister Harjit Singh Sajjan said, "We have to get better at preventing conflict because every time you send our troops into harm's way, politicians have failed." His words echoed those of U.S. President Reagan who said, "Peace is not absence of conflict, it is the ability to handle conflict by peaceful means."

In the past, wealthy people used their riches to build and fund free public services such as parks, schools, hospitals and free housing. When the rich abdicated their public duties, public leaders called for forced taxation.

Human history is the story of human choices. The history of tomorrow is written in the actions humanity takes today. And those decisions are influenced by the collective mind of humanity and how people interpret their long history. There are those who claim higher evolution is achieved through naked self-interest and a 'healthy' fear of others. They are wrong. Despite all the divisions and wars, hatreds and fears of the past 4,000 years, humanity is still driven by its founding culture. People seek peace, friendship, trade, new experiences and new knowledge not death and destruction.

A moral victory is one that sets a noble standard for human behavior. It rewards patience, honor, trust and far-sightedness. A change in thinking is all that is required to once again reward integrity and humanity over greed, arrogance and destruction.

If there is a secret to life, it must be something simple enough for a baby to understand because all things start at birth. According to Hawking, that same truth was comprehensible to the first material particles and fluttering waves of energy. And that singular lesson is this: More can be accomplished by working with others than working alone. That is why the Big Bang did not result in a cosmos of random bits and dust but structures and environments. Everything seeks to socialize and makes use of tools to accomplish their goals. Matter employs its gravity to attract or sling away from other things. Energies are elastic and express their choices in many different ways. And among people, the tool of expression is words.

In the 1950 movie, *Harvey*, Jimmy Stewart's character, Elwood P. Dowd, recalled his mother's advice that to succeed in the world a person must be very smart or very pleasant. "For years I was smart. I recommend pleasant," he said.

To help the world, get in touch with your humanity. Make new friends. Give out friendship offerings and gifts of gratitude without expectation of anything in return. Spread the word that humanity was built by courage, knowledge and friendships, not fear, ignorance and hatred. Be the New Human you want to be. Be courageous and have faith in yourself and the family of humanity.

We have a great history together.

ABOUT THE AUTHOR

Barry Brown is a Pulitzer Prize-nominated Canadian journalist. He has written more than 3,000 articles for 120 news organizations worldwide, including The New York Times, Washington Times, Los Angeles Times, San Francisco Chronicle, Dallas Morning News, Newsday, Miami Herald, Chicago Tribune, ABCNews.com, MSNBC.com, VOA Radio, ABC Radio, CBC Radio, AP, Reuters, UPI, McGraw Hill News Service, Jerusalem Post, Toronto Star, Newsweek, Canadian Business, Asian Advertising and Marketing, Advertising Age and Sky News TV (London).

Testimonials

"Congratulations on this masterpiece of research."
Dr. Abdul Hai Patel
Pres. Ontario MultiFaith Council
Past Coordinator
Canadian Council of Islamic Imams

"An original and brave interpretation of history."
John Saringer
Pres. and CEO
Saringer Life Science Technologies

"Barry, you've discovered the "Rosetta Stone" that unlocks the mystery of the early Bible stories."
Dr. Rev. John Joseph Mastandrea
Metropolitan United Church
Toronto

"You have created a very convincing map of the general unity of Indo-European religions from Hinduism to Judaism to Christianity and Islam as a single and somewhat inevitable path of evolution of human perception of gods. This is absolutely brilliant."
Dr. Mayank Vahia, Astrophysicist
Tata Institute for Fundamental Research
Mumbai, India

"A breathtaking tale of the longstanding companionship and friendship that has followed humanity through the ages. It is a real breath of fresh air from the previously studied views on our journey into the modern world. A fascinating narrative I would suggest to my fellow academics as well as my best friend, because it touches on what seems to be so difficult to encompass for a writer - humanity. Humanity without segregation or fault. It truly is a book for all."
Danniela-Belle Acosta
Editor

"Your book is very thought provoking but without being heavy/academic. I kept reading passages out loud to those around me, stimulating conversation."
Har Grover,
CEO
CannScience Innovations Inc.

"I don't know if you are right or not – my research doesn't go back that far. But I can tell you this: millions of people will be interested."
Prof. Michael Gervais
Ancient Ethiopian History
University of Toronto

"What you say about the Exodus makes good sense."
Prof. (Emeritus) Noam Chomsky
Linguistics and Philosophy of Language
MIT

"I don't know if you are right – you might be.
But, you will change history if you are."
Yaen Vered
Canadian Representative
Israeli Antiquities Authority

"The research of Barry Brown – in light of literary evidence and genetic studies hypothesizing that Jews migrated to Mesopotamia from Indus Valley during its downfall - might be of great importance in structuring Jewish history."
Dept. of Ancient Indian History
Culture & Archaeology
Hindu University Banaras India

"Our study of the Jewish population of India revealed that their maternal and paternal gene pool is linked with the people of West-Eurasia. The literary evidence also strongly supports this hypothesis."
Geneticist Dr. Lalji Singh
Vice-Chancellor Hindu University
Leader of India's genome project

"Barry Brown's provocative redefinition of the past leads us to believe that we were all once one family before we became divided. History as recorded – with motives both good and bad – may need a second looking at."
Bhaktimarga Swami
Hare Krishna Temple
Toronto

"Toronto researcher Barry Brown has discovered some aspects of (Bible) history that are certainly new to me, and most of my friends and acquaintances."
Paul T. Hellyer
Former Canadian Defence Minister
Spirituality is the Missing Link
Postscript to his book,
The Money Mafia: A World in Crisis (2014)

"I like the sizzler reel A LOT! Would love to see the documentary series."
Josh Grossberg
E! Entertainment NY

SIMPLIFIED TIMELINE

14 Billion BC
The Big Womb expansion of the universe begins in dense, hot darkness, gradually cools and thins out.
Light moves freely.
Stars and cosmic structures are created and replaced by a new generation of galaxies, stars, planets and moons.

4 Billion BC
The Sun, Earth and the solar system are born.

2 Billion BC
Oxygen-breathing life fills the Earth's oceans, changing the atmosphere and expanding the number of minerals.

1 Billion BC
Simple sponge-like creatures swim in Earth's warm oceans.

700-650 Million BC
Climate change turns the warm Earth into a Giant Snowball, killing most early life forms and spurring cell specialization.

450 Million BC
Plants begin to emerge from the sea to colonize the land.

400 Million BC
The first predatory animals with hinged jaws, teeth and an adaptive immune system begin to appear.

300 Million BC
Earth's single supercontinent, Pangea forms.

200-100 Million BC
Complex life forms with specialized bodies and behavior appear.

175 Million BC
Pangea, breaks apart and slowly forms the modern seven continents.

66 Million BC
An asteroid impact and other factors cause a severe drop in Earth's temperature and reduction in sunlight, wiping out more than 70 percent of life on Earth, including the dinosaurs.

5-8 Million BC
Hominid ancestor gives birth to two family lines – one evolves into apes, the other to humans.

3 Million BC
"Lucy" is an upright walking, tool-making ancestor of the human family.

400,000 BC
Long distance trade networks among ancestral humans and human cousins are active along the Pacific Ocean shoreline of South Africa.

100,000 BC
The branch of the human family called *Homo Sapiens* ("People with Insight") lives in larger communities and trades more with other humans.
They migrate out of Africa and begin to wander the world.

70-50,000 BC
Human communities spread across Africa, Europe, Asia and Australia.

40,000 BC
A more advanced family of humans called *Homo Sapien Sapiens* or "People with Insight into Insight" use letter-like symbols and painting to communicate ideas and study the world.

33,000-5000 BC
Ancestors of American Indians cross from Northeast Asia to the Americas.
Humans begin living in homes.
Rope and cloth are invented. Early forms of writing spread around the world.

12,000 BC
Gobekli Tepe, the world's first university, is built in southeast Turkey.

10,000-5000 BC
Cow-herding people spread their dairy culture across Europe.

5000-3000 BC
Large scale migration of Austronesian people from Taiwan and China populate East Asia and the Pacific Islands.

4500-3500 BC
Ancient India's "Age of Knowledge" is the world's first civilization.
The Hebrew calendar begins with Year 1 in 3760 BC.
The War at Kurukshetra destroys humanity's first civilization.
Krishna, the inspirational founder of Hinduism, is born.

3000- 2100 BC
Indus River Valley Civilization.
In Ancient Egypt King Narmer rules the north and south of the country after his War of Unification.

2000 BC
The kingdoms of Ancient Sumer and Akkad, Babylon is founded.
The first wars of conquest begin and slavery spreads.
Sargon the Great of Akkad is born.
Sargon's daughter, Enheduanna, creates the first organized religion
Zoroaster is born.

1800 BC
Abraham, patriarch of the Hebrews and inspirational father of Jews, Christians and Moslems is born in ancient Mesopotamia.
Start of Mayan civilization.

1700 BC
The first dynasties of Ancient China.

1300 BC
In Ancient Egypt Pharaoh Akhenaten creates the world's first religious dictatorship.
Moses and the Exodus of Israelites and Hebrews from Egypt.

1250 BC
World's first peace treaty between Ancient Egypt and the Hittites.

850-586 BC
Ancient Kingdoms of Israel and Judah.

700-400 BC
Ancient Greece.

600 BC
Birth of Buddha in India.

500 BC
Birth of Confucius in China.

500-300 BC
The Achaemenid Empire spreads Zoroastrianism.

250 BC
Warrior King Ashoka of India converts and becomes the world's first Buddhist King.

700 BC-400 AD
Empire of Ancient Rome.

7-2 BC
Jesus is born during the Roman occupation of what was Ancient Israel.

300 AD
Roman Emperor Constantine converts and becomes the world's first Christian Emperor.

570 AD
Mohammed is born in what is now Mecca, Saudi Arabia.

1469 AD
Guru Nanak founder of Sikhism is born near what is now Lahore, Pakistan.

1516 AD
The publication of Thomas More's book, *Utopia*.

SHALOMASTE

Shalom (Read right to left)

नमस्ते

Namaste (Read left to right)

Aristotle's quote that the Hebrew people migrated out of India started me on this journey. As a tribute to the history he revealed, I have adopted the word "Shalomaste" for my company and created a logo to evoke its meaning.

Shalomaste, is a combination of the Sanskrit word "Namaste" and the Hebrew word "Shalom." Among intermarried and neighborly Jews and Hindus, this word is commonly used. But no one has defined it.

The root word of Shalom is expressed in many languages including the Arabic *Salaam*, *Sliem* in Maltese, and *Salam* in Ethiopian.

This word has many meanings, including peace, wholeness, welcome, friendship, agreement, justice, truth, reconciliation and the property that comes from widespread trade and exchange.

Namaste is a Sanskrit word that combines the verb "namah," to bow, with the object, "to you." Literally, it means, "I bow and offer my respects and friendship to you." But like Shalom, Namaste carries many other meanings including an acknowledgement of each other's soul, the expression of gratitude, courtesy and politeness, honor and peace.

The logo combines the two "ma" letters. Taken together, Shalomaste means "I welcome you in peace and friendship, and my spirit bows in joyful welcome of your spirit into my life."

CPSIA information can be obtained
at www.ICGtesting.com
Printed in the USA
LVHW02s0829290618
582237LV00004B/4/P